Character and Cops

Character and Cops

Ethics in Policing

Second Edition

Edwin J. Delattre

The AEI Press

Publisher for the American Enterprise Institute
WASHINGTON, D.C.
1994

Library of Congress Cataloging-in-Publication Data

Delattre, Edwin J.
   Character and cops : ethics in policing / Edwin J. Delattre. —
2nd ed.
     p. cm.
   ". . . for the American Enterprise Institute."
   Includes bibliographical references (p.   ) and index.
   ISBN 0-8447-3868-9 (cloth). —ISBN 0-8447-3869-7 (paper)
   1. Police ethics.   2. Law enforcement—Moral and ethical aspects.
3. Police training—Moral and ethical aspects.   4. Law enforcement—
United States.   5. Police—United States.   I. American Enterprise
Institute for Public Policy Research.   II. Title.
HV7924.D45   1994
174'.93632—dc20   94-18150
                                            CIP

ISBN 0-8447-3868-9 (alk. paper)

1 3 5 7 9 10 8 6 4 2

Printed in the United States of America

To my mother, Donna Marie Delattre, and to the memory of my father, Jules Irvey Delattre

The romance of police activity keeps in some sense before the mind the fact that civilization itself is the most sensational of departures and the most romantic of rebellions. By dealing with the unsleeping sentinels who guard the outposts of society, it tends to remind us that we live in an armed camp, making war with a chaotic world, and that the criminals, the children of chaos, are nothing but the traitors within our gates. . . . The romance of the police force is thus the whole romance of man. It is based on the fact that morality is the most dark and daring of conspiracies. It reminds us that the whole noiseless and unnoticeable police management by which we are ruled and protected is only a successful knight-errantry.

G. K. CHESTERTON, *The Defendant*

Contents

Foreword

Edwin Delattre's *Character and Cops* illuminates hundreds of moral problems faced regularly by police officers and managers. It makes a major contribution to the body of knowledge essential for police to play their rightful part in the struggle of society against injustice.

Policing as an emerging profession dedicated to justice under law will be strengthened by these well-reasoned analyses of actual problems of the street and headquarters. This book will stimulate citizens, elected officials, journalists, and, most important, police practitioners to take a harder look at their functions as fundamental elements of a free society.

Understandably, *Character and Cops* is about good and evil. It faces squarely the fact that without individuals of good character and institutions that apply high ideals to daily practice, the goals of liberty, order, and justice cannot be achieved. It offers neither compromise nor comfort to betrayals of the public trust by anyone in government. Professor Delattre is intolerant of double standards and of time-worn excuses for incompetence, avoidable character faults, and corruption.

It is a privilege to be a police officer in a democratic society. Government of the people, by the people, and for the people is possible only with the assistance of the police. In a modern urban industrial environment, the people could not maintain social control with an all-volunteer system. An insufficient number of able-bodied citizens would contribute time to stand guard, to settle disputes, to investigate accidents and crimes, to arrest offenders, to testify in court, to organize communities in the prevention of crime, and to aid the sick, injured, lost, abused, disturbed, homeless, abandoned, and evicted. The tasks are too complex. Highly developed organizations functioning twenty-four hours every day are necessary. Under a government by the people, however, all citizens have an obligation to participate in the maintenance of order, while delegating to police officers, whose salaries they pay, their collective authority to enforce the law.

The patrol officer who orchestrates the contributions of all the people to the maintenance of order is an essential member of the community. Without order, there is neither freedom nor civilization. The neighborhood beat officer can accomplish little alone. She or he gets the job done through others—parents, relatives, neighbors, teenagers, teachers, clergy, social workers, employers, community leaders, prosecutors, judges, and probation and parole officers. The job description of a police officer resembles that of a manager more than a worker. Although the community, not the officer, is the boss, the officer as the one authorized to use force must sometimes resort to intimidation to accomplish the mission.

Since they can have a profound effect on individual lives, such awesome responsibilities should be entrusted only to people of good character, who will exercise discretion in making decisions. Insufficient guidance has been available to those who must grapple with the moral implications involved in resolving disputes, confronting violence, making arrests, issuing citations, detaining disturbed persons, separating families, protecting children, aiding the poor, and other confrontations with unpredictable behavior. This valuable volume sheds light on the nature of the judgment and character required to meet these duties. Wisdom and integrity—and the virtues of justice, temperance, courage, compassion, honesty, fortitude, and restraint—are described succinctly and shown to be irreplaceable in policing.

Yet the decency of police will not of itself accomplish the essential purposes of our country. As the author understands, two hundred years into the "great experiment" American democracy is thriving—except in the inner cities. The dimensions of problems elsewhere are within the normal range for an advanced society. Where the underclass is concentrated in densely populated urban enclaves, however, individuals are deprived of their right to life, liberty, and the pursuit of happiness to an extent that must be considered abnormal. Criminal victimization, disorder, and fear abound, and violent crime rates are many times the national average. People are unable to exercise social control over their neighborhoods. Government of, by, and for the people is not a reality. The 90 percent of the people who are law-abiding are powerless when drug dealers control the streets and use their enormous profits to corrupt and to exert influence.

After the most remarkable achievement in integration in the history of free people, after so many who had been excluded became empowered within the brief period of thirty years, the six largest cities now have four black mayors and five black chiefs. Regrettably their departments—like those of the other major cities—cannot bring justice and freedom to all of their citizens. Since self-government can be realized only when community exists, large concentrations of poor people—weak in the leadership potential of the middle class—look to the police to assist them in becoming a community of free people. They need to be well-informed about crime patterns and resident criminals in order to protect themselves and one another. The police, in partnership with the people, must ensure that criminals do not intimidate them and that the rule of law supersedes the threat of fear.

In practice, individual officers, chiefs, and entire departments are prevented from taking actions that would serve these goals. Improper political interference in police matters by elected officials, political party leaders, or campaign contributors is a common problem. Nepotism and favoritism, as well as discrimination against well-qualified persons in hiring, assigning, promoting, and disciplining are far from rare. Professional standards that might be invoked to correct such abuses or to support highly principled practitioners are not universally available or accepted. Many chiefs are stymied in their effort to provide better service by indefensible provisions of collective bargaining contracts.

The police are the "unprofessional profession." They possess the powers and discretion associated with a profession, but they are not a profession. Although they are making progress, professionalism will remain unachievable until the states and federal government provide a support structure. The most fundamental weakness in crime control is the failure of federal and state governments to create a framework for local policing. Much of what is wrong with the police is the result of the absurd, fragmented, unworkable, nonsystem of more than 17,000 local departments.

Police officers are victims of the nonsystem. Conscientious officers become demoralized and generate the cynicism that permits callousness and indifference. They are frustrated by irrational management and illogical variations in policies and practices. A four-year college degree should be required for every officer to do work that calls for all of the strengths and resources of a profession.

More harm results from the crazy quilt of thousands of uncoordinated, ineffective agencies than from the misbehavior of poorly motivated officers. Many who succumb to the temptations of graft, laziness, and minimal productivity were once highly motivated but were overcome by poor management, weak leadership, and a lack of fulfillment. For the ideal of justice to be faithfully served, police, prosecutors, legal defenders, judges, court systems, jails, prisons, and probation and parole officers must become participants in a system of crime control.

An honest and fully professional police community would acknowledge in its police education the root causes of crime—poverty, unemployment, underemployment, racism, poor health care, bad housing, weak schools, mental illness, alcoholism, addiction, single-parent families, teenage pregnancy, and a society of selfishness and greed. The profession would acknowledge as well that police have in the past routinely served as the instruments of discrimination in American life. They broke their oath of office by depriving people of the protection of the law because of their race. The complicity of the beat officer, the detective, and the chief was necessary to sustain virulent discrimination in housing, education, employment, and public accommodation.

The police are now better educated, more restrained, and more representative of the communities they serve. In the forty-three years since I entered the New York City Police Department, ethical standards have soared. The ability of the police to fulfill their sacred trust will improve as a lucid sense of ethical standards is developed. Professor Delattre's work with and about police is a powerful ally for all in public service and academic life who care about such standards.

Patrick V. Murphy
Former commissioner of the
New York City Police Department
and president of the
Police Foundation

Preface to the Second Edition

In the four years since *Character and Cops* was first published, public confidence in political leaders and governmental institutions in the United States has been subjected to a growing number of assaults. In the executive and judicial branches nominees for high federal office as well as incumbents have been exposed as lawbreakers and as persons of questionable character. Members of Congress have been exposed for conflict-of-interest schemes and sexual predation on subordinates. Bitter disputes have prompted the public to ask whether their servants are genuinely committed to the common good.

These problems are neither new nor unique to the United States. In 1912, H. G. Wells wrote in the London *Times* that the public "behave no longer as though they believe that our political leaders are in the last resort gentlemen, but . . . in the worst sense of the words, lawyers and exploiters."[1]

Policing has not been spared such assaults, as problems of brutality, corruption, and incompetence have been disclosed. Despite what seems to me to be a rising commitment to integrity in many police departments and law enforcement agencies, widely publicized police misconduct in New York, Washington, D.C., Detroit, Los Angeles, and other cities has threatened to taint policing in general. In England, police falsification of evidence and perjury to secure convictions of suspected terrorists have deeply shaken public confidence.

The duty of public servants and their obligation to serve the public with integrity and competence do not ebb and flow with public opinion. Police and other public servants must always hold themselves to high moral and intellectual standards. Still, as James Madison observed two hundred years ago in *The Federalist* No. 49, even "the most rational government will not find it a superfluous advantage to have the prejudices of the community on its side."[2] Police need to be worthy of the public trust, no matter how many other public servants show their contempt for ethics and the public interest.

No single episode in police history has had an impact on public opinion comparable to that of the videotaped beating of Rodney King by Los Angeles Police Department officers on March 3, 1991. The second half of an amateur videotape showing officers striking King fifty-six times with batons while a group of police, including field training officers, stand by was shown on television for months. One nationally known television reporter told law enforcement leaders that the lesson was that the media can make any event a lead story for as long as they want. Of course, this is *not* the lesson to be learned. The power of the media—as well as the intemperance and bad judgment the media often bring to the exercise of power—have long been recognized by police and others. The real lessons of the publicized beating of Rodney King are that some police do not deserve to be police, and that departments must be vigilant about the conduct of their personnel.

If police are to have the weight of law-abiding citizens on their side, including what Madison called "the prejudices of the community," they must make concerted and continuing efforts to reach out to the public. They must make clear that they cannot safeguard the public without public involvement and cooperation, that they are eager to know the primary concerns of the public, and that they want to be known, as individuals, to the members of the community. Such outreach does not guarantee judiciousness and mutual respect, but lack of it sustains a gap between police and public that makes fulfillment of the police mission virtually impossible. At worst, such a gap results in an us-against-them feeling on both sides, to the impairment of the life of police and public alike.

While public attention was riveted on the beating of King and on the trials of the police involved, deeply rooted problems of crime throughout the world continued to worsen. Old and new faces of organized crime worldwide expanded criminal activities in drug trafficking, extortion, bribery, contract murder, money laundering, and other profitable enterprises. In some places, organized crime has become so powerful that it threatens national governments. In the United States, the proliferation of gangs, their evolution into criminal conspiracies resembling organized crime, and the growing crisis of juvenile crime and juvenile career criminals threaten the public interest and safety more than ever. Demands on the resources of police departments and public expectations of police rose, just as public confidence in police declined.

The timing of these developments could scarcely have been worse. When the LAPD officers who beat King were acquitted, riots followed on an unprecedented scale. Despite the destruction, many commentators saw the violence not as a riot but as an expression of rebellion and despair by people to whom justice has been too long denied. While I share the view that many have been denied the blessings of liberty affirmed in the preamble to the United States Constitution, my own inquiries indicate that these riots did not begin as expressions of outrage by normally law-abiding residents. They began near the intersection of Florence and Normandie, where gang members attacked liquor stores and then looted large quantities of weapons and ammunition, their real objective. Only after the riots started, and residents saw on television that the police did nothing to stop the widespread looting, did other citizens take to the streets in search of free goods. Many who were arrested in the second day of civil disarray asked deputies why they were being stopped when television showed so many others freely looting. As University of Chicago Professor Charner Perry pointed out in 1970, "great chiliastic-cataclysmic waves of emotion sweep over large numbers of people . . . , especially where the mass media are highly developed."[3]

After the riots, Los Angeles-based gangs formed an ostensible truce, as gang leaders were legitimized by thoughtless talk-show hosts and other media personalities. National gang "summits" followed, sanctioned and celebrated by civic and church groups. Gang leaders now proclaim themselves civic leaders interested in the welfare of the public, as the credulous media, enamored of their own creations, give license to these lies. As police working undercover in national gang summits in such places as Kansas City have learned, the summits are actually directed toward the organization of nationwide conspiracies to increase profits from drug trafficking and other illegal enterprises.

At the very time the public most needs to understand the emerging patterns of criminality, media trends run counter to their learning what they need to know. There are exceptions; some in the media have worked diligently to present the grim picture of organized crime and gang predation to the public. But proliferation of unreliable accounts makes the work of police more difficult than it would otherwise be.

The United States is now home to upwards of 2 million known gang members. They include white supremacist motorcycle gangs that traffic in amphetamines, Jamaican posses that control much of the crack traffic, and indigenous street gangs that are evolving from instruments of violent territorial power into organized and highly mobile criminal conspiracies. In 1993, law enforcement officials in one city informed me that a gang operating there had a multimillion dollar agreement with a foreign power to shoot down a commercial airliner inside the United States. The plot was stopped when gang members were arrested after purchasing the weapons from undercover law enforcement personnel.

Some of these criminals are stupid; others, even if illiterate, are decidedly not. Most of them understand that juvenile justice systems are generally toothless and that early-release programs for adults are the norm. If as juveniles they can walk blithely from one wrongful act to another, and if as adults they can commit felonies with confidence that they will go unpunished or will never serve a prison sentence in full, then they know that, except for the occupational hazard of being killed, crime pays. It pays in the only coin they value.

The likelihood of transforming large numbers of young people with ingrained habits of criminality into morally responsible members of communities seems to me negligible. Like the rest of us, predators like the habits they acquire. When these habits include remorselessness, sadism, and raw hatred of others, they are staggeringly difficult or impossible to reverse. We offer too little at the start and nothing in the way of sanctions thereafter.

Despite the hazards posed to the public interest, many in America are enamored with irresponsible and immature behavior. Trendsetters speak of legalizing drugs, supposedly to reduce crime, while they romanticize criminals and criminal organizations. The glorification of the gang culture of predation and violence has been accompanied by a dramatic growth in the popularity of "Gangsta" rap music. Such songs commonly include lyrics that denigrate women, celebrate racist hatred, and express a vengeful, even murderous, attitude toward police. Entertainers and producers insist that the themes of misogyny, racism, and violence are just entertainment and that the lyrics have no real meaning or consequences. The indictment of leading rap artists for crimes ranging from illegal weapons possession to rape and murder tells a different story. As Charner Perry explains, many popular artists have never understood the importance of "humor, games, novels, orations, sermons, dramas, and fashions" that are "creative and conserving rather than destructive or perverting." Today, as in the past, "The good society must wait for the renaissance of creative, inspired, disciplined art which can fuse thought and emotion to rebuild the realm of ideals which created civilization and can maintain it."[4]

Unconcerned that the words and images by which we express ourselves influence how we think and behave, advertisers glamorize gang-style clothing and jewelry, portray graffiti vandals as harmless, and signal that the consumption of alcohol and sexual attractiveness go together. Although irresponsibility among those who set styles and make fashions is nothing new, the effects of such irresponsibility in schools and neighborhoods impose impossible demands on teachers and police.

In the United States, 1.2 million babies are born out of wedlock each year. Many of these children will be raised without fathers in densely populated areas where the malign influences of the streets will draw them toward gang membership. Some of them become dangerous to themselves and others at an early age. Viewing such neglected juveniles as a police problem, too many adults will fail to support reforms in public policy and law to combat the patterns of childbirth at the root of so many social problems.

The difficulties facing law enforcement agencies were compounded by the televised horror of confrontation and death at the Branch Davidian compound in Elk Point, near Waco, Texas. After federal, state, and local law enforcement personnel took positions near the compound of David Koresh and his cult, who were known to have stockpiled illegal weapons, agents of the Bureau of Alcohol, Tobacco, and Firearms undertook a raid on the compound on February 28, 1993. Four ATF agents were killed and sixteen wounded in an exchange of gunfire, along with at least six Branch Davidians inside the compound.

A fifty-one-day standoff followed. On April 19, 1993, under instructions from the attorney general, and, apparently, with the knowledge of the president, FBI agents sought to enter the compound by battering down portions of walls and spraying tear gas inside. Koresh and his lieutenants then suicidally set fire to the buildings, killing eighty-five cult members, including seventeen children. While the compound burned and people died, one leading anchorman asked a local reporter, on national television, whether there was reason to believe that the FBI had set the fire. There was then, and is now, no question that Koresh ordered the fire, that Branch Davidians tried to stop it when they realized no FBI agents were actually entering the compound, and that accelerants and wind conditions quickly spread the flames out of control. That newsman's question is a measure of media contempt for law enforcement agencies.

All hands acknowledge that law enforcement leaders made errors of judgment, particularly in February. ATF officials have been heavily criticized for mounting the assault on February 28, when some of them apparently knew that Koresh had been alerted, and two officials were later dismissed for implication in a coverup. Still, dealing with messianic fanatics is an inexact art, not a science, even for those with substantial experience. Experts do not always agree in predicting the behavior of figures like Koresh. Certainly, the hope of the FBI and attorney general that they could use force to end the standoff without large loss of life proved false. Some messianic fanatics, believing that death for them is but a short prelude to resurrection, pose the risk of committing "abstract suicide"—killing themselves and all who are with them in a martyrdom that will be followed by rebirth. For others to try to see things from such a perspective is an arduous challenge. As in other matters where police face the ordeal of judgment, meeting this challenge calls for the wisdom to envision worst possible outcomes.

Members of Congress and the media have treated the public to a spectacle of unrealistic expectations. A number have called for a review of the entire matter to "make sure that no tragedy of this kind ever happens again." Review is certainly imperative; we do need to learn all we can apply to future situations. But to give the impression that anyone can know with certainty how to avert tragedy of any kind is to generate expectations that cannot be met even by the wisest and most conscientious public servants. Such unrealistic expectations invite the belief that when things go unavoidably wrong, someone in a position of authority, such as the police, must be to blame. Such folly promotes cynicism and discourages public cooperation with police for the common good.

While the Los Angeles riots and the Branch Davidian debacle were scarring the country, acts of random massacre and multiple murder also shattered public confidence. Passengers on a Long Island commuter train were murdered in a hail of gunfire; employees in public agencies and private corporations and restaurant patrons have been indiscriminately shot. Private resentments turn into public slaughters. Many law-abiding people have come to believe they are not safe, even in the most mundane circumstances.

Rising public insistence on gun control legislation has been accompanied by fascination with the idea that law-abiding citizens should carry handguns to safeguard themselves. Jeffrey R. Snyder has argued that all crimes against persons and their property resemble rape in the sense that they are "about domination, degradation, and control. . . . [K]idnapping, robbery, carjacking, and assault are not about property."[5] Insisting that self-respecting people would not tolerate abridgments of their liberty and dignity by criminals, Snyder and others conclude that failure to carry a handgun amounts to cowardly disrespect for oneself.

Paradoxically, many people who want gun controls do not expect to be made safe by them; they expect to be safer with a handgun. This phenomenon has the real potential to elevate inordinate fear and escalate violence. Ninety percent of crimes against individuals and their property are committed by criminals who are not carrying firearms. How many will carry guns, shoot first, and rob later if they expect their victims to be armed? If ordinary citizens kill gang members in self-defense, will gangs target their families in reprisal? Will ordinary citizens who shoot others, even justifiably, suffer no emotional hardships? Will citizens who shoot in fear end up in prison or in destructive lawsuits? I concur with the view that self-defense is both a sign and an instrument of self-respect, but not that carrying handguns will restore dignity and safety to the public. Criminals will hardly become law-abiding if they believe their potential victims to be armed. Arming the public is more likely to escalate an arms race with criminals.

All these trends and events confirm that ethics in policing—the continuing elevation of standards of integrity and competence—remains central to the well-being of the country and the public. To contribute to the purposes of policing and to the work and education of police and other public servants, I have added two new chapters to this edition of *Character and Cops*, "Fatalism, Microcosms, and Therapeutic Reductions" and "Ethical Ideals, Youth Violence, and Gang Enforcement."

Chapter 14 addresses the threat to ethics in policing posed by the cynical, yet fashionable, insistence that police departments are mere microcosms of society in general. This excuse for police brutality, corruption, and incompetence is logically indefensible and factually false. The chapter explains how the danger is aggravated by efforts to reduce police education and training to therapy intended to make police sensitive. When the idea that police departments cannot embody high moral and intellectual standards is combined with the notion that police should be trained as if they were patients suffering an illness, their aspiration to high standards is destroyed and their capacity diminished.

Chapter 15 treats ethics in policing that is directed to juvenile crime and gang recruitment and predation. The chapter emphasizes that these threats to public safety, which shake the possibility of justice, liberty, and domestic tranquillity to its foundations, cannot be reduced by isolated police action. Ethics in gang prevention and enforcement requires the highest achievements of character and competence within police departments. Never in the history of America or of the world has the need for police leaders of probity and sophistication been greater. To contend with juvenile violence and gang crime, police leaders must secure trustworthy multiagency task forces, advise political leaders and criminal justice officials, and enlist the cooperation of parents, schools, the media, corporations, foundations, churches, civic and youth organizations, and social service and health agencies. The challenges of sustaining such cooperation over long periods call for police of great fortitude, patience, and judgment. To give in to the idea that youth violence and gang crime are police problems is to dash all hope of improvement.

In 1992, in response to requests from police academies and criminal justice programs, I prepared a teacher's guide for designing academy courses and programs in ethics and for using *Character and Cops* in instructional programs. Containing a brief bibliography for academy and criminal justice libraries, this guide is included as an appendix of this edition of *Character and Cops*. I hope that it and the new chapters will add to the resources of all who bear the public trust.

Notes: Preface to the Second Edition

1. From H. G. Wells, *Your Obedient Servant* (London: 1974), p. 84. Cited by Jacques Barzun in *A Stroll with William James* (New York: Harper & Row, 1983), p. 275.

2. Jacob E. Cooke, ed., *The Federalist* (Middletown, Conn.: Wesleyan University Press, 1961), p. 340.

3. Charner Perry, "Violence—Visible and Invisible," *Ethics*, vol. 81, no. 1 (October 1970), p. 5.

4. Ibid., pp. 20, 21.

5. Jeffrey R. Snyder, "A Nation of Cowards," *Public Interest*, no. 113 (Fall 1993), p. 41.

Acknowledgments

Law enforcement personnel have taught me a great deal about their work and its demands, satisfactions, and hardships. This book could not have been written without their trust and patient assistance.

Personnel from the police departments of Albuquerque, Atlanta, Baltimore City, Baltimore County, Houston, Kansas City (Missouri), Los Angeles, Metro-Dade, Miami, Minneapolis, New York City, Omaha, Philadelphia, and Toledo have been exceptionally helpful. Many FBI Field Offices, the FBI Academy at Quantico, and officials at FBI Headquarters have provided extensive assistance, as have officials of the Justice Department and the Drug Enforcement Administration. Many alumni of the National Executive Institute have discussed portions of the text and brought their experience to bear on it.

Among the people who have given generously of their time and wisdom are Richard Ayres, Samuel Baca, Cornelius Behan, William Booth, Anthony Bouza, Lee Brown, Dana Caro, Lester Davis, Wayne Davis, Patrick Fitzsimons, Robert Gillham, Charles Gruber, Donna Hansen, Daniel Kingston, Joseph Koletar, Nicholas Londino, John Mason, Frank Monastero, Ronald Mullen, Patrick Murphy, Robert Olson, Charles Plummer, Oliver Revell, David Roberts, Walt Sirene, Daniel Sullivan, Edward Sulzbach, Kevin Tucker, John Velier, William Wells, and Donald Witham. I have relied heavily on the guidance of Hillary Robinette, Andrew Tartaglino, Fred Taylor, Anne Verge, and Robert Wadman. And I owe special debts of gratitude to John O'Neill and Edward Tully for their instruction and recommendations.

From the military, Seth Cropsey and James Bond Stockdale have kindly assisted me. From the public policy arena, Douglas Besharov, Michael Cromartie, Terry Eastland, Gary Edwards, Raymond English, Robert Goldwin, and Peter Skerry have done likewise. Kenneth Watson, Patricia Evans, and Noel Augustyn have given valuable instruction about statute and case law.

Colleagues in philosophy have patiently read and reread versions of the text and given me the benefit of insight and experience: William Bennett, John Burkett, John Hardwig, Charles Karelis, Alasdair MacIntyre, Jon Moline, Andrew Oldenquist, John Silber, and Paul Woodruff.

Many undercover agents and officers have helped me extensively. I regret that the confidentiality of their work prevents me from identifying them, for I am deeply grateful. My appreciation is heartfelt as well to the many officers and command personnel throughout the country who took me on patrol with them, showed me the work of their divisions and departments, and raised questions that are central to this book.

The Lynde and Harry Bradley Foundation has generously supported my work throughout the project. I am especially grateful to Michael Joyce, president of the Foundation, for his abiding encouragement and support. The American Enterprise Institute has provided a most congenial setting for my work, thanks to Christopher DeMuth, the resident scholars, and staff, especially Evelyn Caldwell.

Above all, George Brosan, Steven Tigner, and Chuck Wexler have worked tirelessly with me. I have benefited from extended conversation and correspondence with them and from their careful and penetrating scrutiny of the text. I am deeply touched by their devotion to the project.

Robert Royal has served with great skill and patience as editor. Timothy Tigner has served faithfully as my research assistant. Ruth Pilsbury has prepared the manuscript with care and thoughtful criticisms. My wife, Alice, has worked closely with me, and our daughter, Lee, is largely responsible for the book's title.

To all, my heartfelt thanks.

Introduction

Chesterton's description of police activity as romance will strike some people responsible for enforcing the law and keeping the peace as naive, or at least incomplete. Police work involves boredom, suffering, anxiety, danger, and disappointment as much as romance, challenge, satisfaction, and success.

Still, in spite of much literature that describes police as cynical, alienated, disaffected, and unhappy, my own experience with police of all ranks indicates that many love their work and find great fulfillment in it. They understand, with Chesterton, that civilization does not come into existence or survive by accident, and they take seriously their place in sustaining it.

Civilization depends on people who are committed to civility and decency. Not everyone is. People have a mixture of motives; some are high-minded and some are not. Even the best among us have weaknesses. Some of us are downright dangerous—to ourselves, to other people, or to both.

Human beings are neither angels nor beasts, and they differ in attitudes, beliefs, motives, purposes, and ambitions. This makes civilization difficult to create and preserve. For the same reason, there must be "unsleeping sentinels who guard the outposts of society." Simply put, civilization cannot defend itself: people must stand up for it. The specific people who are on the front lines—the police—are thus essential to civilized life, even though there are limits to what they can do.

In the end, of course, the citizens must do much for themselves in their own daily behavior and in educating the young. No police force can safeguard the ideals of civility and decency from a public determined to destroy them or lacking the courage to stand up for them. But even when many citizens are basically respectful of each other and of the law, there is never enough decency, never enough restraint, to enable people to live well together without someone who can step in when civility breaks down. So some of us must be entrusted to guard the public safety, to enforce the laws, to keep the peace, to help the helpless.

The age-old dream of living together free from tyranny is the most daring romance of mankind. We want to be free and at the same time to enjoy security. This is the context in which morality in law enforcement takes shape. We want police and law enforcement institutions that merit our trust, respect, and confidence.

Within this context, I have tried to address the kinds of moral questions most often raised by police and others in the criminal justice system with whom I have worked over the past thirteen years. The chapters are self-contained, but common threads of argument run throughout. I have also tried where appropriate to explain how to think conscientiously about moral questions and public policy issues.

I have addressed the following broad questions: What is excellence of character? Particularly, what are wisdom and integrity, and how are they related to specific aspects of character, such as justice, courage, temperance, and compassion? How does personal virtue figure in the fulfillment of the mission of police? How should problems of infidelity to the public trust—whether in corruption or in abuse of authority, power, and discretion—be addressed? What basic principles of morality apply to police acceptance of gratuities, to uses of deception and force, to treatment of informants, to selective enforcement of the law, to drug testing, and to preparation of reports and testimony? What are just and wise policies for recruitment, selection, reward, and promotion of personnel? How are police to analyze the moral dimensions of public policy debates, such as those concerning the legalization of narcotics? How can police education and training most effectively promote respect for moral ideals? What should decent people do about hard cases where moral ideals seem to be, or actually are, in unresolvable conflict? How can people draw out the best in themselves when suffering heartache and discouragement?

Chapter 1 describes personal character and shows how morality concerns good character and right action. It emphasizes connections between wisdom and integrity in public and private life. Chapter 2 describes the ideals of a constitutional republic and the mission of police in such a republic. Chapter 3 expands on the nature of the police mission by explaining the idea of public trust and describing the kinds of people who are qualified to serve the public. Chapter 4 focuses on the nature, place, and limits of discretion in policing. Chapter 5 discusses corruption, hypotheses about its causes, and the power of individuals to resist it. The chapter distinguishes legitimate higher standards from illegitimate "double" standards. Chapter 6 treats effective uses of authority for reform. Chapter 7 is addressed to departmental leadership, personnel policies, burnout, and affirmative action. It concludes with recommendations for sound recruiting, selection, and advancement. Chapter 8 describes and analyzes the moral dimensions of public policy debates, focusing on the specific debate about legalization of narcotics. It denies that legalization can solve our problems, and it concludes that there are not morally overriding reasons for legalization.

Chapters 9 through 11 are devoted explicitly to police training in relation to good character and good judgment. The chapters proceed from fundamentals of ethics through progressively more subtle deliberation about moral questions to the problems of tragedy and "noble cause" corruption. They emphasize the formation of habits of virtue, including the habit of reasoning well about issues that call for deliberation, and thus highlight the need for command personnel, academy instructors, and field training officers who can bridge the gap between moral ideals and the realities of the streets. Chapter 12 is a reflection on the place of wisdom and character in facing the death of a friend, partner, or loved one; the bereavement of others; and the aftermath of deadly force. Chapter 13 concludes the book with a description of the morality of aspiration by which we take our lives seriously.

Honorable and conscientious police work is performed every day by countless command and patrol personnel throughout America. I have witnessed their work time and again: I have seen police apply patience and good judgment to prevent violent conflict; and I have seen them endure racial and ethnic abuse with equanimity rather than add to tension.

I have worked with departments where officers routinely inform citizens who try to bribe them, "We don't do that here." I have seen officers expose themselves to danger to protect the innocent and seen them suffer harm from sudden violence by the very people they were protecting; I have seen police sprayed with the vomit of homeless drunks rather than let them fall to the pavement. I have observed their efforts to help youths recover their lives from addiction and futility; I have seen police work the streets seeking information to identify and apprehend suspects in violent crimes; I have observed their respect for civil rights even in extended undercover investigations of organized crime; and I have seen them make arrests without force when conflict seemed virtually inevitable.

I have seen police use force to subdue the perpetrators of crimes when no lesser means would suffice and witnessed their anguish afterward, even when there was absolutely no reason for remorse or self-criticism. I have enjoyed their humor when things seemed terribly unfair: for example, an officer who was unjustly attacked by reporters, after a harrowing chase to apprehend a suspect, remarked to me, "Man, what a job we could have done if we had known as much as those reporters." I have been touched by police efforts to bring comfort and assurance to old, mentally frail people who were terrorized by their own imaginations.

I have likewise met sly, greedy, cowardly, mean, unreliable, and brutish police. I have witnessed the effects of individual, rogue corruption and violence and of institutionalized corruption and brutality. I have seen people recruited who were never fit to be police in the first place and learned of their subsequent betrayal of the badge. And I have listened to their excuses and rationalizations for failings, sometimes accompanied by excuses from their peers, departments, and political officials.

I have also learned of the work of honorable judges, legislators, prosecuting attorneys, and defense lawyers and seen the good effects of their probity on the criminal justice system. And I have been taught the scams of corrupt attorneys and judges and their impact on police—as well as the effects of legislative corruption, incompetence, cowardice, and greed.

Accordingly, I have written this book in awareness that policing, like all other walks of life, includes people who are worthy of their authority and responsibilities and people who are not. It is my hope that the book will be of use to police and others in the broad domains of law and politics who seek to bear faithfully the public trust.

1
Excellence of Character

It is a matter of real importance whether our early education confirms in us one set of habits or another. It would be nearer the truth to say that it makes a very great difference indeed, in fact all the difference in the world.

ARISTOTLE[1]

No one who does not already care about being a good person and doing what is right can have a serious ethical question. A person must have achieved a disposition to do the right thing in the right way at the right time for the right reasons before any moral perplexities can arise.

First and Second Nature

No one is born with formed character. Whatever the injustices of the human condition, everyone, regardless of background, race, or sex, enters the world with a full portion of ignorance; and all of us die with much of that ignorance intact.

As infants, we are curious and responsive. Our behavior as babies—such as crying when another baby cries—suggests that the roots of sympathy and social awareness run very deep in us.

At the same time, as infants we are often bent on the immediate gratification of every desire, indifferent to the extent of our demands on others. We have yet to develop a sense of self; our character remains to be formed. We are impulsive. This is what some thinkers call our *first nature* as human beings.

Babies are born with neither good *nor* bad character. Normal people, as they grow, learn, and are trained, develop better or worse dispositions and habits of conduct. They come to have a *second nature*.

Obviously, we are born with a potential for good character—and for the dispositions and habits that make up bad or weak character. Because we are born in ignorance of moral ideals, however, we must be instructed and trained if we are to achieve a good second nature. As the philosopher J. O. Urmson expresses it, "If we are normal human beings and not incapacitated by some abnormal defect, then whether we acquire a good or bad character depends on the kind of upbringing we get."[2]

Aristotle observed that "habit is a second nature" and quoted the Greek poet Evenus: I say that habit's but long practice, friend, And this becomes men's nature in the end.[3] Everyone develops a second nature—whatever becomes natural to do and feel in recurrent situations. The fulfillment of our potential for character excellence depends on the habits "our early education confirms in us."

Environment, however, is not sufficient to *give* a person good character. The habits of feeling, action, and judgment that comprise good character depend on personal self-discipline and powerful aspiration to become a good person, all of which must finally be drawn from within.

Still, children exposed primarily to bad examples seldom acquire good character. They tend to develop habits of self-indulgence and disregard for others, and they often become dangerous.

It is difficult to nurture respect for moral ideals in adults who have not learned self-discipline as children. Adult programs that focus on ethical problems are fruitless unless the students take questions of decency seriously. Without a prior disposition to decency, discussion of moral dilemmas cannot forge a second nature better than our impulsive first nature, and it is not likely to change the bad habits of our second nature.

Anyone who has played sports knows it is easier to develop good habits—hitting a baseball or cue ball—if we have not already developed bad ones. Bad habits are hard to break. Likewise, moral education, training, and habituation have the best chance when they begin early in life, preferably in a setting that emphasizes love and inspires trust. Although the family may be the best setting, an effective sense of kinship, mutual responsibility, nurture, and support can be built into whole communities, as in ancient Greece, in some Israeli kibbutzim, and in some neighborhoods, schools, and churches.

The idea that acquiring good character is comparable to acquiring a skill is not new. Aristotle observed that "people's characters take their bias from the steady directions of their activities. . . . It is these persistent activities in certain directions that make them what they are."[4] J. O. Urmson explains:

> Paradoxical though it may sound, one learns to play the
> piano by playing the piano, and to ride a bicycle by riding

one. Before one has acquired the art or skill one acts in accordance with the instructions of a teacher, who tells us what to do, and one does it with effort. Gradually by practice and repetition it becomes effortless and second nature. In the same way, one is trained as a child (if lucky in one's parents and teachers) to become truthful, generous, fair, and the like. . . . If properly trained one comes to enjoy doing things the right way, to want to do things the right way, and to be distressed by doing things wrongly.[5]

A wholesome upbringing does not, however, lead inevitably to character excellence. But without training and habituation in youth, change for the better is difficult. As the philosopher Immanuel Kant observed, "If a man be allowed to follow his own will in his youth, without opposition, a certain lawlessness will cling to him throughout his life."[6]

Learning—and living up to—high standards is not easy, any more than learning to play the piano is easy. The philosopher John Stuart Mill criticized teaching the young *only* what can be made pleasurable. When the young are not required "to learn anything *but* what has been made easy and interesting, one of the chief objects of education is sacrificed." This system of teaching, he added, was "training up a race of men who will be incapable of doing anything which is disagreeable to them."[7] Learning in youth to control our impulses often is disagreeable, but character education does not otherwise succeed.

Character *can* be reformed later in life. Even mature adults do change habits of alcohol and food consumption, for example. Still, one suspects that they must have achieved some self-control beforehand.

The indispensability of moral habituation to moral excellence as second nature is disclosed in the very idea of character. The philosopher Alasdair MacIntyre writes that a person's character *is* "his set of dispositions to behave systematically in one way rather than another, to lead one particular kind of life."[8] Character excellence, Urmson adds, is the set disposition "to do what reason determines is the best course of action"[9] rather than to allow unconsidered desires and feelings to hold sway. It is made up of habits of feeling and acting in the right way, at the right time, toward the right people, and for the right reasons. Thus, the person of good character will not be inordinately angry about someone's cutting him off in a traffic jam but will be infuriated by the sale of illicit drugs to children.

Such habits are acquired by initiation and instruction from

others—in the telling of stories; the explanation of decent behavior; the introduction to heroes, heroines, and villains; the
exposure to the meaning of fundamental ideals, and the discussion of questions.

This is true not only for children but also for adults and thus
for police. Listening and talking—and frequently reading and
writing—can be basic instruments of moral and intellectual maturation. Political scientist William Ker Muir, Jr., observes in *Police:
Streetcorner Politicians* that grasping "the nature of human suffering" and achieving moral strength "depends in part on developing
an enjoyment of talk."[10] This enjoyment draws us into closer
association and gives us a chance to learn from each other—and to
discern how to meet the moral demands of our work better than
we can in isolation. Great teachers throughout history have emphasized the place of dialogue in education. Socrates told his
fellow citizens that discussing excellence every day is the most
beneficial of all activities.

Habits of virtue are acquired by observation and imitation of
others, by rejection of behavior that falls short, and above all by
practice over time at behaving well.

Character and Police

Obviously, all police and law enforcement agencies want to recruit
candidates of good character and to encourage the best in them,
but how should good character be understood?

The Bad Character. Imagine an officer who comes upon an undetected burglary and can steal goods and blame the burglar, even
if the burglar later denies stealing those goods. A person of bad
character will seek opportunities to profit by victimizing others.
Other people exist for him only to be used for his own advantage.
Whatever he may have been taught about right and wrong has
nothing to do with the conduct of his life. He feels no shame in
abusing his authority. The so-called meat eaters are dangerous to
life and property, they are often shrewd, and they are invariably
rapacious and without conscience. Such persons must simply be
weeded out by background investigations, by observant academy
instructors, by careful field training officers, and so on.

In 1980, Miami, Florida, adopted a policy requiring that 200
new police be recruited immediately, with 80 percent to be minority residents of Miami. Many of the recruits were utterly unsuited
to be police, as background investigations and the warnings of

academy instructors confirmed at the time. Sloppy field training, inadequate supervision, and an ineffective Internal Affairs Division permitted them to behave with contempt for the law. By 1988, more than a third of them had been fired. Twelve members of a group known as the River Cops had been convicted of crimes ranging from drug trafficking to murder. Many of these recruits became police in order to profit from illegal activity with drugs.[11]

The Uncontrolled. A person who is uncontrolled in some aspects of his character may behave like a person of bad character, if his passion for gain overrides his regard for the law. A person who is weak willed and vulnerable to childish temptations may be teachable but does not belong in a position of public trust. Such "grass eaters" cannot trust themselves under pressure from peers or in circumstances of illicit opportunity and may fall into progressively worse behavior. They can be "reached"; they "have a price."

Some of the "Buddy Boys" of the 77th Precinct of the New York Police Department in Brooklyn served with honor for years. When they saw drug dealers making huge profits and flouting the law, however, they began to bust drug dealers in order to steal their money, and they finally stole and dealt drugs themselves. Any habits of decency they had formed succumbed to the temptations of revenge against street dealers and of easy money, as they rationalized their conduct by the timeworn excuse that "others do it."[12]

The Self-Controlled. Persons with greater self-discipline may report a crime, protect the remaining property, and so on, but resent the higher standard of conduct to which they are held. They may be gnawed by feelings that they could have profited and that others are getting away with illegality and enjoying more material goods. Such officers may feel a persistent tension between duty and desire and become desperately unhappy because acquisitiveness draws them even as they do what they *should*. A department should provide support and leadership to foster admirable behavior in the face of temptation and discouragement.

The Excellent. Finally, there are persons of excellent character, who have acquired habits of trustworthiness that have become integral to their lives. They respect and even love honesty, which has become second nature. Such persons behave in the same way as the self-controlled or self-disciplined person in that they do their duty, but they enjoy peace of mind in knowing who they are and what they stand for. Such persons can be said to be truly incorruptible, with no temptation to steal because money is "only green paper." Persons of such character are fit to bear the trust of public office in law enforcement.

In different aspects of their character, individuals reveal themselves to be of more than one of the four types described above. A person may be self-controlled in matters of money, for example, but uncontrolled in drinking. And character in general may range along a continuum from those who are remorseless; to those who cannot resist temptation but are ashamed of it; to the self-controlled, who find little fulfillment and who may be influenced more by fear of detection or sanctions than by duty, regard for others, or honor; and finally to those with an excellence of character, that is deeply fulfilling.[13]

Acquiring Character. The unregulated desires of youngsters for, say, cake can easily overshadow their appreciation for justice and fair play in its distribution. When two children are to share a single portion of cake, we may let one divide it and the other choose the first piece. The first child may cut the cake evenly only to avoid losing the lion's share—motivated by advantage rather than fairness—but by such exercises the child learns respect for fair shares.

We try to give children practice in behaving fairly and in acquiring a sense for the feelings of other people. In games and sports, we witness their frustration when they cannot have their way or cannot do what they try to do, and try to help them find more fun in winning with a fair field and no favors than in ruining the game or triumphing by cheating. We help children mature until they enjoy the fulfillment that comes of treating others fairly and find the peace of mind that accompanies a just life.

A police officer's fitness to wear the badge depends on the acquisition of habits of just behavior. A just officer will see that providing special—even if legal—services in return for gratuities takes time and unjustly deprives other members of the public of the attention they deserve. Officers who respect justice will have nothing to do with racial prejudices, will not exceed their authority in the exercise of discretion, abuse the powers of their office, falsify reports, or give perjured testimony.

None of these considerations is more important than the use of force. William Ker Muir argues that good police officers not only understand human suffering but also resolve the tension between respect for justice and the use of coercion to achieve it.[14] Respect for justice holds them back from using threats when reasoned persuasion will suffice, from force when threats will suffice, and from greater force when lesser force will suffice. Habits of restraint differ, however, from excessive caution, timidity, and irresoluteness.

There is fulfillment in acting with fairness toward others and peace of mind in knowing one has neither exceeded one's authority nor been more coercive than a situation demanded. The use of force is never as satisfying to a person of excellent character as a resolution by persuasion and reason, and a person in whom justice has become second nature reflects this in his behavior.

We admire individuals who resist a strong temptation to strike in vengeance or to deceive for personal gain. But as in the case of honesty, our highest esteem goes to the person who is above such temptation, for whom justice has become second nature.

Another crucial aspect of character formation is associated with temperance. Intemperate people pursue pleasure inordinately—whether through sex, alcohol, food, or drugs. Because pleasure is by definition enjoyable, temperance is self-control in spite of the allure. Temperate persons are not indifferent to pleasure, nor do they reject recreation, relaxation, and amusements, but they choose pleasures that contribute to well-being.

Self-control is also an essential part of courage and fortitude, at least *in extremis*. Courageous officers facing life-threatening situations hardly take pleasure in them, but will not run away and leave a partner or an innocent bystander exposed. They find fulfillment in not allowing fear to dictate their behavior. Shakespeare's insight—the coward dies a thousand deaths, but the brave man only one—holds.

Courage is not only physical, of course. Police officers may know that a partner is corrupt or that some of their superiors are "on the pad," or that fellow officers brutalize suspects. Decent officers may fear the contempt of their colleagues if they refuse to participate or blow the whistle.

Courageous persons will not tolerate such abuses even if they have to blow the whistle covertly rather than openly. To inform on a partner one likes and may admire in other respects and to be rejected and isolated by peers are not enjoyable. No one wants to be thought a "rat" rather than a "stand-up guy," even by colleagues so corrupt that by stand-up guy they mean a crooked cop.

A colleague who *deserves* to be a friend, however, would not compromise a partner. The betrayal of office is an affront to honesty and justice as well as to friendship. Courage here means

11

fearing the right thing—dishonorable conduct—more than contemptible forms of peer pressure.

Balanced Perception. Two kinds of wholeness are related to excellent character. The first consists of a balanced perception of how to make the best of circumstances. On a domestic violence call, police officers must be courageous in ending the violence, just in their treatment of the combatants, temperate in their use of force, compassionate to the victims, respectful of the limits to discretion, honest, timely, and properly equipped and with sufficient backup. But they also need a sense of how all these factors are related. When they conflict, sound judgment of their relative importance is needed.

In a given case, compassion may give a victim comfort that falsely minimizes the danger of future beatings. The unvarnished truth may cause panic. Complete honesty may suggest that the more abusive party has no need to fear the law. And so on. Judgment and a sense of proportion about what the situation calls for may be called *wisdom* in the practical affairs of life.

Integrity. The second kind of wholeness related to good character is integrity. Excellent qualities of character must become integral, not just to certain parts of our lives, but to our entire lives, both public and private. Integrity means wholeness, being one thing through and through, much as homogenization is to milk. Persons of integrity by definition have made certain kinds of excellence integral to all of their lives.

A person of integrity is the same person in public and in private. Accordingly, integrity as an ideal flies squarely against the now-popular idea that we live public lives on one plane and personal lives on another, and that these are essentially separate and subject to different principles of conduct.

Every human life is the life of a person; for this reason, all life is personal life. Personal life has both public and private dimensions, but these dimensions are parts of a single person. Don L. Kooken, who served as captain of the Indiana State Police and chairman of the department of Police Administration at Indiana University, has stressed this point: "Habits that are formed in the home and among working associates are reflected in a policeman's relations with the public. . . . One cannot be a gentleman in public and a cad in private."[15]

But integrity is not achieved just by being *any* one thing

through and through. A person can, after all, be a cad both in public and private. In urban ghettos and elsewhere there are sociopaths, drug dealers, crack addicts, and terrorists who are one thing through and through, the same in public and private, but who are not people of integrity.

The Danish theologian Soren Kierkegaard observed that "purity of heart is to will one thing." Though this is true in important ways, we would not say that a crack addict who wills one thing— his or her next hit of crack—is a person with purity of heart. What then is the wholeness that gives a person integrity?

No one achieves the full measure of integrity whose life falls under the dominion of gluttony, lust, sloth, pride, greed, anger, or envy, to cite a justly famous catalog of self-destroying sins. Moral wholeness cannot be achieved by anyone who commits murder, adultery, rape, theft, or perjury, or who is foul-mouthed, or whose thoughts and feelings are covetous, rancorous, or hateful. Along the same lines, we would not call morally whole a person who is foolish, or unjust, reckless or cowardly, or who is without any sense of charity or has no faith in anything or anybody.

All such flaws are affronts to character excellence as a whole, and therefore to integrity. No one is without fault in every respect, but all the same, the aspiration to achieve integrity as fully as we can is the highest calling of a life well-lived.

A simple test tells us how much integrity matters to us. In *The Republic*, Plato tells the story of the magical ring of Gyges, which can make whoever wears it invisible. The question is, How would you behave differently if you could make yourself invisible? When people do wrong they try to make themselves as invisible as they can; they are motivated more by fear of detection than by integrity. Only a person who is good enough to care about behaving rightly, and not just about being caught, can become better.

The Morally Important and the Morally Problematic

What is morally important must be learned in order to understand what is morally problematic, whether in the moral instruction of children or the professional education and training of police or people in other walks of life. A person who lacks concern for others cannot appreciate moral questions about when deception is morally obligatory, right, or excusable. A person who has no sense of justice cannot understand disagreements about merit and affirmative action in personnel policies. A person who has no ideals

13

cannot understand why they must not be betrayed through cowardice or laxity, or how ideals can conflict with one another.

Police executives, academy instructors, senior officers, and others in law enforcement can, of course, teach how to think through moral questions. We can show how to take stock, make a considered judgment, and respond effectively. We can teach that people deserve to be treated as valuable in themselves, just because they are people, and not merely as instruments. We can teach that we do what is right because it is right and not out of fear of detection or punishment. We can describe the way a fair-minded person deliberates about his behavior, that he is likely to ask, "What if everyone behaved as I propose to behave—would that be possible or would it be self-defeating?"

If a person considers lying for profit, and asks whether everyone could do so, he sees that if everyone lied for personal advantage, then no one would trust anyone else where personal interests were involved, and no one could lie successfully. He can see that his own lie can be effective only if others do not lie, so if he lies he becomes a moral parasite who treats himself as having privileges others do not exercise. No fair-minded person is willing to treat himself with such favoritism. We can explain, as well, that such moral reasons are the most important reasons in deciding what to do.

Yet in teaching how to plan and implement responses to situations, we are, above all, refining intelligence. Powerful intelligence without good character is notoriously dangerous; because it spurns regard for others and for morality, it may be acquired by the successful contract killer, the shrewd drug dealer, or the corrupt public official.

Since the ideal is a combination of wisdom with good character, our instruction must be established by practice. Practice at behaving rightly establishes skillfulness, and with skill comes greater enjoyment; thus does our potential for good character—that element of the dove that is woven into our frame—come into the combination. Such experience at behaving well cannot be replaced by less intimate methods of instruction, and certainly not by holier-than-thou moralizing that implies a person of excellent character must shun every enjoyment of life. Practice and encouragement are necessary to moral wisdom because the proof of the quality of moral life is in living it.

The mission of policing can safely be entrusted only to those who grasp what is morally important and who respect integrity. Without this kind of personal character in police, no set of codes or rules or laws can safeguard that mission from the ravages of police misconduct. No one need choose to be a police officer or to bear the public trust; but those who do so—no matter how naively and no matter how misguided their original expectations—must acquire the excellence of character necessary to live up to it.

2
The Mission of Police

Pride grows in the human heart like lard on a pig.

ALEKSANDR SOLZHENITSYN[1]

The accumulation of all powers legislative, executive and judiciary, in the same hands, whether of one, a few, or many, and whether hereditary, self-appointed, or elective, may justly be pronounced the very definition of tyranny.

JAMES MADISON[2]

The mission of police in the United States, as in the other democracies, is to play a rightful part in the nation's "experiment in ordered liberty."

The Experiment in Ordered Liberty

The United States was established as a constitutional republic in which no person or group could rise to absolute power. Our experiment in government answerable to the public tests whether a country can maintain order *and* protect liberty. Powers are separated among executive, legislative, and judicial branches, each intended to serve as a check and a balance on the others and to be impervious to economic dominion by the private sector, just as the private sector is safeguarded from tyranny of government. Powers are balanced so that no person or agency can function without restraint.

When a country cannot provide order, its people are victimized by factions—whether in the rebellion in Massachusetts in 1786 (which led George Washington to conclude that America was on the verge of anarchy) or in the drug wars in the streets of our cities two centuries later. Yet when order is brought by the destruction of liberty, the people are victimized by tyrants.

Order with liberty cannot succeed if the government or the governed indulge themselves as they wish. Our ordered liberty is an experiment in the rule of laws that are impartial and that apply to governors and governed alike. James Madison, the father of our Constitution, stressed the burden this places on us:

> In framing a government which is to be administered by men over men, the great difficulty lies in this: you must first enable the government to control the governed; and in the next place oblige it to control itself.[3]

Since the rule of law requires the keeping of peace, America's government is also an experiment in law enforcement and peace-keeping. It is an experiment in whether policing can promote security and serve liberty for the sake of what Madison identified as the ultimate purpose of government:

> Justice is the end of government. It is the end of civil society. It has ever been and ever will be pursued until it be obtained, or until liberty be lost in the pursuit.[4]

The drafters of the Constitution were actively concerned about immoderation by both government and individuals. Alexander Hamilton cautioned in 1781 that government must have "a proper degree of authority to make and execute the laws with vigour," for "too little leads to anarchy."[5] Too much, he believed, leads to tyranny. In 1787, Benjamin Rush was even more direct about the dangers of making government too weak to protect citizens from each other:

> In our opposition to monarchy, we forgot that the temple of tyranny has two doors. We bolted one of them by proper restraints; but we left the other open by neglecting to guard against the effects of our own ignorance and licentiousness.[6]

The tension between order and liberty persists wherever men and women care about justice. Though a country dedicated to justice may tilt one way or the other, the experiment depends on the animating conviction, as constitutional scholar Robert Goldwin explains, that while people are not angels, they are still "good enough to govern themselves."[7]

The founders knew that the system they framed was imperfect, that even good people are motivated by self-interest, and that all of us make grievous mistakes. No nation can hope to become perfect, without any abuses of freedom. Efforts to prevent every social evil have often led to worse excesses—including religious and political persecution.[8]

Justice in a society rests on restraint, by government and by the citizenry. Laws provide both a guide and a motive for such restraint for the good of everyone.

Disorder and Injustice

When I describe these American traditions to police, they point to the injustices suffered by many citizens:

> It is not just when perpetrators go free to repeat their crimes, or when victims know that their assailants walk the streets with impunity. Our country cannot be complacent when the bare minimum of civilized order is destroyed in ghettos by drug dealers and street criminals, and when ghetto children are deprived of all opportunity for healthy growth and worthwhile aspiration. It is not just when a known perpetrator in custody possesses information essential to saving the life or sanity of an innocent victim and will not divulge it in interrogation that gives undue priority to the perpetrator's civil rights.

They are right, of course. Immoderation, license, and violence in America are pressing, perhaps now more than ever before. If citizens' rights are largely secure from governmental excesses, they are not safe from individual and group excesses. Although interests and ambitions inevitably conflict among human beings, diversity in America has gone far beyond the legitimate boundaries of pluralism.

Pluralism means the range of views held by reasonable people of good will who restrain self-interest. Today our diversity includes individuals and groups with no regard for civility, decency, and legality. The enforcement of law is a crushing problem in the face of deep divisions over what the laws should be and over the claim of law to our respect. When a country's most privileged citizens break the law—as in public corruption and white collar crime—and crime rates in urban areas put the entire public at risk, the situation is very serious.

Street crime has become mindlessly vicious in our time:

> The most disturbing aspect of the growth in "street crime" is the turn toward viciousness, as well as violence, on the part of many young criminals. A lawyer who was a public defender noted for her devotion to her clients' interests, as well as her legal ability, speaks of "a terrifying generation of kids" that emerged during the late 1960s and early 1970s. When she began practicing, she told me, adolescents and young men charged with robbery had, at worst, pushed or shoved

a pedestrian or shopkeeper to steal money or merchandise; members of the new generation kill, maim, and injure without reason or remorse.[9]

Police, along with many ghetto residents, are exposed to this violence every day. Describing the Henry Horner Homes on Dameon Street in Chicago, Adam Walinsky wrote:

> Dominant authority is exercised by the gangs: organized groups, led by men of thirty or forty, organizing and recruiting down to the age of eight. . . . The gangs engage in regular and constant warfare for control of the drug and vice trades . . . armed with pistols, rifles, automatic weapons, and occasional grenades. . . . Children dodge machine gun crossfire as they leave school. . . . Women and children are mugged by youths of all ages. . . . Eight-year olds, serving as drug salesmen, have been shot in the foot to encourage greater effort. . . . Children grow as in the midst of a war. . . . The children almost routinely witness friends and acquaintances shot and bleeding to death in the street. . . . The neighborhood has no place to buy food. . . . Move out? This is not the worst housing project in Chicago. Even if there is room in another, the Housing Authority assigns better apartments only when bribed. . . . In Detroit, the police do not keep count of shot children; the newspapers counted 270 last year.[10]

These citizens live and die deprived of the liberty and justice the Constitution is intended to secure for them. They live, in Chesterton's words, "in an armed camp . . . a chaotic world" in which "criminals, the children of chaos," visit tyrannical terror upon them every day.

The *Wall Street Journal* has noted the rise of vigilantism in America in the burning down of crack houses in Detroit, Miami, and the South Bronx, and in the lethal beatings of muggers:

> Vigilantes return . . . whenever citizens come to believe that the law enforcement agencies don't work. Right now, the vigilantes are back, especially in this country's most beleaguered, drug-infested central city neighborhoods. . . . The police fail because the lawyers won't let them succeed. The lawyers prevail because liberal jurists, cheered on by columnists and editorial writers intent on expanding their notions of civil rights, have erected a vast legal jungle gym of evidentiary procedures, subjected police conduct to extensive second-guessing, and eliminated nearly all discretion from the cop on the beat—for example, by outlawing vagrancy laws. . . . The system of criminal justice . . . is failing the people who need it most.[11]

Although police can still exercise discretion on the beat, the problems of the criminal justice system are real. Many officers—and prosecutors—consider specific laws self-defeating. When police officers arrest a person who throws his narcotics to the ground, the officers may momentarily lose sight of the package. But if they testify in court that they did so, the case is likely to be dismissed. Some officers perjure themselves rather than lose the case. If an officer admits he lost sight of the drugs, some police, attorneys, and judges infer that his testimony has been bought by the dealers.

Lawmakers sometimes present police with unenforceable laws or fail to provide the funds necessary for enforcement. Courts issue rulings that impose unreasonable standards of proof, undermining public respect for law. Greater wisdom in legislators and judges will be required to square the balance between order and liberty, together with more communication to the public by police organizations, as in the growing opposition to easy purchase of cheap handguns. Convincing testimony by the public about the erosion of its safety must be joined with widespread participation in the electoral process.

Since inefficiency cannot be entirely avoided, however, the system will remain imperfect. Safeguarding rights of due process interferes with efforts to detect criminal activity, apprehend perpetrators, and secure convictions. The separation of powers does not place a premium on expediency. Tyranny does—and the results are terrifying.

Against Tyranny

The Marxist Sandinista government of Nicaragua fails to provide any economic security—or hope—to its people. Students carry their desks to and from school to prevent their being stolen; school toilets are stolen. Robbers armed with AK47 rifles prowl neighborhoods stealing everything from manhole covers to clothes hung out to dry. Neighbors kidnap each other's dogs for ransom.[12] Yet so tyrannical is the government that at a ceremony "opening the sugar harvest Agrarian Reform Minister Jaime Wheelock threatened a gathering of sugar workers. . . , 'If anyone raises a strike banner here, we will cut off his hands.'"[13]

In Iran, under the Ayatollah Khomeini, mass executions and torture are routine. Iranian government documents confirm approximately 12,000 executions in the second half of 1988. Women are executed, or beaten until the skin falls off their feet, raped by

police, and disfigured with acid—and their children are slaugh-
tered—for appearing in public with their faces uncovered. Public
officials extort bribes for release from prison: $125 for the crime of
an exposed lock of hair; $900 for wearing fingernail polish.[14]

This remorseless arrogance of power is not new, though tyrants of our time may exercise greater dominion by their use of
modern bureaucracies and technologies. Such perpetrators of evil
seem capable of immense self-deception, persuading themselves
that whatever they do is justified by circumstances.

On the strength of his experience under tyranny, Aleksandr
Solzhenitsyn maintains that "to do evil a human being must first of
all believe that what he's doing is good."[15] William Parker said
something similar when he became chief of police of Los Angeles
in 1950:

> As practicing policemen we are familiar with the fact that the
> average criminal does not believe that he is doing wrong. As
> he views the situation, he is doing right. However faulty his
> premises, however weak his logic, and however transitory
> his beliefs, he acts in accord with his own concepts.[16]

Although these statements omit that right and wrong are
simply of no consequence for some people, they do highlight
human capacities for self-deception and self-aggrandizement, and
for judging oneself favorably. Awareness of these tendencies lies at
the base of America's doctrine of separation of powers. When self-
righteousness or remorselessness joins with unrestrained power,
injustice and terror become inevitable. By restraining the power
that resides in any individual or group, the worst horrors may be
avoided.

Many tyrants, as in the post-czarist Soviet Union, celebrate
the unrestrained exercise of power. Solzhenitsyn explains,

> The supreme accuser—in other words, the Prosecutor Gen-
> eral—informs us that the All-Russian Central Executive
> Committee. . . "pardons and *punishes*, at its own discretion
> *without any limitation whatever.*" For example, a six-month
> sentence was changed to ten years. . . . All of this, Krylenko
> explains, "shows the superiority of our system over the false
> theory of the separation of powers. . . . It is very good that
> the legislative and executive power are not divided by a thick
> wall as they are in the West. All problems *can be decided
> quickly.*"[17]

Those who want to unite the powers of government believe that its
purpose is to perpetuate itself or extend its power. This is why the
Soviet secret police—the Cheka—was empowered to do anything

to preserve the dictatorship (ostensibly, in the interest of the public) and why the Communist party, led by Lenin, claimed that its mistreatment of the people was necessary for the revolution. The viciousness of this dogma continues to be seen today in the Soviet Union as dissidents are imprisoned, freedoms of religion and press denied, and due process mocked in show trials. The United States was established in opposition to such arbitrary deprivation of life and liberty.

Still, we may be tempted by expediency in order to "decide things quickly," without a lot of technicalities and restraints. Confronted with merciless criminals who savage innocent victims, we may feel justified in taking illegal shortcuts.

But expediency pushes us onto dangerous ground. Expediency of the worst kind insists, "the end justifies the means" and "might makes right." In a setting such as the Soviet Union, the courts are not concerned for justice, law, extenuating circumstances, or guilt or innocence. They proceed "on the basis of considerations of expediency," as Solzhenitsyn explains. "That was the way it was in those years: people lived and breathed and then suddenly found out that their existence was inexpedient. And it must also be kept in mind that it was not what he had done that constituted the defendant's burden, but what he *might* do if he were not shot now. 'We protect ourselves not only against the past but also against the future.' "[18]

This is how unrestrained power works. Expediency favors punishing the innocent to ensure that the guilty do not go free; it presumes the guilt of the accused, and it accuses anyone whose ideas or behavior are inconvenient to the tyrant. It imposes punishments that do not fit the crime. But punishing the innocent does *not* ensure that the guilty will also fall into the net. The presumption of guilt is therefore not only unjust but also impractical.

In fact, the presumption of guilt and the power to punish without due process may not even be significant deterrents to some kinds of crimes. Sir Leon Radzinowicz, director of Oxford University's Institute of Criminology, reports that "no national characteristic, no political regime, no system of law, police, justice, punishment, treatment, or even terror has rendered a country exempt from crime."[19] This point is confirmed by figures released in August 1988 by Igor Karpets, director of the All-Union Scientific Research Institute of Soviet Legislation. Karpets describes a high incidence of embezzlement in the Soviet Union in the 1960s and 1970s "when many people confused their own pockets with those of the state." In 1987, 95,000 were convicted of hooliganism, and nearly 5,000 were convicted of premeditated murder for the first half of that year.[20]

In America, we have chosen the presumption of innocence out of regard for justice and for the importance of the individual. For all its deficiencies, our system exhibits greater respect for the dignity of humanity than any other ever devised. Within it, police are charged to respect the lawful liberty of the people while applying authority, good judgment, and power to see that order and peace do not collapse under individual or group excesses. The role of police in the experiment in ordered liberty must be respected to grasp the specifics of their mission.

Mission

Some authorities, politicians, and citizens' groups say that the primary work of police is crime prevention. Others emphasize peacekeeping and maintenance of order. Some stress the enforcement of the law and the apprehension of perpetrators; others stress social services. Some scholars are especially interested in police work with juveniles, while other scholars and practitioners claim this work should be done by separate agencies. Social movements, as during Prohibition, cast the police as enforcers of morals, and legislation can have the same effect. And some people expect the police to combat every social ill.

The police cannot do everything expected of them by everyone. In ghettos where social ills are worst and street crime is relentless, the problems require extreme remedies, which go far beyond anything the police can deliver. Citizens who appeal to the police suffer reprisals from the gangs, which are so powerful that enforcement of the law and protection of the public are largely impossible.

Attitudes have changed since the late James Baldwin characterized police in the ghetto as an occupying army. Because of drugs, gangs, and guns, many ghetto citizens want more and better police protection, not less. More crime is intraracial than interracial—simply because of the proximity of potential victims—and the innocent victims of ghetto crimes know it.

The desperation of ghetto residents makes their expectations of the police unrealistic. In the South Bronx, I once accompanied police to a tenement where a woman had been bitten by a Great Dane. Other residents were frightened, and the owner of the dog—which never had any shots for distemper or rabies—wanted

23

it removed. Children skated noisily through the halls on discarded metal food containers. As the police arrived, residents assured each other, "It's all right now, everything will be OK now, the police are here."

Of course, it was not all right. Emergency calls were coming from other areas of the precinct; the victim expected police to transport her to a hospital that was within easy walking distance; and the residents expected the police to substitute for the ASPCA and take the dog away. The two officers explained what they could and could not do, saw that the dog was confined, told the victim how to get to the hospital, and notified the ASPCA to collect the dog as soon as possible. Then they rushed to another call.

Unrealistic expectations of the police are not confined to ghettos. In 1988, citizens of Tampa, Florida, learned that a convicted rapist, who had cut off the arms of a victim, was living among them after being released from prison in another state. In televised proceedings, many citizens became abusive when police explained that they could not violate the man's civil rights and drive him away. "I pay your salary, and you're supposed to protect me," they said. "It's your job."

Most knowledgeable accounts of police mission stress law enforcement, peacekeeping, and delivery of social services. The Police Foundation, for instance, observed in 1972, "The Foundation fully realizes that improved police services must strike a *balance between effective crime fighting and humane efforts to keep the peace.*"[21] David A. Hansen, who served as supervising captain of the Daly City, California, Police Department affirmed this view: "The keeping of the peace and the protection of life and property by those who are police officers—this is the police function."[22] Professor Lee W. Potts rehearsed data confirming this view in actual practice:

> One of the common findings of the volume of data developed on the police in the late 1960s and early 1970s was the falseness of the belief that law enforcement dominates police work. . . . Rather than being primarily a law enforcement officer, the average policeman is primarily a peace officer. His time is spent performing public services such as directing traffic and escorting vehicles or performing social welfare services such as dealing with the mentally deranged, attempted suicides, domestic crisis intervention, and neighborhood disputes.[23]

Potts added that this multiplicity of responsibilities can cause tensions for officers, since law enforcement duties may require "their

24

coercive role to be paramount" while "as peace officers, they most often find their public servant role to be paramount."[24]

As Potts suggests, the mission "To protect and to serve" is not so simple as it may appear when emblazoned on a patrol car. The two functions require common skills, but they require distinct and separate skills as well. Furthermore, law enforcement frequently involves legal and institutional guidelines more rigorous than do police duties in peacekeeping and other social services.

In 1936, August Vollmer, a pioneer of modern American policing, wrote that "the original purpose of police organizations was protection against the occurrence of major crimes and the apprehension of perpetrators of such offenses." Although he believed that this remained the primary duty of the police, he insisted that

> police departments are also called upon to perform every conceivable kind of service. No federal or state law or city ordinance is passed which does not call for the attention of some police organization. Responsibility for sick, injured, and missing persons, for the insane and the feeble-minded, as well as the investigation of suicide cases, is assigned these public agents. At any time of the day or night, citizens may report suspicious persons or circumstances and request action by the police. In times of disaster, strikes, or riots, it is the duty of the police to preserve, if possible, or to restore, peace and order.[25]

In 1978, Charles Silberman described how the diverse functions of the police are interrelated, in terms of work by sociologist Egon Bittner:

> There are common denominators to almost all the situations I have described that make them uniquely a police responsibility. To begin with, the police are called because they are available—twenty-four hours a day, seven days a week. . . . More important, the police are called because of a sense of urgency; what unites the various situations with which police deal is the fact that someone thought emergency help was needed to prevent injury, loss, harm, disorder, or inconvenience. [Egon] Bittner writes that whether a police officer is preventing someone from jumping off a bridge, rescuing people from a burning building, dispersing a crowd that might hamper the firemen, settling a domestic dispute or barroom brawl, breaking up a robbery in progress, or arresting a suspected burglar, the incident involves "something-that-ought-not-to-be-happening-now-and-about-which-someone-had-better-do-something-now". . . . Most important of all, the police are called into urgent situations because they, and

25

only they, are empowered to use force to set matters right. . . . Much of the artistry of police work lies in the ability to handle explosive situations *without* resorting to force. But the fact that the police can use force is uppermost in the minds of those who call on them for help; it also directly affects the way other people behave.[26]

Within this rough consensus about manifold functions are many disagreements about priorities. But police are expected to fulfill their obligations "professionally"—that is, competently and honestly, and with accountability to supervisors for their performance. Disagreements abound about the appropriate levels of autonomy and authority of police administrators, elected officials, and citizen review boards, and of the public itself.

Still, the law enforcement community and scholars of policing agree that the police cannot fulfill their mission without effective communication with the citizenry and without public support. Maintaining the best relations with the public, however, and having a near monopoly on the legitimate use of force make police walk a fine line. Both police and scholars recognize with Bittner, that "no amount of public relations work can entirely abolish the sense that there is something of the dragon in the dragon slayer."[27]

Police often sense that people draw into themselves when they are around. This is, perhaps, why the social life of many police officers centers on the companionship of other officers. They share in the tradition of St. George, because they have the authority to use force, even deadly force, though for most officers the need is rare.

But police must remember that their mission is more complicated than St. George's, and if they work well, they will convey much more to the public than the image of a mere slayer of dragons. Police, after all, work in a chain of command; they abide by laws, departmental policies, and court rulings; they cooperate with internal affairs units; and they make reports. Moreover, they have to enforce laws, prevent crimes, maintain order, deal with the media, use informants responsibly, provide a range of services to those in need, testify in court, and be alert to the safety of their colleagues as well as of the public. Any police officer who conveys an image of being solely a dragon slayer causes needless risk to himself and to everyone around him.

Public Confidence

Some problems *cannot* be solved by sensitive communication. No one can be persuaded by reason to be reasonable—a person must be predisposed to reason even to listen. Even in intellectual debates, passions run so high as to make civility impossible. Discussions about abortion, arms control, federal policy, or constitutional reform are as likely to exacerbate as to relieve differences. We must be realistic to grasp the demands of police work.

The history of war and violence is not simply a history of failed communication. Some wars occur because nations *do* understand each other and know that they cannot be brought into harmony by diplomatic means. This was the case in World War II. In private life and in police work, self-defense and the protection of the innocent sometimes require immediate and sufficient force, both in the enforcement of the law and in dealing with the domestic and neighborhood disputes. The distinction between law enforcement and peacekeeping can never be absolute.

Public trust depends not only on communication but on many kinds of performance by the police, including the use of such powers as are minimally required. Ineffectiveness in protecting, for example, abused wives and children is as likely to erode trust as failure to communicate with sensitivity.

In early 1988 while riding with patrol officers in Atlanta, I asked what had been the best thing to happen to police in the past two years. The reply, interestingly, had nothing to do with salaries, benefits, or other personnel matters. Without hesitation—and with the concern for protection of the public that typifies fine police officers—one responded, "The Domestic Violence Act." He explained that many women abused by husbands or boy friends would not press charges out of fear of reprisals. Domestic violence statutes enable police to become complainants and make arrests when they believe that assault has been committed, without action by the woman.

In such cases, arrest (and possibly prosecution) may be no more effective as a deterrent than separation and counseling, despite research studies that indicate otherwise.[28] But the legislation increases the alternatives to sensitive communication immediately available to the officer and surely safeguards some victims in a way that communication cannot.

Obviously, police civility, freedom from prejudice, realistic patience, and so on are essential to communication and to fulfillment of mission, but critics who fear police use of force above all else have missed an essential point. We allow police to use force because we prefer a disinterested party to have this authority, rather than allow those impassioned by involvement to use force against each other. The use of reasonable force by an authorized official for a legitimate purpose—even if extreme force is required—is not the same as the brutal use of force or as police brutality. Undue reliance on communication when force is needed jeopardizes innocent citizens *and* police officers.

Police necessarily exercise some discretion in their duties. Not only do they decide which available methods are most useful in a given situation; they must also decide which laws to enforce and when. As the President's Commission on Law Enforcement and Administration of Justice observed in 1967, "the police do not have the resources to enforce all criminal provisions equally." Every police officer quickly learns that he cannot enforce every law to the letter and still enjoy public support. People who generally obey the laws resent excessive strictness. Since laws, as well as policies and procedures, are often ambiguous, police officers must often "make [their] own resolution instantly, under stress, and often without advice" in matters that only years of litigation may ultimately resolve.[29]

In 1947, Elijah Adlow, an associate justice of the Boston Municipal Court, wrote, "Police problems are immediate. The policeman . . . must make his decision right now. His judgment is called into play now. His discretion is taxed. He cannot reserve the matter for some future time."[30] Similar discretion is exercised by— and similar ambiguities are set before—police executives.

How important are these duties and their conscientious fulfillment to the "experiment in ordered liberty"? August Vollmer goes too far in saying that "democracy's strongest reliance is the police."[31] Democracy's strongest bulwark is the citizens themselves and their self-governance in a constitutional republic. Vollmer himself observed that "laws never have been an effective substitute for human virtues."[32] He echoed the observation of the ancient Roman statesman Cicero, "Laws without habits are in vain."

The importance of citizens' virtue to a constitutional republic has never been more beautifully captured than by Joseph Story, a founder of the Harvard Law School, who served on the Supreme Court from 1811 until 1845. His *A Familiar Exposition of the Constitution of the United States* (1840), perhaps the greatest book ever written for teaching high school civics, concludes:

> Let the American youth never forget that they possess a noble inheritance, bought by the toils, and sufferings, and blood of their ancestors. . . . It may, nevertheless, perish in an hour, by the folly, or corruption, or negligence of its only keepers, THE PEOPLE. Republics are created by the virtue, public spirit, and intelligence of the citizens. They fall, when

the wise are banished from the public councils, because they dare to be honest, and the profligate are rewarded, because they flatter the people, in order to betray them.[33]

Though the people are the ultimate basis for the experiment, the behavior of government officials—especially those visible as the police—has a profound effect on public attitudes. The citizens are unlikely to escape cynicism if government officials routinely show bad judgment, prejudice, or greed. As Charles Silberman puts the matter,

> If street crime threatens the social fabric of American life, governmental crime destroys the political fabric by undermining the trust and belief in the legitimacy of government on which our entire political system is based. "Our government is the potent, the omnipresent teacher," Justice Louis D. Brandeis wrote. "For good or ill, it teaches the whole people by its example. Crime is contagious. If the government becomes a lawbreaker, it breeds contempt for the laws; it invites every man to become a law unto himself; it invites anarchy."[34]

Honorable, competent, fair performance by police, however, is no guarantee of public confidence. Since current images of police are drawn largely from television programs bearing little resemblance to reality, public expectations are bound to be unrealistic. Furthermore, some people are convinced that all public officials are everywhere corrupt, cowardly, ambitious, or interested only in political survival.

A person or an institution should not be preoccupied with public image. Inordinate concern for it can lead to indifference about how well we are *actually* doing. Public opinion may be uninformed and irrational and may be manipulated by demagogues.

The sportswriter Grantland Rice named Knute Rockne's Notre Dame running backs after the Four Horsemen of the Apocalypse, and other sportswriters picked this up. Fearing his running backs might grow overconfident, Rockne put in a scrub offensive line. When his backs were stopped cold by the defense, Rockne shouted, "Show 'em your press clippings, boys, show 'em your press clippings!"

Wise leaders will not assess their performance simply by media coverage. They should ask themselves, "If my critics knew everything I know—all the facts and relevant evidence, some of which are confidential—would they believe that a conscientious public servant could do the things I am doing?" If the answer is yes, then they have good reason to continue their course of action. If not, then they should conduct a serious review.

Policing has become more professional since the 1930s, when Vollmer said, "Law enforcement agencies are usually held in contempt and law enforcement is [taken as] one of our national jokes."[35] But a constitutional republic must be able to survive adverse public opinion toward government in general and police in particular. If our nation were too frail to survive governmental malfeasance or unjustified public mistrust of government, it would have collapsed already. Although many citizens have realistic expectations of police, police and other government officials are obliged to conduct themselves so as to give no reason for public mistrust. By example, they teach respect for law, liberty, peace, and justice. Every day, they must face the plight of victims, the anguish of the helpless, the inevitability of unsolved crimes, the ambiguity of the laws, the limits of what reason and persuasion can accomplish, the necessity of using coercion and force, and danger, including possible death—and they must do so in a manner that inspires public confidence. They must stand in harm's way for people who by national tradition distrust authority and power.

This is a challenge that, like most ideals, can only be approximated in practice. Consider the kind of person it takes to live up to it. As Leonard V. Harrison observed in his 1934 study, *Police Administration in Boston,*

> There are few vocations which, if adequately performed, require so much of a man—physical courage, tact, disciplined temper, good judgment, alertness of observation, and specialized knowledge of law and procedure. . . . Not only physical courage but strong moral fiber is required of the policeman. He is at war with thieves, fences, and sharpers of every sort who will stop at nothing to avoid interference by the police. These underworld characters are skilled in every form of trickery and deception needed to compromise a weak policeman. . . . But physical courage and moral stamina are not enough. A policeman may be courageous in the face of danger, or have strong defenses against corrupting influence, and yet be too indolent or too ignorant to perform many kinds of work which make no demands on his admirable qualities.[36]

Codes of Ethics and Personal Character

Harrison has described the good police officer as a professional, a person of fine character and specially trained abilities. The spirit of such professionalism is captured in the Law Enforcement Code of Ethics, published by the International Association of Chiefs of Police.

LAW ENFORCEMENT CODE OF ETHICS

As a Law Enforcement Officer, my fundamental duty is to serve mankind; to safeguard lives and property; to protect the innocent against deception, the weak against oppression or intimidation, and the peaceful against violence or disorder; and to respect the Constitutional rights of all men to liberty, equality, and justice.

I will keep my private life unsullied as an example to all; maintain courageous calm in the face of danger, scorn, ridicule; develop self-restraint; and be constantly mindful of the welfare of others. Honest in thought and deed in both my personal and official life, I will be exemplary in obeying the laws of the land and the regulations of my department. Whatever I see or hear of a confidential nature or that is confided to me in my official capacity will be kept ever secret unless revelation is necessary in the performance of my duty.

I will never act officiously or permit personal feelings, prejudices, animosities, or friendships to influence my decisions. With no compromise for crime and with relentless prosecution of criminals, I will enforce the law courteously and appropriately without fear or favor, malice or ill-will, never employing unnecessary force or violence and never accepting gratuities.

I recognize the badge of my office as a symbol of public faith, and I accept it as a public trust to be held so long as I am true to the ethics of the police service. I will constantly strive to achieve these objectives and ideals, dedicating myself before God to my chosen profession . . . law enforcement.[37]

Some police object to portions of this code as too demanding or too vague. They point to the great difficulty—or impossibility—of safeguarding lives and protecting the innocent from deception and the weak from intimidation *and* of simultaneously acting within the laws in respecting everyone's right to privacy and liberty. They add that in extreme danger, they are not calm, even though they may act with courage. Some police ask whether an "unsullied" private life means that they should not live with a lover. Some insist that they cannot prevent feelings from influencing their decisions, that they have to compromise on crime in order to maintain informants, and that acceptance of small gratuities is customary.

The code expresses ideals whose demands must be weighed

with the wisdom of experience and tested judgment. Police should do all that they can to safeguard the public within the limits of their authority. They should try to form habits of self-control in dangerous situations that reduce the likelihood of panic even if they do not produce calmness. Police can ask whether their private lives impair their performance in office, compromise their authority, or force them to live a lie. If others knew, would they be ashamed, and would their colleagues question their decency? Not all feelings need be excised. Decisions ought to be influenced by the feelings of a person of good character, by habits of justice, courage, compassion, and so on. And the proper uses of informants and the acceptability of gratuities should be thoroughly treated by departmental policies.

So understood, the code is trustworthy as a general guideline, conveying the spirit of fidelity to the public trust, although no code can take the place of good character and wisdom. At the request of police commissioners, I tried in 1987 to capture this spirit in a concise way that would provide guidance both to newcomers and to experienced patrol and command personnel:

> When a citizen pins on a police badge, he *voluntarily* agrees to bear the public trust. He is entrusted to protect the safety and the rights of his fellow members of society.
>
> To provide these protections, the officer is given special authority and powers. He has the authority to investigate other people, to abridge their normal liberties, and to use force when necessary.
>
> There are two basic limits to the rightful use of his authority and powers by the police officer. First, it is wrong for the officer to use his office for personal profit or gain, wrong for him to accept any favor that places his own advantage above the welfare of the public. Second, it is wrong for the officer to violate the Constitution or the laws in the performance of his work.
>
> Some officers are offered favors by citizens who hope for preferential treatment at a later time. Those who accept such favors dishonor themselves and the badge. Likewise, officers are confronted with monstrous crimes and rightly want to get perpetrators off the streets. But they have no right to behave illegally to accomplish this purpose. The police officer must abide by the laws guaranteeing citizen rights to the fullest extent of his training and understanding of them.
>
> Beyond these requirements, the officer must bring personal qualities to his work that the badge cannot provide for him. The most important qualities are common sense and

common decency. He should never expose himself needlessly to danger, he should maintain his physical fitness and his skillfulness in the use of the tools of his work, and he should pay attention to the needs of the people he serves.

Living up to the public trust is demanding work. It can involve disappointment, weariness, and stress. These are the facts of life in police work. But this is the work each police officer has chosen for himself.

The (City) Police Department is obligated to provide the best possible training and support for its officers throughout their careers. When the officer pins on the badge, he becomes a public servant, but he also becomes a member of the Department.

Although persons in official life find guidelines useful, codes of ethics do not motivate people to behave well. They assist only people who already want to do so. Public office holders, such as police, need genuinely to want to serve the public and to become good at their work. They cannot eliminate self-interest from their lives, nor can they be infallible. But they must be of reasonably good character, and they must know their mission and be dedicated to it.

Both individual character and codes of ethics must be sustained by departmental policies and by the conduct of command personnel. Even when men and women are virtuous, even when they behave with high standards of conscience, they benefit from responsible supervision and instruction designed to help them become better. They deserve superiors and peers who assess their performance with care and make departmental expectations clear. If the leadership and the experienced personnel do not show that they take ethics violations seriously, their codes will be treated as worthless platitudes.

3
The Public Trust and Probity

Friends and Fellow Citizens,

The period for a new election of a citizen to administer the executive government of the United States being not far distant . . . your thoughts must be employed in designating the person who is to be clothed with that important trust. . . . In the discharge of this trust, I will only say that I have, with good intentions, contributed towards the organization of the government the very best exertions of which a very fallible judgment was capable.

GEORGE WASHINGTON[1]

In his Farewell Address to the People of the United States in September 1796, George Washington emphasized that a public office is a public trust. He recognized that no person is expected to be infallible; indeed, to suppose that anyone *can* be infallible in the conduct of public or private life is arrogant and dangerous. The public trust, rather, calls for "good intentions" and the "very best exertions."

Public servants must *intend* and *resolve* to put the public good above private advantage for anyone—self, family, friends, political allies, factions, or interest groups. They are obliged to identify the public good and to serve it; this is the sort of "exertion" that public office demands. John Adams wrote that such devotion to the well-being of the public interest "must be Superior to all private Passions. Men must . . . be happy to sacrifice their private Friendships and dearest Connections, when they stand in Competition with the Rights of Society."[2]

On this account, public office is a high, demanding calling, which calls for the very best from us. To appreciate trust in public life, we begin with its place in private life, where nothing is more basic.

Private Trust

Trusting persons is a serious matter, since it gives other people the power to affect by their words and actions our feelings, interests, and well-being. Accordingly, we choose friends, husbands, and

34

wives whom we believe we can trust; our most intimate bonds to others are forged of many things—chemistry, affection, shared interests, common ideals—but trust is always present. Indeed, genuine intimacy cannot be imagined without trust. We can be sexually involved with people we do not trust, and enjoy the company of rogues, but lust and mere companionship are far from the genuine intimacy that joins our lives to the lives of others.

Betrayal thus causes deep resentment, anger, and heartache. To trust others is to believe they will not forsake us—not that they will be perfect or infallible, but that they will use good judgment with us—and that they will neither sacrifice us for some private advantage, nor use us as mere instruments of some hidden desire, nor neglect to consider us. We believe that those we trust will treat our interests and feelings as though they were their own. Few disappointments run deeper than that of misplaced trust, and few lives are as barren as those from which mutual trust is absent.

We also entrust important interests to our doctors, lawyers, priests, ministers, rabbis, and teachers. We expect them to serve as trustworthy agents of our well-being and to behave in our behalf as we would behave for ourselves if we knew enough—that is, as professionals.

We are rightly resentful when they let us down. A doctor who brings a hangover to work, a lawyer who gouges, a minister or teacher who takes sexual advantage of others offends us. We trust professionals to give us their best, in the spirit of the Hippocratic Oath: "Whatever houses I visit, I will come for the benefit of the sick, remaining free of all intentional injustice, of all mischief, and in particular of sexual relations with both female and male persons, be they free or slaves. Whatever I see or hear in the course of the treatment . . . I will keep to myself."

Much of daily life depends on trust in strangers. We can decide where we will live, but we can seldom decide who will share a sidewalk with us, or a bus or subway ride, or the lanes of a highway. When strangers—such as drunk drivers—disregard our well-being, they betray the trust required for people to live together securely. Few experienced people trust strangers any further than they have to, but persons cannot live together when they cannot trust each other at all. People who survive without trust do so in a condition resembling war.

The Public Trust

Just as we cannot all be our own architects, electrical contractors, doctors, and lawyers, we cannot serve entirely as our own government. Even in a constitutional republic where the people are the ultimate repository of authority, we must delegate that authority to public officials. People cannot live together without government, or promote the common good—or even the common defense—without government. If private life without trust is barren, our common life in liberty without trustworthiness in government is impossible.

Because the people must rely on government, the persistent questions throughout history are: How should government be constituted? and How should public officials be authorized to hold office? The people have often had little choice in the matter; government has consisted of hereditary monarchs or of tyrants whose only claim to authority was power. Even today, many governments rest mainly on military or economic dominion.

America, by contrast, derives authority from the consent of the people. "No man is good enough to govern another man without that other's consent," as Abraham Lincoln expressed it. "I say this is the leading principle—the sheet anchor of American republicanism."3 If we must trust those who govern us, we should be able to decide who they will be.

Since most of our government officials are strangers to us, we cannot choose them as we do doctors or lawyers, let alone friends. Elected officials are rarely chosen by a majority of the people or even of the eligible voters. The majority of those who do vote generally compose a small portion of the population. Appointed officials, such as judges and police, are even more distant from any direct public choice.

The spirit of service essential to avoiding majority or minority tyranny requires that every official seek to deserve the public trust he may not actually possess. However effective the checks and balances of government, however extensive the prevention of abuses of power by government, the government itself will be less than trustworthy unless individual officials try to be worthy of the trust they bear.

As James Madison wrote to Thomas Jefferson in 1788, while the Constitution was being considered for ratification by the states, "Wherever there is an interest and power to do wrong, wrong will generally be done, and not less readily by a powerful and inter-ested party than by a powerful and interested prince."4 Laws and sanctions cannot always prevent individuals from using the powers of office for private gain, so we must trust to the quality and decency of our officials.

Appalling incompetence and dishonor undermine private as

well as public institutions. Fraud in savings and loan companies has been said to have reached epidemic proportions, for example, and allegations of bribery and the illicit use of inside information has been charged against defense contractors and the Pentagon itself.

At a Roofers Union racketeering trial in Philadelphia, tape recordings revealed an elected municipal court judge, a top official of the federal Occupational Safety and Health Administration, and two police officers accepting bribes while in office.[5] An Atlanta-based Drug Enforcement Administration agent was arrested in Washington, D.C., after police observed him buying drugs on the street.[6]

After the conviction of three elected Philadelphia judges and the naming of sixteen others in various investigations, Senator Arlen Specter called for judges to be appointed because so many judicial candidates are on the ballot that the public cannot be informed about them.[7] At the same time, twenty-eight New York City restaurant inspectors were accused of extortion.[8] The *New York Times* has reported, "There are now more than 100 cases each year in state and federal courts in which law enforcement officials are charged or implicated in drug corruption."[9]

Few have ever maintained that human beings can be trusted to behave well unless they are held accountable. In the eighteenth century, republican agrarian John Taylor of Caroline said "The more a nation depends for its liberty on the qualities of individuals, the less likely it is to retain it. By expecting publick good from private virtue, we expose ourselves to publick evils from private vices."[10]

This skepticism seems less realistic than the position of the British historian Lord Acton, who observed that "power tends to corrupt, and absolute power corrupts absolutely." A century earlier, the American Founding Fathers established absolute limits on absolute power in our Bill of Rights. Notably, both they and Acton said, not that power corrupts but that power offers temptations to corrupt that some resist. They believed that the well-being of a constitutional republic *does* depend on the virtue of citizens and their officials. John Adams believed strongly in the necessity of good morals and manners for republican government: in 1776 he wrote to a friend that there was "so much rascality, so much venality and corruption, so much avarice and ambition" among men *"even* in America" that there might not be "virtue enough to support a republic."[11]

The propensity to misuse authority led the eighteenth-century Scottish philosopher Francis Hutcheson to write that "the constituting of civil power is *the most important transaction* in human affairs," and for that reason, we have a right to insist that the obligations of public servants are "very high and sacred."[12] "The rights of rulers," he said, are "less divine than those of the people, as the former are destined for the preservation of the latter."[13]

While realizing that corrupt governments that treat the public with disdain or that permit anarchy do immense harm, Hutcheson also recognized that even well-structured governments rely on officials to respect the public interest. Crimes by public officials are so pernicious, he said, that they warrant more severe punishment than private crimes. Although he approved of pardons and legal immunity for ordinary criminals, to break up gangs and to secure useful information, he urged that "for crimes against the publik rights of a people, or for gross abuses of power . . . there should be no impunity."[14] In a word, violation of the public trust is unpardonable.

Many officials, however, have never succumbed to temptation at the expense of the public. Federal agents, for example, regularly walk away from bribes greater than their lifetime earnings. This better side of human nature often emerges in police conduct, as indicated by the wife of Jim Giza, a street cop in Baltimore:

> When he puts on his uniform he creates a barrier between himself and the rest of mankind. And he does that out of choice and a willingness to risk difference because he believes he can make a difference. . . . So when I hear critical, accusatory, and snide comments about police, I react. Police are not freaks, they are people like the rest of us—with families and mortgages, taxes and car payments. The only difference is that they have chosen a profession that puts them in daily contact with those elements of society we would like to forget, a profession that few of us would choose but which all of us depend on.[15]

Joanne Giza tells as well of "the shootings, the cuttings, the rapes, the drugs, the life he witnessed with its poverty and hopelessness and fear."[16] She confirms the willingness of some to bear the public trust faithfully while their families share in their sacrifices, unsung and uncompensated. Their lives bear out the novelist Tom Wolfe's observation that cynicism is "a cowardly form of superiority," because it implies that *I* do not have to try my best, on the false grounds that nobody else tries.

The demands of fidelity to the public trust for police today may be greater than in earlier periods. Much of what is worst in America today grows in a poverty that many free people—not slaves—in Colonial America were spared. Forrest McDonald writes, "The vast majority of American families held a comfortable amount of land, and poverty of the depth that was common in Europe was all but unknown."[17] Historian Marvin Meyers adds that the founders knew the experiment in ordered liberty itself could be threatened in the future by poverty:

> The republican remedy for factional violence, injustice, and confusion was far from perfect, Madison recognized; and it would meet its real test in the future when America, like other nations, accumulated a propertyless mass of citizens.[18]

Poverty has come to a portion of the American people with a vengeance, frequently accompanied by disenfranchisement, ignorance, brutality, and alienation from government. The poor are likely to feel powerless to call government to their aid. Such feelings and circumstances make them mistrustful of the police. James Madison observed that "the most rational government will not find it a superfluous advantage to have the prejudices of the community on its side."[19] Where circumstances are dreadful, prejudices run the other way, so police must make the greatest effort to serve this public and to be worthy of their trust, not out of charity but justice. Although police cannot by themselves deliver the benefits of a just society to those who are helpless through no fault of their own, they can offer service and respect. And they must resist not only bribes and the like but the temptation to give up as well.

The daily experience of police confirms the positions of Hutcheson, Madison, and the others on offices of public trust. Their philosophic points apply in practice.

Competence

As many cases show, a police officer without an understanding of people will not deal competently with conflict, while one who has it can calm adversaries and ease tension.

A particularly well coordinated and mutually trusting team, consisting of an older officer with more formal education and a very observant learner, was called late one afternoon to a domestic disturbance in a trailer park. A woman with her small daughter, inquiring about a trailer rental, had parked in a tenant's space. Upon returning from work, the man flew into such a rage that she fled into a trailer and was afraid to come out. When we arrived, the police escorted her and the child to their car and directed them to another parking space. Then the officers approached the tenant, a big man who was obviously tired. He assured the police that he had politely asked the woman to move her car and could not imagine why she called the police.

Arguing with him about the facts or suggesting he was a liar might make future problems for the prospective tenant. Instead, the senior officer said, "I really don't know how you did it. When I come home from work, I'm bushed, and if somebody parked in my space, I'd be so damned mad, I'd probably raise hell." The man grew red in the face and spewed out his real feelings, using the grossest profanity, until he realized that he had given himself away and stopped abruptly.

The police might have rubbed it in but did not. The senior partner paused and then said, "Look, we know everybody has to put up with a lot of crap. We do, you do, and so does that woman over there. She's desperate for a home for herself and her daughter, and none of the spaces is marked, so she didn't know it was yours. She seems like a person who wouldn't do it on purpose. Maybe you could give her a break."

By not putting the man in a defeated position, the police gave him the opportunity to walk over to the woman and apologize. She apologized in turn and thereby led the way to a decent resolution of the conflict. But the man's wife arrived and interrupted with a diatribe against police in general, while insisting that her husband never was abusive, never used foul language, and never threatened anyone. After the police cocked an eyebrow, however, the husband shook his head, and the reconciliation continued.

This kind of competence is indispensable to serving the public well. In this instance, it also prevented any tension that might have arisen from the fact that of all the people involved, only the senior officer was black. I have seen other officers become involved in pointless arguments that only made people stick to their stories no matter how absurd.

Trustworthiness

Much police literature stresses common sense as the basis of competence. More to the point is the good sense in allowing others to keep their self-respect rather than humiliating them needlessly. This is a simple application of the golden rule.

Undercover police have been reported to let prostitutes undress before arresting them for solicitation. Mature people do not use their positions for foolish self-indulgence, however, or allow prurience to interfere with their judgment.

Albert Seedman, who served for thirty years in the New York City Police Department, from patrolman to chief of detectives, tells of his colleagues' habitual decency:

> Ray McGuire, the captain who had run the squad for years, was famous for his integrity. . . . One Friday, just before Christmas in 1947, Seedman helped lug into the Safe and Loft office dozens of cartons of toys that had been recovered from a hijacking case. There were dolls, teddy bears, stuffed animals of all kinds.
>
> Ray McGuire, busy overseeing the operation, suddenly looked up and saw that it was close to three o'clock. "I'm never going to get to lunch," he said. "I was going to stop at Macy's to pick up some toys for my girls." One of the detectives mentioned he had to do the same at Macy's. McGuire handed him a twenty-dollar bill. "Pick up a pair of dolls for me, will ya?"
>
> If there were two dolls in that office, there were two thousand. . . . Yet I doubt it ever occurred to McGuire that a pair would never be missed. Or that the owner would be delighted to make them a gift.[20]

The habit of not even considering greedy behavior, of not speculating about ways to profit from office, prevents such conduct from "ever occurring" to us.

The same habits apply to bribery. An offer of a bribe is deeply insulting. That someone believes you can be bought is enough to stir anger (which must be concealed to prosecute the suspect). For any decent person, rejection of the offer requires no deliberation.

For anyone tempted by such offers, the central questions are: Is this behavior worthy of me? Is it consistent with the reasons for which I respect myself? Do I have a price? If such questions are not sufficient, more compelling questions are, Am I willing to be viewed with contempt, however tactfully, by the person who has bribed me, and to deserve it? Am I willing to be bought—for I am being bought, not merely rented—by such a person? What would the people who love me think? What about the people whose respect I cherish and want to deserve?

As Elijah Adlow explained,

> The policeman who accepts a gratuity or solicits a bribe from a racketeer must remember that he is dealing with a man who is not renting his soul for a day but is taking title to it for

life. Once his hands are tainted he can no longer assert his authority with dignity and without restraint. . . . For a policeman who weighs the offer of a bribe it is wise to remember that only a consciousness of freedom from the taint of suspicion insures true peace of mind.[21]

For people of mature habits of trustworthiness, these reflections are unnecessary, but for people who aspire to such maturity they can be useful. And for people who are greedy—or intemperate in other ways—they are not likely to serve as much of a constraint. People who conceal their own greed from themselves usually are good at other kinds of self-deception and live comfortably with other betrayals of the public trust. For those without conscience, the only remedy is to cast them out.

Similar points can be made about self-pity, cowardice, and injustice. Like intemperance, these faults arise from inordinate self-love. Those who pity themselves—who believe, for example, that their jobs are too hard, or that the world is not sufficiently sensitive to their needs and desires—probably do not think straight about how to do their jobs well and how to live up to the trust others place in them.

Self-pity tends to obscure the importance of earning one's own respect. As one police officer remarked after he had been imprisoned for burglary: "The real truth is, after ten years on the force, I'm afraid I had reached the point of feeling, 'Nobody else cares, and why the hell should I?' "[22] The answer to his question is simple: You should care because it is your life, not theirs; your self-respect that is at stake, not theirs; your oath of office that is in the balance, not theirs. By allowing self-pity to influence us, we give away control of our lives. Self-pity is that tempting voice that says, It's all right . . . go ahead . . . nobody cares.

Cowards betray their obligations and forsake other people because they are inordinately concerned about their own survival, be it physical or occupational. They do not rise to their duties, because they fear the consequences. Failure to control fear, rather than fear itself, makes them cowards. They fear death more than dishonor, fear losing their jobs more than failing in their duties, fear suffering harm more than causing harm to others by their neglect or flight.

People can be unjust in many ways, but all of them involve failure to consider others. Whether it takes the form of prejudice, racism, sexism, pursuit of more than a fair share, or indifference to facts and evidence, injustice is an affront to decency.

In summary, immaturity and self-indulgence are incompatible with the trust of public office. We all have weaknesses, of course, but we also have obligations to root them out when they impair our capacity to serve faithfully. Individuals must do this for themselves; no laws or policies can do it for them, although specific institutional policies may either encourage our best or indulge our worst selves.

We can help each other to become worthy of the public trust. Seedman saw that Captain McGuire's honesty about the children's dolls was so natural that it was unforgettable to his colleagues: "One example like that is better than a year's supply of lectures, memos, and threats from the Commissioner's office on the need for honesty in the ranks."[23]

Policies and procedures for accountability are, however, important. Patrick V. Murphy, the commissioner of police in New York City who established the policy of cooperation with the Knapp Commission investigations of police corruption, stresses that institutional improvement cannot be based simply on conscience: "In reality, the [detective] bureau was an independent breakaway entity, with its own laws, customs, and marching orders. From the reform's point of view, accountability meant nothing to the detectives if they only had to answer to their consciences."[24]

How people behave, however, usually matters more than what they say. Even children sense hypocrisy. Officials whose behavior belies their words get the contempt they deserve from their colleagues. Moreover, moralizing can be offensive and tiresome and may sound self-righteous. Paying attention to the behavior of others is less likely to breed resentment.

In this regard, the English novelist Thomas Hardy was right to say, "Persons with any weight of character carry, like planets, their atmospheres with them in their orbits."[25] They do so naturally, not by pretension, as Captain McGuire did.

Able leaders understand that nobody can really serve as an example by *trying* to do so. When we see an attempt to set an example, we suspect it is phony and not deeply rooted. People become real exemplars, trusted and looked up to, by being what they appear to be.

The Roman thinker Cicero pointed out, "Socrates was perfectly right when he declared that there is a direct shortcut to winning a reputation: 'Make yourself the sort of man you want people to think you are.' "[26] The Greek historian Xenophon reported that Socrates gave this advice, "If you want to be thought good at anything the shortest and safest and most reputable way is to try to make yourself really good at it."[27] And James Madison wrote of his brother, "If he wishes to estabish himself in the good will of the County, the only durable as well as honorable plan will be to establish a character that merits it."[28]

4
Discretion

"You see," he [King Arthur] said, "Might is not Right. But there is a lot of Might knocking about in this world, and something has to be done about it. It is as if People were half horrible and half nice. Perhaps they are even more than half horrible, and when they are left to themselves they run wild . . . without reference to justice. Then the horrible side gets the uppermost, and there is thieving and rape and plunder and torture. The people become beasts."

T. H. WHITE[1]

Discretion is the authority to make decisions of policy and practice. In policing, discretion often includes command or patrol authority to decide which laws shall be enforced, and when, where, and how. It also includes authority to decide which means of helping the helpless, maintaining order, and keeping the peace are best suited to particular circumstances. Discretion is a special kind of liberty—the freedom to make decisions that affect the lives of others, which other citizens are not empowered to make. Special liberties entail special duties.

Judgment and Rules

Just as liberty should not indulge what is worst in human beings, neither should discretion indulge the unrestrained exercise of might. Might does not make right; if it did, the powerful could tyrannize over the weak, or the evil over the good, without objection.

Police are granted discretion because no set of laws and regulations can prescribe what to do in every possible circumstance. The possibilities are too numerous for us to have rules for everything that may happen.

Trying to make a rule for everything demeans our ability to apply our intelligence. When a bureaucracy becomes rule-bound, it is like a person who is muscle-bound; it can do less because it lacks flexibility.

Those who believe that people should be bound by institutional rules and mandatory responses neglect the complexity of our lives. They sometimes ignore the facts that must be taken into consideration to achieve justice, and they seem to believe that people cannot exercise good judgment.

When Mahatma Gandhi committed acts of civil disobedience in hope of reform in India, he was convicted of sedition. Eager to show British rule at its worst he asked for the severest penalty from the court. But the judge understood that Gandhi was a man of exceptional civility and decency. A harsh sentence would *appear* as unjust as it actually was and would therefore be both morally wrong and politically foolish. He therefore chose a lesser penalty, one within the limits of his discretion.

The fear of discretion in government in general is strongest in regard to police discretion. According to Professor Herman Goldstein, of the University of Wisconsin-Madison Law School, this fear arises from concern over "the awesome power of the police," their reputation "for exceeding their legal authority," and their abuse of "existing discretion."[2] Many high-ranking police in America say in private that police themselves have brought on such criticisms. The history of policing in America does include disregard for the limits of discretion, violation of civil rights, brutality, and arrogance. Some police know of problems of sadism among their fellows as well.

These issues are crucial. Their importance is reflected in their emphasis at the very beginning of the 1984 *Standards Manual of the Law Enforcement Agency Accreditation Program:*

> Written policy should set forth the enforcement policy of the agency, define the limits of individual discretion and provide guidelines for the exercise of such discretion. Because the concept of discretion defies rigid codification, officers should be trained in how to exercise the broad discretionary authority they have been granted. . . . The written directive should identify the authority of sworn officers to use alternatives to arrest (e.g., citations, summonses, referral, informal resolution, and warning) to address the variety of problems they confront. . . . The directive should encompass the use of all types and kinds of force . . . [A]n officer may use deadly force only when the officer reasonably believes that the action is in defense of human life, including the officer's own life, or in defense of any person in immediate danger of serious physical injury. . . . Definitions of "reasonable belief" and "serious physical injury" should be included. . . .[3]

Some command personnel cite the *Miranda* ruling as an example of judicial reaction to police excesses and believe that policing is better for it. Goldstein describes positions taken by other institutions, some of which reject "the concept that police can and must exercise discretion." For example,

- A local chapter of the American Civil Liberties Union challenges the policy of a police administration intended to regulate the use made of street interrogations, arguing that police have no basis for questioning citizens unless there are grounds for making an arrest.
- A state supreme court finds a law enforcement officer guilty of nonfeasance for his failure to initiate a criminal prosecution where evidence of the violation came to his attention.
- A state attorney general holds that a police chief cannot limit the authority of his personnel to use deadly force within the bounds of existing statutes.
- A newspaper editorial condemns the local police chief for rising above the law in setting down guidelines that would result in his officers arresting curfew violators only under certain conditions.
- Another newspaper editorial condemns a chief for pointing out that the enforcement of a newly enacted ordinance regulating massage parlors will have to compete with other demands for police manpower.
- A group of citizens in Berkeley, California, in 1973, obtained enough signatures to have an ordinance placed on the ballot that in effect instructed the Berkeley Police Department to give a low priority to the enforcement of marijuana laws. After its adoption, however, the state attorney general filed suit.[4]

Such actions usually stem from the belief that the accountability of police to the public is best preserved by minimizing discretion from the outset. Accountability is stressed, for example, in the 1987 report by the Philadelphia Police Study Task Force, *Philadelphia and Its Police: Toward a New Partnership:*

> The police are agents of the community and are therefore accountable to it. . . . Implicit in this relationship is the expectation that the police will feel morally responsible to the community, not just to themselves.[5]

The report does not suggest that the principle of accountability in itself reduces discretion. Virtually everyone agrees with the principle as such. The issue is not whether the principle is right, but how it should be applied, and whether the positions taken by the ACLU and the others above are wise applications of it.

Because its explicit mission is to protect liberty, the ACLU tends to obliterate the distinction between grounds for questioning and grounds for arrest. If we focus solely on protection of liberty, we neglect the public safety, so we must pay heed to both liberty and public safety, which sometimes conflict. For this reason, discretion cannot be eliminated in distinguishing between grounds for questioning and grounds for arrest. The ACLU protects liberties, but takes too narrow a position on police discretion.

The instance of the state supreme court seems to deny that some cases of lawbreaking should not be prosecuted—or at least that police can make that judgment. Its concern is probably to avoid favoritism and discrimination—a worthwhile purpose, but again, too narrow. For if police could make no such judgments, enforcement would be unconditional, and therefore unjust. It would offend public sentiment and thus render police ineffective. The newspaper editorial about curfew violations is too narrow in its perspective in the same way. The second editorial, about regulating massage parlors, is too narrow as well, because resources and manpower are always limited. The writer presumes that all legislation is accompanied by funding adequate to enforce it.

The state attorney general's objection to a police chief's making departmental limits on the use of force more confining than existing statutes takes law seriously. But it risks impairing police performance by assuming that laws are always clear. And the Berkeley ordinance about marijuana tells the police that the will of the majority is above the law.

In each case, the perspective is too narrow to accommodate the range of ideals that morality must take into account. Such steps do not promise a citizenry that laws will be enforced justly or wisely, peace kept securely, or safety maintained effectively. They lead not to a government of laws that is just but to one that treats everyone the same, no matter what. Sameness is not justice, for justice is sensitive to differences in context and detail. Justice is blind in the sense that it knows no favorites, not that it spurns evidence. An officer who does not arrest when a crime has been committed in a barroom brawl where no one is competent to offer reliable testimony, or when a summons is as effective for the public safety, has exercised judgment. Laws and regulations cannot possibly cover every instance with sensitivity to the circumstances.

Properly conceived, laws and regulations are not cynical, but realistic. They set boundaries to discretion; they frequently say what divides rightful and wrongful uses of authority. But they leave broad domains within which to decide which alternative is the best.

As Kenneth Culp Davis, professor of Law at the University of Chicago, observed, "A patrolman should not have discretion about overall enforcement policy but should have discretion to do the needed individualizing in applying the policy made by his superiors to the facts and circumstances of each particular case."[6] Most law enforcement studies have reached the same conclusion. As mentioned, the Commission on Accreditation of Law Enforcement Agencies did so in 1984, the President's Crime Commission did in 1967, and the American Bar Association's Project on Standards for Criminal Justice and the Law Enforcement Assistance Administration's National Advisory Commission on Criminal Justice Standards and Goals did in 1973. Since the late 1960s most such groups have also advocated the establishment of rule-making procedures within each department, so that rules are not idiosyncratic, unilaterally alterable, or so secret that the public cannot learn what they are. The International Association of Chiefs of Police, the Arizona State University Project on Law Enforcement Policy and Rule-Making, and others have provided guidance for both substance and procedure.

Command personnel must establish departmental policies in writing to avoid discriminatory performance by subordinates. They must make policies that take into account the facts of daily enforcement, and they must have the courage to say what they mean. The policies cannot be false, tongue-in-cheek, or so unrealistic that they cause disbelief, such as one that requires total enforcement of all criminal laws. Limited manpower and budgets, proper use of informants, public sentiment, and policies of prosecutors and judges must all be taken into account in deciding what a department should enforce. Full enforcement is unrealistic and impracticable. As Davis wrote in *Police Discretion,*

> The plain reality is that from the beginning of American government, a gap has existed between statutory law and enforced law. When legislative bodies learn that enforcement officers are enforcing something less than the enacted law . . . they generally express their appreciation to the enforcement agencies for contributing to a sensible system. Almost all legislators are fully aware that the system would not be sensible if every criminal statute were enforced according to its letter.[7]

He added that "the police accomplishment in escaping the full enforcement legislation is a very considerable one, for which the police deserve much credit" and without which "the system of criminal justice would be insufferable."[8]

Some argue that the police usurp the authority of the legislature by determining which laws to enforce. If police enforce laws that are unpopular or foolish, it is also argued, then adverse public reaction will motivate the legislature to change the laws. Normally such arguments imply that selective enforcement leads to corruption, in that unpopular laws against prostitution, gambling, double-parking, after-hours sale of alcohol, and the like may be manipulated by the police for bribes and payoffs.

Such arguments seem unpersuasive, partly because in most places resources are insufficient for total enforcement. Furthermore, adverse public reaction to enforcement is much more likely to be directed at police than at lawmakers, who are often slow to admit, let alone correct, their mistakes. Although selective enforcement can deteriorate into uneven, unjust, and corrupt enforcement, the elimination of discretion is a poor preventive.

As with enforcement, truthful policies within which officers can responsibly exercise discretion are a basic obligation of command. Fulfillment of this obligation enables openness and obstructs corruption by increasing the possibility of acting on the words the department says it lives by.

In policing, as in all public service, the place where discretion ends must be known and respected. Two factors are involved. A person can know he is not allowed to go beyond a certain point, respect that limit, and still show bad judgment when he has the authority to decide. And a person can know how to handle difficult situations and still be contemptuous of limits. The challenge is to achieve respect for the limits and wisdom in acting within them.

Respect for Limits

Respect for limits is a matter of fundamental attitudes, which have been succinctly drawn by the theologian Reinhold Niebuhr in *The Children of Light and the Children of Darkness*. He distinguishes people who will do anything, at anyone's expense, to accomplish their purposes—good or bad—from people who restrain themselves in the pursuit of their goals. The former he calls the children of darkness—for example, the Nazis—and the latter, children of light.

Obviously, no children of darkness belong in policing or anywhere else in public service. But in the tradition of America's founders, Niebuhr stresses that a child of darkness in each of us— our passions and desires, our ambitions and commitments— tempts us all toward excesses. No children of light can be trusted in public service either, if they believe they have no capacity for misconduct, no propensity to excess.

In a way, naive children of light are as dangerous as the children of darkness. Their naiveté about the tendency of power to corrupt limits their own humility, obscures to them their own fallibility, and may lead to the kind of prideful self-righteousness that typifies tyrants.

Persons who can be trusted to exercise discretion are the children of light who are wise about human nature as it exists in themselves. They respect limits and recognize that they may be tempted to exceed them.

Respect for limits cannot excuse laxity, indifference, laziness, or timidity in the exercise of rightful authority. Public officials who are too lazy to do their duty, or too fearful of confrontation or controversy to use their authority, may not be as dangerous as those who violate the laws and the rights of the citizens, but they endanger all the same. Intemperance in the exercise of discretion is like other forms of intemperance—it consists of doing too much or too little.

Citizen complaints and departmental investigations of police performance involve accusations of both excess and deficiency. In New York, after the racial violence in Howard Beach, one Harlem priest referred to the police as "a bunch of thugs gone wild."[9] Police everywhere are familiar with complaints that they fail to respond to calls quickly enough.

No amount of conscientious performance will satisfy everyone. Not even heroic diligence will transform the world and eliminate its evils. Even after police officers give up their early expectations to "help change things" and "get drugs off the street," and after they reach a point where they realize "that's not gonna happen,"[10] they are still obliged to deliver their best every day.

Few actions erode the confidence of the public or of the police in their own department as much as the indifference of command officers to misconduct by their personnel. Stories are commonplace of police who are protected while drunk on duty. A former New York officer, now a major city chief, tells of a New York cop who "had a notorious drinking problem; he would pass out on the sidewalk, like the grimiest wino, in full uniform and in broad daylight. His colleagues would haul him in to the station house time and again, protecting him and coddling him."[11] Other police tell of their own excesses being indulged by fellow officers. One estimates that "fellow officers stopped him for drunken driving fifteen times. Not once . . . was he arrested. Fifteen times he was taken home, followed home, or allowed to drive home. 'The job afforded me lots of ways to stay active in alcoholism,' he says."[12]

Confidence also erodes when officials play favorites among their personnel. A 1987–1988 investigation in Washington, D.C., compelled the police chief to reprimand two high-ranking officials for actions beyond their authority, including possible falsification of data, that "contributed to the perception that there are improprieties and favoritism in the department's drug-screening process."[13]

Policies and Laws

Some policies and laws—such as a law against robbery or a policy prohibiting conflict of interest—are established to reinforce behavior that would be automatic for a decent human being. They clarify the limits to rightful action, which if not obvious to common sense or decency, need to be learned. A police officer needs a sense of relevant laws, regulations, and departmental policies in order to abide by them. Their proliferation, therefore, can reduce respect for limits, if the lists become so long that officers cannot learn them. They are then as likely to sneer at the whole business as to try to identify the fundamentals.

As every parent knows, if rules make a show of being complete, someone will respond to novel circumstances with, "You didn't forbid it, and so I will do it." Too much attention to the letter can kill the spirit. At the opposite extreme, vague and ambiguous laws and policies, conflicting laws at different levels of government, and laws, regulations, and policies that impede the performance of duty tend to have the same effect. Most destructive are laws that require unreasonable standards of proof to dispel reasonable doubt. Yet, since vagueness, ambiguity, conflict, and difficulty are unavoidable, they do not excuse intemperance in the exercise of discretion. No one can blame his own failures on the imperfections of the system.

Public officials are nonetheless obliged to reduce or avoid imperfections to the extent possible. Legislators should draft laws as lucidly as they can, consulting members of the executive branch about problems in enforcing them. Law enforcement officials must identify ambiguities and conflicts and advise their personnel about departmental expectations. Leaving everyone to his own devices is trusting to luck.

Clearly, some conflicts of law cannot be resolved by police alone, as shown by "kidnappings" by parents of their own children in custody disputes. A woman who won temporary custody of her son in California, for example, moved to Louisiana where she was granted permanent custody at the same time her husband was awarded custody by the California courts, so he kidnapped the boy. This dispute could be resolved at the federal level, only if new legislation is enacted by Congress.[14] Until then, police in different states will be called upon to enforce conflicting rulings.

Other problems arise over court rulings on the Fourth Amendment. In 1985, for example, Judge Patricia M. Wald of the United States Court of Appeals for the District of Columbia argued that the Supreme Court had "rewritten fourth amendment law"[15] in two cases:

> In *Illinois v. Gates*, the court discarded all the old rules for deciding what constituted probable cause sufficient to obtain a search warrant and adopted a new "common sense," non-technical, omnibus rule based on the "totality of circumstances" in each case. In *United States v. Leon*, the Court held that evidence obtained in an unconstitutional search could still be admitted . . . if the police officers, however mistaken, did not act dishonestly or recklessly in drawing up the affidavits submitted to the magistrate and if they could reasonably have believed that probable cause existed for the warrants, even if in fact it did not.[16]

Judge Wald observes that the "totality of circumstances/reasonable belief" standards will lead to lengthy deliberations in the lower courts over "whether the police behaved reasonably in conducting unreasonable searches."[17] Obviously, police are required to exercise discretion in seeking warrants for arrest, in assessing probable cause for warrantless arrests, and in the "balancing of the competing interests"[18] in stopping and frisking a suspect. As Judge Wald observes, "in some of these contexts, courts have worked out rules interpreting the concept of reasonableness. . . . In others, such as determining whether an officer's observations will support probable cause for an arrest, the great variety of situations in which the problem arises has made this task more difficult."[19]

Their trend may increase the discretion of judges in lower courts more than discretionary authority elsewhere. It will not make judgment easier for police in the streets, because it will not make explicit any general guides to conduct.

Many codes of conduct and commentators on police work

echo O. W. Wilson's "Square Deal Code" of Wichita, Kansas, in advocating a policy "never to arrest if a summons will suffice; never to summons if a warning would be better." The lesser means is conceived to be the most temperate and justifiable, the least likely to exceed the limits even where they are vague.

Determining whether a lesser means "will suffice" or "would be better" depends on what is to be accomplished. Means are sufficient or not to the achievement of specific ends, and judgment is required to establish which ends are to be pursued in specific circumstances.

Howard Cohen, associate dean of the College of Arts and Sciences at the University of Massachusetts, Boston, emphasizes that police authority "can be, at once, highly specific and exceedingly vague. It is specific insofar as it is conferred by statute with respect to law enforcement . . . and vague in the areas of peacekeeping and public safety where the variety of activities expected of the police is, typically, not legislated."[20] The tasks of police, says Cohen, do not come with convenient labels that identify them as cases of law enforcement or peacekeeping or public safety. Police "regularly step into situations in which neither their objectives nor their functions are particularly obvious."[21]

He refers to the case of George Kirkham, a university instructor who decided to become a police officer. While patrolling a ghetto, Kirkham's field training officer, D'Angelo, calls two men, whom Kirkham cannot see, out of an alley and orders one of them to get "on the car" in position to be searched. When he tells Kirkham to do the same with the other man, Kirkham hesitates, even though the second man's hands are in his pockets and he acts confused. D'Angelo then orders the man, at gunpoint, to "get on the car." After his search of the first man uncovers a revolver, D'Angelo handcuffs him while Kirkham searches the second suspect and feels a soft, spongy object in his sock. He asks D'Angelo whether to run a record check before releasing him, but D'Angelo orders him to find out what is in the sock. "We can't do that," Kirkham objects, thinking of the restrictions against further search implied by the Supreme Court decision in *Terry* v. *Ohio*. D'Angelo then removes the spongy object, which he identifies as a plastic bag filled with small packets of heroin, and arrests the second man.[22]

Cohen's analysis is that Kirkham

> understood this encounter primarily, if not exclusively, in terms of law enforcement. . . . D'Angelo, on the other hand . . . seemed to be treating this encounter as a matter of

public safety. . . . He was not . . . acting from ignorance of the law. . . . D'Angelo saw two dangerous people, one of whom turned out to be armed. All of his street sense told him they were probably drug users and dealers. . . . A gun and a small quantity of heroin were removed from the street. D'Angelo . . . was exercising his authority as a peace-keeper in the name of public safety.[23]

Cohen finds Kirkham's behavior unquestionable, but he does question whether D'Angelo's actions are justified, whether his means can appeal to the end of public safety. This is a specific instance of the general question whether ends justify means.

He offers four standards that must be met for an end to justify means: (1) The end itself must be good. (2) The means must be a plausible way to achieve the end. (3) There must be no alternative, better means to achieve the same end. (4) The means must not undermine some other equal or greater end.[24]

These standards are implicit in O. W. Wilson's injunction to use lesser means that "will suffice" to achieve their ends. They make explicit a general theory of means and ends within which practitioners do their work.

Cohen concludes, at least for some circumstances, that D'Angelo's behavior satisfies the first three conditions: public safety is good, as is removing heroin from the streets; illegal searches by experienced officers are likely to turn up enough heroin to make them worthwhile; and confiscation of drugs is sometimes a more effective control than legal arrests and convictions that end in suspended sentences, probation, and the like. Thus, Cohen concludes that the real issue is whether D'Angelo's behavior is consistent with criterion four: The means must not undermine some other equal or greater end.

What ends are at risk in D'Angelo's conduct? "First, the enforcement of law, including the law of search and seizure and narcotics laws; and, second, police adherence to, and respect for, due process of law." These ends are betrayed, but are they of equal or greater status than the end of public safety-heroin control? Cohen argues as follows:

By undermining the legal process of administration of the law of search and seizure and narcotics laws, D'Angelo contributes to the conditions of secrecy and police isolation that foster corruption in narcotics enforcement and, presumably, further entrench the use of heroin. Even if D'Angelo is an honest and well-intentioned officer, his methods, if permitted to flourish, undermine his own goals. I conclude that

55

D'Angelo has overstepped his peace-keeping authority and is not justified in doing so.[25]

Hardly a surprising conclusion. Although extraordinary steps are sometimes demanded, police work can scarcely be rendered exempt from the constraints intended to protect citizens from routine suspension of their rights.

Police, including beginners, should learn that serving multiple purposes will not justify riding roughshod over any of them, especially when limits are so fundamental to police authority. Cohen's four tests can be useful for the routine treatment of the public, including dope dealers and other suspected criminals. But in unpredictable circumstances, the simpler principles of lesser means and respect for law may have more application.

Most law enforcement executives I have worked with take Cohen's analysis for granted. They instruct personnel that ends do not justify means, and that violation of citizen rights is rarely professional or effective. Furthermore, one excess often leads to another. If officers violate citizens' rights, they must conceal their behavior alone or bring others, including superiors, into complicity with them. If convictions are sought, false reports, perjury, and cynicism and self-contempt may follow. Deception undermines trust among colleagues and disrupts efforts at conscientious performance. Moral wisdom includes recognition that excess begets excess; once on it, they can find the slope very slippery.

Kirkham's regard for legal rights was admirable, but what of his hesitancy and second-guessing of his partner? When D'Angelo called the two men from the alley, one was armed, so the other could have been as well. Yet when Kirkham hesitated with the second suspect, whose hands he could not see, D'Angelo drew his revolver and took control—even though he was already dealing with the first suspect. Kirkham's embarrassment and dallying placed his partner and himself in jeopardy. His concern about *Terry* v. *Ohio* should not have left him or his partner exposed. Once in a situation, two officers should not be at cross-purposes, at least not until the immediate danger is addressed. If disagreement is unavoidable, so be it, but not during risk of violence.

In an analogous situation in private life, I once ate with a friend at an oyster house and gave a $10 bill to the counter man, who returned change for $20. When I persisted in trying to correct the error, I learned that he understood little English. His boss heard me, rushed up to us, and began shouting recriminations at the man, threatening to fire him. As my friend and I left, he turned to me and said, "Ed, I never saw one man risk so much harm to another out of concern for his own character."

His analysis was instructive; I had been so determined to be honest that I neglected the harm I might do to the counter man. I could have left the extra change on the bar and gone quietly. Then, when the error was detected at day's end, the counter man would have had the money to make it up. My end was worthwhile, but my means, though well-intentioned, were inappropriate.

If the stranger at an oyster bar deserves such consideration, our colleagues at work deserve even more. Police who work as partners have an absolute necessity for mutual trust, and one must not needlessly jeopardize the other out of concern for his own character. Kirkham should have got the situation under control first, and then thought about what to do next, especially since D'Angelo's decision to stop and frisk was legitimate. Otherwise, character can be damaged by failure to meet the trust of a colleague and to see to a partner's interests as though they were one's own. Perhaps D'Angelo should never have thrust the inexperienced Kirkham into the situation, but once there, each person must give priority to the danger to the other, as well as to the suspects. Allowing a situation to get out of hand jeopardizes them, too, though Kirkham ignored this.

Most police would not view the question of whether D'Angelo's behavior was excessive and unproductive as a difficult one. They are, however, concerned about discretion in the use of force, especially deadly force, and how police should be instructed in it.

In one of my classes on ethics in law enforcement, an experienced uniformed officer said, "You know, Mr. Delattre, most of us don't want to shoot people. We don't even like to hurt people." Most of my work with police confirms this. For example, two patrol officers with whom I was riding were called about 8:00 P.M. to a bar between white and black sections of a midwestern city. Violence had occurred there before, and the owner had killed a patron.

In this case, the owner had thrown out a man who threatened to "go home and get my rifle and come back and kill you." The owner called the dispatcher and said that he would have to shoot the man if he returned.

The officers entered the bar from opposite ends, then joined the bar owner in scanning the street. The man was walking toward the bar with a long object in hand, concealed in brown wrapping paper. When he saw the police and ran, one officer ran after him while the other took the car and started up the alley behind the bar. The foot patrolman informed him by radio that the suspect had entered a Camaro driven by another man and that they were coming down the alley. As the police car blocked the Camaro, it slid to a stop sideways in a small parking area; the foot patrolman ran to within a few feet, drew his revolver, and ordered the suspect from the car, while the other officer covered him. The driver came out with his hands up, shouting that he knew nothing, and threw himself face against a wall. The suspect hesitated, then came slowly out of the car, raising the object until it pointed at the shins, the knees, and then the midsection of the officer. Both officers shouted, "Drop it, drop it, drop it!" Finally, the suspect dropped the bag, which as it rattled to the pavement disclosed not a rifle but a long iron bar. Back-up patrol arrived and took the suspect downtown.

The officers continued their tour shaken by the episode, but did not discuss it until after the shift. I had believed that the suspect had a rifle or shotgun in the bag, and so had they. The officer who had allowed the suspect to point the object and apparently threaten his life said, "Well, I wasn't sure he had a gun, but I thought he did, and I thought he was going to shoot." Then he added, "At the end, I was pulling the trigger. I honestly thought I was pulling it hard enough to fire, but I released it as he dropped the bag. I was lucky—that he didn't have a gun, and that I didn't shoot him."

He meant that he was lucky, not because he had escaped media fall-out or a departmental investigation, but because he did not have to live with his having shot an unarmed man. Even though he exposed himself to grave danger and had every reason to believe the man to be armed, he "didn't want to shoot people."

This officer was in no sense soft on crime or an apologist for criminals, and he held no social theories that rendered people blameless for their conduct. Though young, he had several years of experience and a fine record. He simply tried to avoid ever using more force than necessary in the performance of his duty. And so he held out against firing, hoping against hope that the suspect would not shoot.

In that confrontation, I believe he exposed himself to the threat of being killed beyond anything required by duty or prudence. I remember vividly my cold fear of what seemed about to happen to him. The event unfolded very fast, but it seemed endless.

I have met other police like him. Some have never needed to draw a weapon. A few have been hurt trying to quiet domestic fights without hurting anyone. Some have successfully ended gunpoint confrontations without firing. Some have given enormous benefit of doubt to suspects, erring, if they err at all, on the side of danger to themselves.

Other police show few signs of such excellence. Much police literature, both popular and scholarly, focuses on excess use of force, including deadly force. For many who have reached middle age, visions of police brutality against nonviolent civil rights demonstrators are indelible, as are memories of the 1968 Chicago Democratic convention. And no one who follows the news can be unconcerned about errors of judgment, or apparent ill will, in policing.

Force and Deadly Force

Since police departments have very different records, we should look at laws and policies that may reduce the use of inordinate force and at attitudes about force that do not belong in policing.

Roger Wertheimer, a Ph.D. who served as deputy sheriff of Multnomah County, Oregon, drafted a general code of conduct that "tries to clarify the most general do's and don'ts of police use of force. For example, one paragraph categorically prohibits threatening or causing harm for the purpose of retaliation, or as a means of coercing a suspect, or in response to verbal abuse or exhibitions of disrespect, or as a means of procuring information or evidence."[26]

In offering these prohibitions, Wertheimer echoes the injunctions of the Wickersham *Report on Lawlessness in Law Enforcement*, completed in 1931. There, August Vollmer wrote with respect to third-degree techniques in interrogation:

> While third-degree methods are most frequently practiced by policemen and detectives, there are cases in which prosecuting officers and their assistants participate in them. To the contention that the third degree is necessary to get the facts, the reporters aptly reply in the language of the present Lord Chancellor of England (Lord Sankey): "It is not admissible to do a great right by doing a little wrong. . . . It is not sufficient to do justice by obtaining a proper result by irregular or improper means." Not only does the use of the third degree involve a flagrant violation of law by the officers of the law, but it involves also the dangers of false confessions, and it tends to make police and prosecutors less zealous in the search for objective evidence. As the New York prosecutor quoted in the report said, "It is a short cut

and makes the police lazy and unenterprising." Or, as another official quoted remarked: "If you use your fists, you are not so likely to use your wits." We agree with the conclusion expressed in the report, that "The third degree brutalizes the police, hardens the prisoner against society, and lowers the esteem in which the administration of justice is held by the public."[27]

Recognition by police of the need for binding limits is essential to their education and training. But many statutory provisions on police use of force are either so permissive or so vague, Wertheimer says, that they leave police in need of clear and useful departmental policies. "Few citizens have any realistic conception of how much and what kinds of force are necessary to accomplish certain tasks safely," he says, and "still fewer citizens appreciate that a policeman is not likely to respect a rule he views as a threat to his own self-respect because it bars him from effective action."[28]

Wertheimer cites Oregon's ORS 163.100 as a typical case of inadequate legislation:

> The killing of a human being is justifiable when committed: (1) By public officers or those acting in their aid and assistance and by their command: (a) When necessarily committed in overcoming resistance to the execution of a legal duty. (b) When necessarily committed in retaking persons charged with or convicted of crimes who have escaped or been rescued. (c) When necessarily committed in arresting a person fleeing from justice who has committed a felony.[29]

And ORS 133.280 read,

> Means of Effecting Arrest: If after notice of intention to arrest the defendant, he either flees or forcibly resists, the officer may use all necessary and proper means to effect the arrest.[30]

The second statute offers no guidance about the meaning of "necessary" and "proper." The first does not oblige an officer to shoot at a felon or escaped prisoner who flees, but it functions within "a statutory requirement that the department and its officers faithfully execute their duties and fulfill their functions."[31] Thus, the first is largely useless with respect to the discretion of officers, who need to know what their departments expect. The second, to the extent that it suggests that fleeing felons are to be stopped, militates against restraint.

In this context, Wertheimer's revision of his department's rules and procedures manual included the following paragraph:

Members will use deadly force with *maximum restraint*. . . .
The use of deadly force against a human being is unwarranted unless there is a preponderant evidence that the
person will attack another human life.[32]

It also specified the particulars of the two circumstances permitting the use of deadly force.

The first circumstance is that the officer "has no reasonable
alternative means of protecting himself or another person
against a clear and present danger of death or serious injury
from an unjustifiable attack." The second and more debata-
ble circumstance specified is that the officer has no reasonable alternative means of preventing an escape or effecting
an arrest and capture and (a) he has good reason to believe
that the subject is a violent and dangerous public menace,
(b) the arrest, capture, or prevention of an escape is lawful,
(c) the subject is known to be an adult, (d) the subject is
known to have committed a felony, (e) the officer exerts
every reasonable effort to make known his authority and
purpose to the subject.[33]

Wertheimer cautions that these policies are imperfect. They
are compromises, efforts to take into account, for example, concerns about imminent peril *and* about the age of offenders, the
protection of innocent life *and* regard for the life of the felon. They
were drafted in part on the rationale that Oregon had abolished
capital punishment, and that past misdeeds alone could not therefore justify the use of deadly force. He denies that such departmental policies could be implemented everywhere, and he insists
that each department should review with care its own legislation,
past policies, and history of the use of force to determine where
problems persist. Wertheimer's policies are in accord with standards of the Commission on Accreditation of Law Enforcement
Agencies. They say, for example, that "a 'fleeing felon' should not
be presumed to pose an immediate threat to life in the absence of
actions that would lead one to believe otherwise, such as a previously demonstrated threat to or wanton disregard for human
life."[34]

Finally, the manual gave officers the discretionary authority to
decide whether to use deadly force when the circumstances permitted it.

Even when a member is permitted . . . to use deadly force,
he may refrain from doing so if he deems it advisable in a
particular case. A member will not be censured if a subject is
not apprehended after all reasonable methods except deadly

force have been used, and the member deems the use of deadly force inadvisable.[35]

The idea, clearly, was that error on the side of restraint is better than error on the side of excess.

Critics may think that this allows too much discretion, or that it does not rightly identify all the cases where deadly force might be used, or that it allows too little discretion, or is imprecise about imminent peril, and so on. What matters most, though, is that the department met its obligations to address fundamental issues of policy in a way that both respects limits and advances the exercise of discretion within those limits. For the wise implementation of law and policy in the daily work of police, this kind of con-scientiousness is irreplaceable.

Anticipation and Planning

Crises in judgment and discretion can be avoided by anticipating situations in which questions of duty and rightful conduct arise. Facing them when there is time to think can result in better reactions when there is no time and can forestall dilemmas about what to do, not only in uses of force but also in other police work.

For example, in 1988, northwest Washington, D.C., had been the scene of fourteen sexual attacks in four years for which one man may have been responsible. The crimes showed similarities, as did descriptions of the attacker. The *Washington Post* reported, "In the aftermath of each attack, there has been another similarity: District Police issued no immediate statement warning residents, even though the assailant remains at large."[36]

The police were uncertain that there was a single attacker. The *Post* said these cases "underscore a debate over whether and when it serves residents to warn them that a serial criminal is preying on a community. 'It's always been one of the most difficult issues to deal with: When do you go out and make a public release?' " one police official asked. "While police warnings can raise community awareness . . . they can spawn 'copycat' crimes or merely cause the assailant to change the method or location of his attacks."[37]

The police were criticized by residents, who noted that other departments, as in Fairfax, Virginia, and Prince George's County, Maryland, operate on a different policy: "If we think there's a pattern, we put it out to the public." The public may respond with heightened awareness and take precautions to avoid the circum-stances of the attacks—by locking doors and windows, for example, or staying away from certain neighborhoods or streets. These gains seem to the departments to outweigh the risk that apprehension of the criminals may be made more difficult.[38]

The issue was taken out of the hands of the D.C. police when the media gave it attention. Whether the police were right or wrong not to publicize the cases, they then faced the same result as if they had gone public except that they also became the subject of public criticism.

To avoid such results, police officials can review the effects of policies on the apprehension of perpetrators, the protection of the public, and so on. They can make continuing efforts to secure good, candid relations with the media, community leaders, and neighborhood associations. By making these routine, they can explain their policies when no specific case is in progress, as well as find out the opinions of those they serve. They can ask the media to cooperate in stressing police warnings to the citizenry.

Such steps are better than having no clear policies or policies the public does not know. When the steps are taken apart from a climate of fear, they may be less newsworthy in the eyes of the media, but they are a conscientious means of parrying the charge that the public had no way of knowing how police operate.

Finally, law enforcement personnel sometimes object that the standards they are expected to meet in their use of authority and discretion seem unfair. A few have complained to me that although others are innocent until proven guilty, police seem to be presumed guilty by the citizens and the media whenever accused.

Some people are simply prejudiced against police and any other form of authority. Others are prejudiced in favor of them. When authority, power, and discretion are granted to public officials, however, rational people presume that they will not use more than they need for their legitimate purposes, because rational people would never grant more authority or discretion to abridge liberty or use force than they believed necessary. The presumption is not of guilt but of official respect for restraint. Citizens expect public officials to justify their uses of authority or power when questions arise.

As Wertheimer insists, citizens may be naive in assessing how much authority and force are in fact needed. For this reason, the education of the public—not only by police, but by other public officials, schools, and others—is essential. But citizens are right to expect restraint, because each one risks being victimized by official excess.

Since prejudice is always unfair and presumption of guilt is prejudicial, it is therefore unfair. But there is nothing unfair in a presumption of respect for limits and an expectation that the burden of proof will be met by officials who have authority and use it. This presumption amounts to insistence that might does not make right, that officials will bear the public trust faithfully, and that they will accept the onus of showing they are doing so. Those who have no stomach for such ordeals of the public trust should choose another line of work.

5
Public Corruption for Profit

Richard Rich. But every man has his price!
Thomas More. No-no-no.
R. Rich. But yes! In money, too.
T. More. (with gentle impatience) No, no, no.
R. Rich. Or pleasure. Titles, women, bricks-and-mortar,
there's always something.
T. More. Childish.

ROBERT BOLT, *A Man for All Seasons*[1]

The only thing that is incorruptible is personal character that refuses to be corrupted. An incorruptible person, as Aristotle observed, "is truthful in word and deed just because truthfulness has become second nature with him." Such a person, "who is truthful even in matters where nothing depends on his veracity, will be still more careful of the truth when something does depend on it."[2] The person of incorruptible character has no price.

Incorruptibility

Good character includes a conception of what is worthy of oneself. Persons who truly have no price consider it beneath them to give in to temptations for illicit gratification or profit. Peer pressure, weakness in others, impulse, opportunity, and personal rationalization or consolation do not excuse lapses of character.

A person who is incorruptible, and who respects ideals of due process and limits to the rightful use of power is different from a fanatic. Fanatics, such as terrorists on suicide missions, cannot be diverted from their purpose, but they disdain the restraint essential to justice, liberty, and decency in law enforcement.

Incorruptibility is a form of personal freedom that consists in control of one's life in accordance with standards of excellence and self-respect that are more important than anything else, including life itself. No other disposition makes our lives our own, and no other disposition can make anyone trustworthy to the very end.

Although few of us may ever reach full incorruptibility, we all should keep its nature clearly before us.

Cynicism and Consolation

Complaining that no one is incorruptible, that everyone has a price, is a timeworn excuse. If the cynicism were true, then our experiment in ordered liberty simply could not long endure. Neither could we identify any trustworthy public officials except by assuming that their price had never been offered.

A popular little book of counsel to young men and women explained in 1797:

> Men who transgress the rules of Justice are not destitute of palliatives for their conduct. "In these times," they say, "the practice of every kind of dishonest trick is so universally prevalent, that were we scrupulously to abstain, inevitable ruin would be the consequence." Be it remembered, this libel . . . is not ours; it is quoted from men who . . . urge it as an excuse for conduct their own hearts do not approve and their tongues will not otherwise justify.[3]

History is full of stories of persons who have had the character to resist all sorts of powerful temptations. When the ancient Athenians put Socrates on trial, he could have persuaded them to spare him if he repented asking philosophical questions in public and promised never to do so again. Socrates told them, however, that his accusers might have the power to banish him or to kill him but not to do him real harm. Since betrayal of his convictions about his duties as a citizen would have made him a worse man, he declined to make a deal. They executed him, but they could not "reach" him, even by offering him life.

Thomas More, in Robert Bolt's play, was beheaded by Henry VIII on the strength of perjured testimony by Richard Rich. Rich had a price, but More did not. To save himself, More had only to put his hand on a Bible and tell a simple lie, but he remained silent.

In the 1960s and 1970s, hundreds of American POWs in Hanoi were offered freedom to return to America if they would provide information and false "confessions" of war crimes. They refused except after torture, and then said only as much as they had to. Many suffered in solitary confinement, manacled, for years rather than betray themselves, each other, or their country.

Thousands of police officers similarly cannot be reached by temptations to forsake duty for profit or for personal safety. The natural desires to live, rather than die, and to live in some comfort have not eroded their sense of duty. They own their own lives, and they will not sell them to anything or anybody. Each of them is incorruptible, certainly in the sense described by Frederick Elliston and Michael Feldberg: none will accept "money or money's worth for doing something he is under a duty to do anyway, that he is under a duty not to do, or to exercise a legitimate discretion for improper reasons."[4]

Many who do have a price cushion their weaknesses in false consolation. As the novelist-philosopher Iris Murdoch writes:

> The chief enemy of excellence in morality is personal fantasy: the tissue of self-aggrandizing and consoling wishes and dreams that prevents one from seeing what is there outside one. . . . Almost everything that consoles is a fake.[5]

We human beings, of course, show remarkable capacity to excuse our worst excesses and negligence and to console ourselves that we are blameless for our own misdeeds. We blame our parents for how we were raised or embrace social and political ideologies that tell us "the system" is always to blame.

Corrupt public officials—including corrupt police—in particular seek consolation by blaming "the system" for their own misconduct. Some police say that planting evidence, obtaining confessions illegally, submitting false reports, and committing perjury are necessary to take criminals off the streets, but even if they were, they would be inexcusable lawbreaking. Respected command personnel throughout America flatly deny that such means are necessary. They, like experienced patrol personnel, know that criminals continue to commit criminal acts and, if not apprehended for one crime, will often be apprehended and convicted—legally—for another.

Self-consolation attends laxity and negligence as well. Some police may be lax in enforcing traffic laws on the excuse that many traffic violations go undetected and unpunished and that competent patrol officers would never engage in a pursuit that constituted a greater hazard than the violation did. That is no excuse for laxity, however, when it is safe and prudent to stop and warn, ticket, or arrest violators.

Higher Standards and Double Standards

Some police seek consolation by claiming that they are victims of a double standard, unfairly discriminated against. For instance, police complain that random testing unfairly identified them as drug users because airline pilots, railroad personnel, and heavy-equipment operators are not similarly tested. The point, however, is that certain drugs are illegal, and that those in a position to endanger others impair their capacities by using them. If airlines, railroads, and other industries are lax about such matters, so much the worse for all of us; their laxity must not determine the trustworthiness of private or public officials. If police departments insist on higher standards than others, they are better institutions.

Those who serve the public must hold to a higher standard of honesty and care for the public good than the general citizenry does. Anyone likely to pursue self-interest and public or private excess—even in ways tolerated among the citizenry—does not belong in government.

A higher standard is not a double standard. Persons accepting positions of public trust take on new obligations and are free not to accept them if they do not want to live up to the higher standard. A higher standard as such is not unfair; granting authority to an official without it would be unfair to the public.

Since double standards are unfair standards, the distinction between them and higher standards should be maintained by command officers and teachers. Otherwise they lose their justification for legitimate standards of performance in public office.

When police complain about double standards (and are not just confused about legitimate higher standards), they may refer to standards for police that differ from those for other officials. Police who enforce the laws, they say, should have the same standards as legislators who make the laws.

Some public officials fuel this resentment, as Senator Patrick Leahy (Democrat, Vermont) did on March 31, 1988, on the Mac-Neil/Lehrer NewsHour, when he insisted that the attorney general, under investigation for possible illegal and unethical conduct, should either resign or take a leave of absence. "This is not a case where he is running the Department of HUD or something like that," the senator said. "He embodies the justice system in this country. He's the chief law enforcement officer of this country." The senator was then asked, "If you were the subject of an investigation, which you thought was in some way tarnishing your office that you hold, or the public respect for your office, would you step down, or resign, or step aside temporarily, if you knew in your heart that you were innocent?" He replied, "If I was running the Department of Justice, with the responsibility of that, of course I would have to step aside."

By implication, Leahy proposed a double standard that calls for greater trustworthiness from law enforcement than from other executive branch officials and from legislators. But if law enforcement executives cannot fulfill their duties because of high levels of public mistrust, neither can others in government. Lawmakers are impaired in representing their constituents.

One difference, however, is relevant. A senator can be voted out of office, but a police officer or attorney general cannot. For this and other reasons, many thoughtful people believe that all who bear the public trust cannot be judged—and punished—by the same standards and methods. They argue that a police officer should be judged by a higher standard than a legislator because police carry weapons and are more dangerous. Police "make law in the streets and can more readily violate rights." Also, police are more visible to the public and "the example they set is more important."

Police do apply distinctive powers to the lives of citizens and are much more visible than many other government officials. The powers of judges or legislators are, however, no less important and have no less impact on the public. Legislative and judicial regulation of institutions and individuals reach further now than ever before into American life, and the example they set matters no less; much of the cynicism of school children and college students stems from classroom study of media reports of corruption and bad judgment in high elective office. The behavior of lawmakers sets an example for them—and for police. If lawmakers and judges care how police behave, they should not behave in ways they consider wrong for police.

Although police should not be judged and punished differently, the work of law enforcers does differ from that of lawmakers. Some of these differences suggest the appropriateness of different responses to misconduct.

When a police officer falsifies a report in order to preserve a chain of evidence, he is subject to departmental discipline. A legislator who manipulates data to the point of lying in floor debate is not subject to discipline. He is made accountable by the rebuttal of other lawmakers—if they take their jobs seriously—and by voter rejection. The methods of accountability differ because the work of police and lawmakers is not the same. Although it is wrong for both to lie, the institutional remedies are necessarily different. Neither set is entirely effective, since many police and many lawmakers are not actually held accountable for lies.

Stressing such differences is an argument not for double

standards but for appropriately different policies and procedures in different institutions. That some public servants will inevitably betray the public makes it more essential that others not do so. Immoral behavior in government is not an excuse for others to imitate it but rather a compelling reason not to. Under such circumstances, high moral aspiration is needed more than ever.

Still, rationalization and self-consolation accompany even the worst kinds of behavior by police. Gerald Clemente, a former police captain in Massachusetts, who stole and sold police promotion examinations and also became a bank robber, said: "I became corrupt by going on the police force. . . . [T]o be a part of that police force . . . you had to be a thief. You had to steal. Otherwise, they want nothing to do with you."[6] Officer Bob Rathbun, one of the Buddy Boys of Brooklyn who stole money and dealt in drugs, was frustrated by his job and his superiors.

> They destroyed me mentally. They did. 'Cause every time I did something good, they did something to turn around and say no good. . . . I looked around . . . and I saw who was doing what, and they're getting away with anything, and they seem to be getting along with every boss. So I must be doing something wrong.

A fellow officer, Henry Winter, who rationalized that stealing money from drug dealers was "a means of getting back" at them, said he learned from his own corruption "never to become a cop, not in the City of New York, no never. Never get involved, never. Don't get involved. That's the lesson."[7]

Although such police may succeed in deceiving themselves, they were a disgrace to the badge, and their explanations are a fake. Public officials occupy a station of trust, which entails incorruptibility. Nothing like greed is compatible with the trust of other people.

All trustworthy command and patrol personnel grasp the difference between policing and the criminal justice system. They have duties of law enforcement and peacekeeping irrespective of the outcome of their work. Whether or not the suspects they arrest are prosecuted or receive only a nominal penalty is absolutely irrelevant. Emotional involvement in cases is dangerous because it encourages bitterness when they do not turn out as desired. Resentment can turn into the self-deception and self-consolation of the Buddy Boys.

The best police tolerate abuse from the citizenry without personal animosity that tempts them toward retaliation and self-indulgence. Their character protects them from self-destructive frustration. An experienced black police officer described a not unusual situation in which a terribly frustrated individual, in tears of rage at his mistreatment by another person, screamed, "pig" and racial epithets at the officer: "Look, I know how he felt, and I figured he would be swearing at anybody who came on the scene. It wasn't anything about me, or my color, or even my uniform. I was just handy." In this instance as in "more dangerous situations in the [housing] projects," he explained, a police officer has to recognize that people are often pretty close to their own limits of tolerance and self-control. "You have to try to give people enough room to do what you want them to do and not press the issue in a way that just makes things worse. Even very dangerous people who prey on others have feelings of pride and anger like the rest of us, and you have to allow them some room."

I am often told that we cannot expect everyone in public life to be like that, nor can we recruit police for that level of self-mastery. After all, history also reveals that decent people at the highest levels of government fall into corruption and suffer a decline of personal character and the loss of moral purpose. The real issue, it is said, is to try to eliminate those things that corrupt or at least to combat their effects. But efforts to prevent corruption that rest on changes in environment, external inducements to honesty, and sanctions against dishonesty are poor substitutes for personal character. They cannot take the place of the deep and unshakable conviction that corruption is dishonorable and that dishonor is truly worse than death.

Hypotheses about Corruption

If greed is simple, the variety of temptations to which police and other public officials succumb is not. Hypotheses about the causes of corruption abound, together with the array of proposed remedies. The main positions are that police corruption is caused by society at large, by influences within police departments, or by a disposition toward corruption in individuals who become police. I call the first position the society-at-large hypothesis, and scholars call the second the structural, or affiliation, theory and the third the rotten-apple, or affinity, theory.

The Society-at-Large Hypothesis. O. W. Wilson gave voice to the society-at-large view in accounting for the history of police corruption in Chicago.

This force was corrupted by the citizens of Chicago. . . . It has been customary to give doormen, chauffeurs, maids, cooks, and delivery men little gifts and gratuities. . . . It is felt that the level of service . . . depends on these gratuities.

Now, there was little difficulty in transferring the concept from servants to *public* servants. It was natural to include policemen. . . .

Unfortunately, it was easy to extend this to the offering of gratuities to policemen who would perform little favors that were not legal. . . . A certain progression of events follows. Some of the more grasping policemen would, shall we say, make themselves available for gratuities. Businessmen and others came to understand that the policemen now *expected* the gratuities.[8]

Such practices led to small bribes, Wilson explained; truckdrivers, for example, would clip money to their drivers' licenses to avoid traffic citations. As petty bribery became commonplace, police would make frivolous traffic stops to get the bills.

The practice of accepting payoffs from businessmen and drivers was extended to more serious crimes. If a policeman caught a burglar with a big haul, he would take part of the haul and let the burglar go. "If I arrest this man," the policeman would rationalize, "he will be released on bond. The money will go to a bondsman and a lawyer to fix up the case." The officer reasoned that he might just as well have that money himself. Now we come to the final act of the grim business. . . . Suppose you caught a thief with no money. You could bargain with him. You could get him to perform future burglaries with you or for you, and offer him protection in exchange for a share of the haul.[9]

Wilson was warning, too, of the slippery slope (or moral career) hypothesis: that corruption begins with apparently harmless and well-intentioned practices and leads over time— either in individuals or in departments as a whole—to all manner of crimes-for-profit. When Wilson became superintendent of police in Chicago in 1960, he told the people of the city that "the same kind of special consideration that they were buying for small amounts, could, by the same logic, be purchased by criminals and crime syndicates for larger amounts. . . . When people realized that they were part of the pattern of corrupting Chicago police, they cut it out."[10]

Although Wilson's belief that citizens stopped seeking "special consideration" is not confirmed by the facts, his analysis shows how a police department can be hurt by the desire by ordinary citizens for special services and then for illegal ones. His description of police rationalization shows how corruption becomes routine when police believe other parts of the criminal justice system are corrupt. When police believe that a violator will buy relief from a corrupt judge, they may sell relief themselves. Oliver Revell, executive assistant director of investigations at the FBI, has described such judicial corruption as "a significant problem in causing police corruption" because "where the judges are corrupt, police corruption has virtually always followed. It is nearly inevitable."

Wilson saw that cleaning up the Chicago police would require a strong and systematic method of addressing citizen complaints and a powerful internal affairs division to investigate charges. Such a division must be as assiduous in its defense of falsely accused police as in its disclosure of corrupt ones; Wilson understood that presumption of the guilt of his own men was self-destructive and self-defeating.

Believing that remedies for corruption could not be found outside police forces, he opposed political intrusion and civilian review boards:

> Discipline . . . is a function of command. It should not be divorced from operational responsibility. The answer to the problem of police misconduct and corruption is not the creation of an outside disciplinary agency. The answer is the creation of the right kind of a system within the force, consisting of men who know and understand police work, to protect the innocent and punish the guilty.[11]

Even those who concur acknowledge that external investigations in Chicago in the late 1960s show that Wilson's methods were not altogether successful. Still, with few exceptions, police officials find truth in the slippery slope hypothesis. The prevailing view in my experience is that corruption must be nipped in the bud by policies prohibiting *all* gratuities.

This policy denies that there is "honest graft," a notion advanced, in typically self-serving fashion, by George Washington Plunkitt of Tammany Hall. Rejecting blackmail, extortion, and bribery in public life, he attempted to justify the use of political office—and especially insider information—for profit. He believed that politicians could rightfully give contracts to friends, indulge cost overruns, and buy up land where parks or roads would be built. "Ain't it perfectly honest to charge a good price and make a profit on my investment and foresight?" he asked. "Of course it is.

Well, that's honest graft."[12] As one former police official put the point, however, "There is no honest dollar except your salary. Everything else compromises you somehow."

Police everywhere know that the symbol of the gratuity is the free cup of coffee. A rather jaded police captain, upon learning that I was writing a book about police ethics, said, "Oh, God, not another book about the free cup of coffee." We shall return to the issue of gratuities below.

The Structural or Affiliation Hypothesis. The society-at-large hypothesis bears a strong resemblance to the structural (or affiliation) hypothesis. Arthur Niederhoffer, author of *Behind the Shield: The Police in Urban Society,* writes,

> Actual policemen seem to accept graft for other reasons than avarice. Often the first transgression is inadvertent. Or, they may be gradually indoctrinated by older policemen. Step by step they progress from a small peccadillo to outright shakedown and felony.[13]

Niederhoffer appeals to the account of "a Denver policeman involved in the police burglary scandal of 1961," who claims to have learned from senior officers when he was a rookie to take payoffs.

> So the rookie . . . is turned over to a more experienced man for breaking in. . . . He knows he is being watched. . . . He is eager to be accepted. . . . The older man stops at a bar, comes out with some packages of cigarettes. . . . He explains that this is part of the job. . . . So he, the rookie, goes into a Skid Row bar and stands uncomfortably at the end, waiting for the bartender to acknowledge his presence and disdainfully toss him two packages of cigarettes.
>
> The feeling of pride slips away, and a hint of shame takes hold. One thing leads to another for the rookies. . . .[14]

Niederhoffer shares the widely held view that police loss of faith in mankind generally spawns individual and departmental corruption. He concurs with William A. Westley that

> the policeman's world is spawned of degradation, corruption, and insecurity. He sees men as ill-willed, exploitative, mean and dirty; himself a victim of injustice, misunderstood and defiled. He tends to meet those portions of the public which are acting contrary to the law or using the law to further their own ends. He is exposed to public immorality. He becomes cynical. His is a society emphasizing the crooked, the weak and the unscrupulous. Accordingly, his

morality is one of expediency and his self-conception one of a martyr.[15]

According to Niederhoffer, these conditions lead to anomie in police departments, to which the "typical adaptation" is cynicism: "It consists of diffuse feelings of hate and envy, impotent hostility, and the sour-grapes pattern." Cynicism is "a state of mind in which the *anomie* of the police organization as a whole is reflected in the individual policeman."[16] Niederhoffer's position is traceable to the sociologist Emile Durkheim's account of anomie, a pathological condition of alienation from society and its constraining influences of law and morality. It means loss of any sense of solidarity with the collective sentiments and positive norms of society.

The structural account of police corruption is described by its advocates, the sociologists Julian B. Roebuck and Thomas Barker:

> Police corruption is best understood not as the exclusive deviance of individual officers, but as group behavior guided by contradictory sets of norms linked to the organization to which the erring individuals belong, i.e., organizational deviance.[17]

The view is that corruption emerges among police because deviant behavior is regarded as appropriate within the police department. Many studies confirm that young police are socialized by their senior colleagues in traditions of corruption within the department. According to this view, corruption depends on secrecy; thus, police reform can be achieved best by external review, by civilian boards, or by elected and appointed public officials. Police commissioners often lack sufficient authority and resources, however, to combat corruption from within: "Very few police expect repercussions from their involvement in corrupt exchanges. They are not deterred by the law enforcement apparatus of which they are a part, nor do they fear departmental sanctions for their illegal behavior."[18]

Mark Pogrebin and Burton Atkins add that external remedies also encounter obstacles:

> The assuredness of punishment either on the part of the district attorney or another outside investigative body is usually lacking, therefore permitting corrupt activities on the part of police to endure. Internal control appears to prove insignificant and external control has proven to be successfully challenged by local Police Benevolent Associations.[19]

The hypothesis of structural deviance and the attendant perplexity about remedies are not complex: (1) If a young person of high ideals but little exposure to realities that challenge naive expectations of human decency (2) enters a world that exposes the worst in people and (3) is trained and influenced by senior colleagues who have lost faith in police work, and (4) if the young person must establish some mutual trust and reliance with colleagues who use their work to line their own pockets and to get their share of what all others are grabbing as fast as they can, and (5) if their superiors are unlikely to support efforts to behave honorably, and (6) the likelihood of sanction for corruption is negligible, (7) *then* the young person will probably accept the status quo and join in corrupt practices, perhaps with initial feelings of shame, but ultimately without remorse. The difficulty of remedy is equally transparent: when cynical persons on both sides of the law profit from an alliance, and when the ability of police command to force the issue is constrained, those persons will use any means to preserve the status quo and to prevent reform from outside.

No one has to conduct massive studies to know these things. They are amply demonstrated in history and political theory and in daily experience. Still, they do not confirm that police are universally cynical; clearly a great many are not. Nor do they show that disappointed expectation is sufficient to make anyone corrupt. Many patrol and command personnel whose expectations of people have been lowered by years of experience would never take a dime that did not belong to them. Not even great disappointment in the citizenry in itself can make police corrupt; to become corrupt, police officers must give up on themselves, not just on others.

The Rotten-Apple Hypothesis. Some argue that the affiliation (or structural) hypothesis neglects important roots of corruption. The Chicago Crime Commission, for example, "placed an emphasis on the type of police officer on the force . . . in examining the major causes of police criminal behavior. . . . The commission concluded that poor recruitment methods permitted many men to enter the department who were not suited for law enforcement work. The commission recommended that all police candidates be subjected to a complete character investigation."[20] This "rotten-apple" hypothesis, critics reply, ignores socializing influence within departments and is too individualistic, like "the analogous free-will explanation of criminal behavior."[21]

The rotten-apple argument has, however, been confirmed repeatedly by cases of corruption within departments—for example, the discovery of the River Cops and others in Miami, Florida, which was expected to lead to removal of a tenth of the department. By the early 1980s, Miami had become a volatile city: "A savage turf war among cocaine traffickers provided a daily litter of corpses. And that was just one of the developments that left a shell-shocked citizenry screaming for more police. Another was that Cuban neighborhoods were becoming explosively over-crowded." In May 1980, "a race riot ripped through the black Liberty City ghetto."

In that year, officials decided to double the size of Miami's police department; within two years, two hundred new officers were hired. These newcomers were not adequately trained or supervised; officers with less than a year's experience became field training officers and made recommendations whether newcomers should pass probation. Seventy-five percent of the officers "since accused of wrongdoing or complicity have come from this poorly trained group. . . . Ten . . . have pleaded guilty to murder-conspiracy or drug trafficking charges."[22] After two more officers were convicted of racketeering, cocaine possession, and conspiracy, a police official said that he was "proud of the jury" and that more arrests would follow.[23]

The crimes included robberies, burglaries, millions of dollars in profits, and conspiracy to murder a drug dealer who became a state's witness. According to a former chief, "The rush to expand . . . seems to have led to a willingness to overlook past behavior in background checks that at other times would have been judged unacceptable." The president of Miami's Fraternal Order of Police, adds, "When you're on the line offering your life for $25,000 a year and you see these cocaine cowboys getting off on light sentences and getting off on probation, it becomes opportunity for the employee who's a little weak-willed."[24]

Few, if any, of these police were corrupted by more experienced police, who had little contact with them. Instead the newcomers continued to frequent bars they had patronized before becoming police, the haunts of drug dealers. Supervision was lax, even nonexistent.

The frenzy of indiscriminate hiring, inadequate training, and poor supervision eroded personnel standards of the Miami Police Department until even illiteracy was no disqualification. Such betrayals of standards would have the same effects on any police department, regardless of the ethnic background of the newcomers, because so many thoroughly unfit individuals became police.

Neither the structural theory nor the rotten-apple theory is adequate by itself, nor are they mutually exclusive. The variety of corruption in public life gives plausibility to each in specific circumstances. But neither must we therefore accept Niederhoffer's account of anomie or the structuralist idea that men and women are not free to avoid corruption. The incompleteness of each position is clear; the structural argument cannot account for those who remain uncorrupted in corrupting environments; and the rotten-apple argument fails to explain how decent persons fall victim to circumstances. It also fails to account for those who lose their moral standards because they lack the imagination or intellect to control corrupting environments.

Some corrupt police are remorseful and tell the truth when they say they "just didn't know how to say no" to partners who led them to corruption. Others had no idea what to do when they discovered corruption in their command structure. Part of their moral decline may be a matter of practical ignorance. In a few cases, I believe it occurred partly because they knew too little about how to acquire power within institutions to combat abuses by supervisors, not because they were predisposed to corruption. For the clean members to join together to reverse peer pressure and to constrain others from corruption is a sophisticated political art, never learned by many police, especially at the patrol level. Standing for high principle need not mean standing alone, as students of politics know.

Departmental Supervision

Departmental structures and administrative policies can teach officers of integrity that they are not alone. Appropriate policies can thwart temptations toward corruption.

Bob Leuci, the subject of the book *Prince of the City* in New York, started on the road to corruption when he and his colleagues secretly used illegal wiretaps on drug dealers. When this surreptitious information enabled them to find drugs and make arrests, their successes led to accolades, to lack of supervision, to extensions of their tours of duty in narcotics, and to an insulated, cocoonlike environment. The officers then began keeping the money they found when arresting dealers, and later they kept and sold the drugs.

Closer supervision of the officers by command personnel

might have prevented the wiretaps at the outset. Routine examination of informants by supervisory personnel could have served as a check on police activities. Mandating rotation of personnel assignments could have prevented insulation and the misconduct it made possible. Reassigning personnel whenever they are promoted and assigning them on the military model to fixed terms known at the beginning to be three years or so would have been useful. The expense of such practices in giving greater training to more people is small compared with that of corruption in law enforcement. If followed all the time as a way of safeguarding the police, these practices will not be seen as merely distrust or a reaction to corruption.

Although departmental structure does make a significant difference, especially in assignment and supervision, the structural hypothesis goes far beyond that. Its greatest weakness is to suggest that we are mere creatures of circumstance, that we can be courageous, honest, just, and temperate only so long as our circumstances do not become too difficult, and that we can have integrity only so long as it does not cost too much.

In my experience, many have greater fortitude than that. There is truth in the venerable beliefs that "fortitude even conquers fortune" and that "the art of living well consists principally of bringing good out of evils we may have to encounter."[25]

Still, such mature character is a great deal to expect of a teenager or someone in his early twenties. Habits of excellence can be developed by that age, for many young people do behave justly, courageously, honestly, and temperately, but their inexperience can make them too credulous toward senior colleagues whose good faith they take for granted. Misled about what qualifies as decent behavior, they may enter on a slippery slope. Their moral and emotional fortitude may be untested as well, even if they are disposed toward right conduct, but their main weakness is likely to arise from inexperience. These facts have implications for recruitment, education, training, and supervision. To forestall the young from stepping onto a slippery slope, two admonitions by former New York City Police Commissioner and Police Foundation President Patrick V. Murphy should be stressed: Except for your paycheck, there's no such thing as a free buck[26]; and, Eliminating or reducing police corruption was always more important than convicting organized crime figures, even the overlords—the dons.[27] If this position is made clear, recruits may learn from the first day that behavior accepted by police personnel is not always acceptable.

79

Gratuities and the Slippery Slope

As we have seen, O. W. Wilson, Patrick V. Murphy, and many other experienced officials believe that the slippery slope of corruption begins with any gratuity, including the well-known free cup of coffee. Many officers disagree, as do some scholars. The historian Michael Feldberg, for example, says that "small vices have small effects, and we need not begrudge police officers their free cup of coffee, half-priced meals, and the sense of welcome that they convey. . . . They are a relatively innocent transaction in a work universe in which the standard form of reciprocity . . . is extortionate rather than hospitable."[28]

Some restaurant owners do intend the free coffee or the reduced meal-price as a kindness to police they judge to be underpaid, but others, more or less subtly, expect something in return. Some clearly want the police presence, but others want illegally parked customers to be left alone, and so on.

Police have told me that insurance companies reduce theft and robbery premiums on restaurants with a visible police presence and raise them where gratuities are prohibited. Although these officers believed that, a survey of major companies suggests they were wrong. Insurance companies sometimes prefer to insure restaurants with a central alarm system or with a security guard, but rates are not affected (even when off-duty police are hired as guards). Restaurant owners may tell police otherwise, but they are never so motivated.

Some police view the free coffee as a hospitality, and others view it as their right. Some always leave a tip as large as the price of the coffee plus the normal tip and expect nothing in return; others leave no tip. Most shopowners and waitresses can tell the difference in police attitudes, and so can the police themselves. Some restaurant personnel clearly believe the police would be rude to refuse their hospitality, and so do some police. But the police who think they have a right to the coffee do not much care about rudeness.

My experience leads me to conclude that, for some police, the small kindness—like making fresh coffee when the police arrive in the middle of the night—is just that. It is not like a tip for a bellhop, and it is not the beginning of a slippery slope. Since the intentions of the restaurant personnel are often equally innocent, police acceptance and appreciation are not illicit. Other police believe themselves deserving of special consideration because they feel underpaid or burdened with too much hardship in their work. If this attitude resembles self-pity, it can be a sign of vulnerability to a slippery slope. The free coffee may not cause the vulnerability, but it may, by indulging it, lead to worse things.

What, then, should be a department's policy? It should tell the truth: not everyone who accepts free coffee steps onto a slippery slope that leads to more serious corruption, but some do, and some is too many. Although Wilson and others may not be entirely right about bellhops and maids (if they do a poor job unless tipped, they probably will not keep their jobs long), they are right that members of professions do not take gratuities. If police want the status of professionals, they should view being tipped as a threat.

Accordingly, departmental policy should treat all gratuities as unacceptable. They undermine public respect and cause resentment—costs that police in general must pay. In this sense, the free coffee is much too expensive. Young officers should take nothing except their compensation, rather than be faced later with questions about how far to go. Once that becomes the issue, the matter has gone too far.

Some police departments compromise by permitting officers to accept free coffee and meals within their assigned districts but not elsewhere. This practice risks injustice in the distribution of benefits to police and jealousy among them over areas of assignment. If police departments require officers to sign these checks, many restaurant employees do not bother to submit them. Some police mock the policy by routinely signing illegibly or by writing the name of the chief or someone else.

Under a chit system, if a restaurant provides free coffee to an officer, it can seek reimbursement from the city. Thus, the officers retain the free coffee, but the city, not the restaurant, is the benefactor. The system is supposed to remove incentives to corruption. I would rather have the city and the police department make known that gratuities are prohibited. Any money available for a chit plan can be placed in the salary pool for police, who can decide how to spend it.

The question of where the slope begins is no more emphasized in police literature than where it ends. Lawrence Sherman of the Crime Control Institute offers a hypothetical moral decline, beginning with the acceptance of minor perks, such as the free cup of coffee, which leads to complacency about accepting a free drink after hours from a bartender, to bribes for traffic violations, then to money from gamblers and prostitutes, and finally to graft from narcotics. Sherman insists that such a decline presupposes circumstances that enable it, and he concurs with Ellwyn Stoddard's suggestion that "most policemen stop at a certain stage of deviance on the basis of group definitions of 'limits.' "[29]

But what makes up the "group" that defines the "limits"? Surely not the police force as a whole, or the Buddy Boys could never have accepted their final limits. Once a group begins to push to the limits, they may continue to press until few, if any, boundaries are left.

Furthermore, Sherman's identification of the coffee as a perk begs the question. By definition, a perquisite is a legitimate benefit, "expected or promised, held or claimed as an exclusive right" by virtue of a job, such as a residence for a college president. If a police officer thinks of the coffee in this way, he may think the same way about other benefits to which he has no right. A kindness is not a perquisite and therefore cannot suggest other perquisites except to a person who is confused about rights. Still, for those who can never have too much of a good thing, bad thinking can turn little vices into bigger ones.

According to the Knapp Commission in New York City, many police stop at a certain point on the slippery slope and go no further.

> Corruption, although widespread, is by no means uniform in degree. Corrupt policemen have been described as falling into two basic categories: "meat-eaters" and "grass-eaters". . . . The meat-eaters are those policemen who . . . aggressively misuse their police powers for personal gain. The grass-eaters simply accept the payoffs that the happenstances of police work throw their way.[30]

But why do police become grass-eaters at all, if they lack the greed and contempt for decency necessary to become meat-eaters?

Character and Free Will

Herman Goldstein reports the commission's view, endorsed by Mark Pogrebin and Burton Atkins among others, that "the grass-eaters may not, in a corruption-dominated department, be acting out of free choice. . . . One strong impetus encouraging grass-eaters to accept relatively petty graft is, ironically, their feeling of loyalty to their fellow officers. Accepting payoff money is one way for an officer to prove that he is one of the boys and that he can be trusted." Officers who refuse such payoffs may not be "fully accepted into police fellowship."[31] As one former police executive put the point to me, "You know a department is in trouble when 'He's OK, you can trust him' means 'He's on the take, too.'"

Some officers say they became corrupt because they feared for their lives if they did not. They feared that others would not assist them in an emergency or that active reprisals would be taken against them. Officer Crystal Spivey, who was videotaped accepting a $500 payoff to protect a drug dealer in the Buddy Boys scandal, said: "I'm a victim here . . . because of [Officer] Henry Winter coercing me, over several months, to get involved in some kind of a dirty deal. . . . I began to feel afraid that being on his bad side would put me in a very life-threatening situation." She could not complain to IAD about corrupt senior personnel, she said: "There were pretty big connections . . . that guys had in the precinct, who were corrupt, with the Internal Affairs Division. And if you made a complaint against them, they would know about it."[32]

William Phillips, a corrupt cop who became a witness for the Knapp Commission, said that it is "true everywhere" that "a stand-up cop won't be an informer" because deviation from the corrupt norms of the department will be "punished, promptly."[33]

Even if one accepts these rationalizations (and many experienced command personnel do not) and even if police do slide into corruption for peer approval, to say they are "not acting out of free choice" is bad sociology.

When police find that they cannot enjoy the approval of their fellows—and cannot rely on others for protection in dangerous situations—unless they are willing to forgo honesty, they are faced with a choice. No matter how great the pressure, it is their choice, and they are responsible for making it.

It is not their fault that the department suffers from corruption, and it is disgraceful that any police should be faced with such a choice, but it is a choice, and they must make it. Freedom of choice does not mean freedom from pressure or from conflict of loyalty, conflict of desire and duty, or conflict of one felt duty with another. If freedom meant that, our only free choices would be those made in a vacuum, and we are never in a vacuum.

A person subjected to torture who can bear no more and must yield has no choice. But a person who has much to lose from choosing honor over peer approval—in the circumstances the Knapp Commission described, for example—does have a choice and, one way or the other, makes it.

This is not to say that being incorruptible is easy or safe. Most of us face difficult choices of this sort in public and private life: who has not wanted to protect a friend from the consequences of some error of judgment or misconduct? And who can fail to understand the temptation of a chief of detectives who allegedly falsified reports to make his son appear to be working as a police informant when he was arrested for drug dealing? Making such choices is evidence that we are free, not that we are not responsible for our conduct under pressure.

We teach children when faced with peer pressure in favor of promiscuous sex or dangerous drugs to "just say no." Children yearn for peer acceptance at least as strongly as adults do, and yet we expect them to have what it takes to say no to behavior that would shame or harm them. We insist that they are free to choose, even though the choice may be hard.

Children are exposed to tremendous peer pressure not to be tattletales, sometimes reinforced by adults who suspect they are becoming whiners who "run to Mama" whenever they cannot get their way. But we try to combat peer pressure that conceals bad behavior within the group. We may not sufficiently explain to children that, if playmates are doing dangerous things, we want to be told, and that this differs from "telling mommy" about every dispute over a toy. As a result, some reach adulthood unable to distinguish tattling from rightful disclosures of misconduct that require courage. They think of all disclosure as a sign of weakness, even when it reveals the serious misbehavior of others, and they overlook that their duty in accepting a position of public trust implies a refusal to tolerate corruption in silence.

This confusion also arises among college students at institutions with honor systems, which require students to behave honestly and to inform officials whenever they witness a violation. Honor is understood to include intolerance of dishonor in others. Some might feel like a tattletale to tell on someone else and might fear that others would blame them for what happened to their friends.

The honest reply is that tattletale is a dirty word if it refers to whiners or cowards or to those who lack the strength to make their way with their peers. But if it means a person who has the courage to disclose serious wrongdoing, then it is not. Others may blame that person if their friends are punished for misconduct, but refusing to tolerate dishonor is neither whining nor cowardice. It is near the heart of our conception of honorable life, which includes the courage to accept contempt from those who should know better. Those who behaved dishonorably are responsible for whatever happens to them, not the person who would not yield to dishonor by silence.

Those who bear the public trust must see the difference between a refusal to tolerate dishonor and "tattling" in the bad sense. And those who bow to peer pressure at the expense of fidelity to the police mission are bad risks for the laws and the people, even though disclosure of police misconduct may require immense courage—and may destroy the whistle-blower's career.

But won't there always be some who take the path of least resistance? Of course. And won't there always be those who truly believe that their obligations to fellow officers override their obligations to abstractions, like the laws, the public, and the public trust? Probably. And given the things police suffer together, given the need for high morale and mutual trust, how can we have both mutual loyalty and whistle-blowing?

Loyalty among specific men and women is something to be prized, but it is not the purpose of law enforcement; and it must be subordinate to the purposes for which police are given authority and power. If colleagues had a duty to conceal each other's violations of office, it would make the duties of office subordinate to personal kinship. Upsetting the order of duties in this way is as misguided—and contemptible—as would be a command officer's thrusting an inexperienced patrolman into peril in order to spare a more qualified friend. If the command officer said later, "I did it out of loyalty to my friend," we would conclude he was unworthy of command, that he played favorites, and that he was more interested in protecting his friends than in protecting the citizens, as he and his friend were obliged to do.

Someone might reply that the command officer jeopardized people, but routine corruption jeopardizes no one. As Albert Seedman explains, however, some investigations of dangerous felonies are impaired because police cannot seek information from other police for fear word will reach the suspects. Of one murder case, he observes,

> Normally, I'd have called the local police routinely to find out what they knew about a suspect, but bookmaking was the one line of work where I didn't dare. . . . A bookmaker could not operate without at least tacit approval of local police. Like the folks who bet, most cops just do not regard gambling as a genuine crime. That's why so many of them

can justify not enforcing the law in this one area. In any event, I was afraid that asking the Suffolk County Police about [the suspect] would be like shouting in his ear.[34]

Corruption has long tentacles, which may cause harm at unpredictable times and places. Blithe tolerance of "harmless" corruption should therefore always be avoided.

"But my *life* depends on my fellow officers. I don't want to be betrayed as Serpico was, or left to die for lack of assistance." The judgment of Patrick V. Murphy and others is that "there was never the slightest speck of evidence" suggesting that New York police officers were trying to rub out the whistle-blower Frank Serpico. "His shooting was . . . thoroughly investigated by all of the people who obviously would want to make hay out of it, like the District Attorney, the FBI, reporters, and the police department's own internal affairs division."[35]

Even so, any officer cast into the wilderness by endemic corruption deserves great compassion. The most hardened command personnel ought to be unwilling to allow this to happen. To prevent it, they must root out corruption ruthlessly, out of feeling for their fellow officers as much as justice. No person's life ought ever to be on the line for the sake of graft.

6
Authority and Reform in Controlling Corruption

Everything secret degenerates, even the administration of justice; nothing is safe that does not show it can bear discussion and publicity.

LORD ACTON[1]

Corruption has few easy remedies. According to an old truth, if the bad cannot corrupt the good, it will seek to drive it out or destroy it. The bad seeks ways to cloak itself in secrecy, among police as much as anyone else.

The historian James F. Richardson has written about departments where corruption has run deep:

> The habit of secrecy came from the policeman's sense of public pressure and hostility, which required solidarity among the police to protect themselves. . . . Men were not to talk about department business to outsiders, and, above all, they were not to inform on a fellow officer. In the department Westley surveyed, many policemen were willing to commit perjury to avoid informing on colleagues guilty of a felony.[2]

When things reach this stage, public service has collapsed into self-service, and little or no trustworthiness remains.

What can be done from within a department to prevent corruption from taking hold and to reduce it where it has a hold? And what can be done from outside? No remedies are likely to be effective unless they face both issues—how to avoid rotten apples and rotten structures in policing.

The general answers are not difficult. To avoid rotten apples, police need high standards for recruitment and selection, the capacity to attract candidates of high quality, and good educational programs both for newcomers and for experienced personnel. To avoid rotten structures, police need leadership that will not tolerate corruption, institutional procedures for accountability and for systematic investigation of complaints and of suspicious circumstances, commonality of purpose and moral ideals among command and patrol personnel, and a decent political and governmental environment. Like most general answers, however, these provide scant practical counsel.

As administrators in all walks of life learn, reform of recruitment and selection, training, policy, practice, and attitude is never easy. Institutional habits run deep; they are often tied to uncritical acceptance of the inevitability of the way things have been done. People set in their ways resent efforts to change anything, not only in police work but also in education, business, and government. An old saw in education is: It is harder to reform a curriculum than to move a graveyard.

In police departments, as Jack Goldsmith suggests in *The Police Community*, "a discernible *patrolman* subculture is found within the broader police subculture,"[3] but reform depends on initiative and commitment at the command level. In *An Anti-Corruption Manual for Administrators in Law Enforcement*, Richard Ward of the University of Illinois and Robert McCormack of the John Jay College of Criminal Justice describe analyses showing that "the level of misconduct or corruption is generally related to the quality and style of management . . . and the chief's commitment to eliminating such conduct."[4] Many patrol officers have told me that they care more how command personnel treat them—and speak publicly about them—than about public opinion or media coverage.

The Authority to Lead

To effect reform, administrators must be masters of the art of politics. No one can sustain reform who cannot survive in office, yet no one can stand for high principles who is not willing to lose a job over them. No person working alone—no matter in how high an office—can generate durable reform; and few administrators can implement reform unless they can generate pressure from outside the institution.

The strategy and tactics of reform must be built on these lessons. Failure to heed them leaves in place the fundamental obstacle cited by Lincoln Steffens in his *Autobiography*, the belief that "reformers are no better than others, that they lack the knowledge, efficiency, and machinery to establish permanent reforms,"[5] and that the prudent course is to wait until they move on. Ward and McCormack stress that "the facts of political life cannot be ignored . . . and a chief must recognize the importance of developing a political climate in which an anti-corruption campaign will not collapse and result in the chief's removal. Forces in political life and in organized crime support corruption, and they are frequently powerful enough to destroy an anti-corruption campaign."[6]

Before accepting a position, top administrators should learn what they can of a department's history and present condition from federal and state officials, as well as others in nearby police departments, courts, and the media. They should review departmental policies, procedures, and budget and discuss pending lawsuits and related matters with departmental legal counsel, including consent decrees. The expectations of the mayor or governor in making the appointment ought to be discussed candidly.

Whether orally or in writing, top administrators need a clear sense of the nature and purpose of their appointment. The charge should make clear their authority to change structures without hindrance, since reform can seldom be achieved without structural revision, and it should give the authority to assign and reassign personnel. In some cases, prospective chiefs will want a guaranteed minimum term of office and an explicit account of causes sufficient for removal. They will want to know how many specific leadership positions in the department may be filled or vacated at their discretion and whether this is subject to revision.

Obviously, not all these items can be expected in some settings, but as many should be sought as possible. Too many candidates for executive positions in law enforcement try to get the job first and worry about management prerogatives later. They make themselves vulnerable to political interference from politicians who will buy labor peace at any price. "The real bottom line of police reform," one chief recently said to me, "is control of personnel matters. The elected official who appoints you has a mandate and you have to be prepared to cooperate with him. But without authority for personnel decisions, you're finished before you start."

Longevity in office is not sufficient for reform, but it is almost surely necessary for it. When unconvinced that a chief or commissioner has staying power, the members of a civil service bureaucracy can resist by lying low and waiting for the next one. They can also commit sabotage without much fear of disciplinary action.

Because top administrators have many daily responsibilities that draw them away from close supervision of subordinates, they must have colleagues in the command structure they can trust, whether drawn from existing personnel or brought from outside. No administrator can accomplish much without them, especially in the chief's anti-corruption program, as Ward and McCormack stress:

> The sensitive and controversial nature of corruption makes it difficult to find administrators who are willing to assume responsibility for an anti-corruption program. . . . [T]he individual selected to supervise an anti-corruption program must have the complete trust of the chief. He must be willing to accept the "flak" that goes with the position, and he should be accepted by the rank-and-file as an individual who is fair but firm.[7]

The chief must make explicit that all command personnel—no matter who appointed them—are accountable for corruption and its control. Patrick V. Murphy insists that "despite civil service restraints, the chief must find ways to make his subordinates in management actively participate, and hold them strictly accountable, for a positive approach to the control of corruption."[8]

Accountability is essential in all areas—lawfulness, conformity to institutional policy, prudent exercise of discretion, and fidelity to the best departmental traditions. To control corruption, a police department should be responsible to the public in direct and identifiable ways, subordinates should be responsible to their superiors, and command personnel to the honest members of the rank and file.

Accountability—like authority and power—depends on information. After informing the public and police about policy, the leadership should show that it means what it says, by rewarding honesty and punishing corruption. Since information must be acquired from the public and from police about what is actually going on, command personnel at the highest levels must be accessible. Where the police leadership has established conversations among all ranks about problems and has done something about them, police performance is palpably improved, corruption minimal.

Policies and practices must appeal both to what moves the best people, their character and sense of public service, and to what moves the worst of them, fear. Fear alone cannot motivate all people. Command personnel must develop internal and external flows of information to appeal to motives of every kind.

Chiefs who take this counsel seriously must be willing to make dangerous and resolute enemies. Unless their own conduct is above reproach, those enemies will besmirch their reputation to undermine their authority. At the same time, chiefs should keep in mind the adage, When you shoot at a king, you must kill him. When enemies attack, a chief is wise not to let things fester but to act to excise a cancer before it grows beyond control. Such action often forces hidden enemies to declare themselves; if the chief is in the right, enemies are better faced in the open.

Alliances

Although some anti-corruption work is bound to be adversarial, enemies should not be made needlessly. Alliances should be sought in the department, the media, the broader political structure, and the general public.

Such alliances are more likely where people are genuinely disgusted with the corruption. A portion of the public wants corruption, whether graft for double-parking, gambling, or some other form. Whatever the jurisdiction, however, two fundamental points are on the side of reform and must be driven home in public and in the department: (1) the public always pays for corruption; and (2) corruption condemns honest and dedicated police to anti-police prejudice, harassment from colleagues, and dangers that can become life-threatening.

A significant number of people inside and outside government say that some corruption is part of the cost of doing business. Herman Goldstein observes that some people "consider the problem of corruption unsolvable."[9]

The response should be, Which problems? Although no country, city, or sizable institution has ever entirely eliminated corruption, the issue is which specific problems can be addressed and solved. Recognizing this is one antidote to apathy about corruption. Countless instances prove that corrupt individuals can be weeded out: law enforcement officers who have extorted money from defendants, for example, have been indicted or forced to resign. Police have been caught in the sale of drugs and in the use of illegal wiretaps in extortion schemes. Police who profited from scams have been convicted of income tax evasion. And police whose relations with informants were in violation of policy have been suspended or fired. Some departments have changed structures for the better. Even if some corruption is inevitable, specific problems of corruption can be identified, isolated, and solved.

The costs of corruption must be explained to the public and to the police themselves. When people are convinced that they are personally the victims of corruption, they are likely to be supportive, and when they sympathize with other victims, such as honest police, they can be made allies.

Former Police Commissioner Don Pomerleau of Baltimore learned in 1972 from police officers of a "possible lack of integrity on the part of some members of the department."[10] For the first time in the history of the city, he sought assistance from the FBI and U.S. Attorney in undertaking an extensive investigation. In January 1973, eighteen civilians and six active and two former police detectives were indicted for violations of the Organized Crime Control Act of 1970. In the next six months, five detectives were convicted, and other command and patrol personnel indicted. Pomerleau said at that time:

> Corruption is corruption, and like a cancer its malignancy spreads. . . . But one thing should be clear now: Baltimore is not permissive when it comes to paid winks at wrongdoing. The lowliest patrolman on the beat should feel at this stage that he can blow the whistle on payoffs, no matter who is involved, and that he will be backed up. His badge is just as big as anyone else's. . . . Members of the force . . . have been consistently reassured, as I reassure you, of my wholehearted support of this most important endeavor—the ferreting out of those few among us who violate their public trust and solemn oath of office. It is our individual and collective, moral and legal obligation to do so.[11]

One of his former colleagues says, "Don Pomerleau witnessed many abuses by the police and many abuses of the police. He felt he could make a meaningful contribution. He did, and many of us owe him a debt of gratitude. He had a difficult job to do here. He did it well. He did it his way. As others like him, he paid a price."

Although the chief must take local circumstances and history into account, he can guarantee his honest subordinates that they are not alone and that command personnel will initiate internal affairs investigations of evidence that police, as in Miami, are living far beyond their means. If political patronage or perversion of the civil service system have rendered internal investigations impossible, assistance can be sought from the FBI and other agencies.

A chief can provide command support and encouragement to honest officers by seeing that reports of corruption are investigated. A chief cannot necessarily guarantee confidentiality of disclosure of corruption by officers, which may be limited in trials by the Sixth Amendment. If corruption runs deep, the anonymity of informants may be difficult or impossible to protect. Chiefs should not falsely minimize the risks of breaking the code of silence, but they can reduce these risks.

Annual in-service training should be required for every patrol and command officer, with special focus on the temptations of vice and narcotics assignments. Supervisors in every department should know their subordinates thoroughly, so that they can detect any striking changes in cars, houses, clothes, and so on. With today's higher police salaries and with the increase in employed spouses, these changes may be more difficult to detect than in the past. A strong disciplinary code is essential, even if it leads to high levels of attrition. Such measures can elevate the morale of the police who matter most—the honest ones. They are indispensable to penetrating what Goldstein and others call "the most formidable barrier to eliminating corruption: the blue curtain—the conspiracy of silence among police."[12]

Conspiracies of Silence

The conspiracy of silence is not unique to police. Televangelists have apparently kept silent about corrupt practices for fear of reducing financial support. In education, faculty and administrators who know that others are taking sexual advantage of students turn away rather than risk criticism or public repercussions. The medical profession closes ranks against criticism, and in business and government, too, some choose silence rather than go out on a limb.

"Insider" groups that feel beleaguered in one way or another try to safeguard themselves by keeping outsiders ignorant of their practices. Some persons find strength in feeling that they have a special understanding of "how things really are." Ignoring the opinions and judgment of anyone outside the group is, however, a sign of weakness. If widespread, it lends support to all manner of corruption as fear always does.

Police studies, however, address the curtain of silence more frequently and extensively than any other field, perhaps because of the history of literature about police. In its monopoly on the use of force, undercover investigation, and so on, police work is distinctive but probably no more subject to corruption than other activities. Some police departments are corrupt to the core, and others are scarcely corrupt at all. Some individual police are corrupt; many are not. The same can be said of ministries, businesses, educational institutions, industries, retirement centers, hospitals, and government agencies.

Opportunities for corruption exist in all walks of life. Conspiracies of silence are different in policing only in degree, if at all.

Reform

Leadership seldom achieves much without a clear agenda, known within the institution and by key outsiders, that leaves no questions about the highest priorities. It cannot be effective if it is framed in platitudes or if it is vague.

In addressing corruption, commentators propose techniques after the pattern of guides to management. Ward and McCormack stress that corruption in its various forms must be defined unambiguously. Borderline cases do not deserve emphasis in an agenda, which must make clear that even if day shades imperceptibly into night, noon can easily be distinguished from midnight.

They also urge that administrators "realistically consider community norms when defining corruption and formulating policy."[13] Some officials emphasize that indifference to conduct in the community establishes an untenable and self-defeating double standard for police. In Ward and McCormack's view, administrators must then identify the extent and level of corruption and develop manuals of procedure and guidelines for internal affairs investigations, all in the context of an anti-corruption policy that is "realistic, manageable, and continually reinforced." The administrator can then "develop a program to implement and enforce his policy";[14] he may find it useful to establish "an ethics committee which is representative of the department. The committee should make recommendations about minor misconduct to the chief, but, ultimately, the chief must determine the policy."[15]

Although these are steps any competent administrator would plan, no one can responsibly allow community norms to dictate policies. Public opinion may have a bearing on enforcement of laws, for example, where strict enforcement of a law against drinking on a public street would cause immense disruption and antagonism and would be ineffective in any case. Although the standards of the community deserve serious attention, community expectations of police behavior may be so low as to be worthless. If the public expects police to accept gratuities, failure to set a higher standard would be tantamount to licensing corruption.

Police leadership should not leave a community in ignorance if it does not know how much can be accomplished by a truly fine police department. Teaching and showing what can be done, in an effort to raise community expectations, is better than taking community standards as immutable. If expectations are low, they may reflect dreadful past service and loss of confidence. Police can hardly achieve good community relations by concurring in this expectation.

A higher standard is sometimes the only means of improving a situation; great schools are built by discipline and aspiration that exceed the norm, and so are great athletic teams, great armies, great businesses, great countries, and great individuals.

Combating Mediocrity

No one remedy serves for all the varieties of corruption, as may be seen in the case of the Philadelphia Police Department, which according to the *New York Times* has "long been considered one of the worst in the country."[16]

On July 19, 1988, seven current or former narcotics officers were indicted for racketeering, drug dealing, and perjury after seven others had been indicted earlier.[17] Investigations also confirmed widespread judicial corruption, long known to the Philadelphia police and suspected by federal agencies. Where police corruption is widespread, internal reassignment, expanded powers for internal affairs investigations, improved recruiting and training, and so on, are useful, but insufficient to clean house. External investigative agencies that cannot be compromised by local political powers and departmental pressure are also needed.

Other kinds of corruption—petty graft, "cooping" (sleeping on duty in a secret place), trading favors with local merchants, and the like—can be signs of mediocrity in general, which may be susceptible to less direct treatment. In Philadelphia, efforts to improve policing through broad cooperation with citizen groups became the byword of reform under Commissioner Kevin Tucker.

William B. Eagleson, Jr., the leader of a citizens' group overseeing improvement efforts, said that advances in the last year had "proven wrong those who believed that the Philadelphia Police Department was so entrenched in its mediocrity that change was impossible to accomplish and would indeed be unwelcome."[18] An earlier panel appointed by Tucker confirmed that "years of complaints about mismanagement, corruption, and brutality were justified." Police cooperation with the two panels led to the establishment of foot patrols, programs to assist crime victims, and three "small satellite stations or precinct houses to 'provide a police presence that is different from the abstract links created by the 911 telephone system and patrolling automobiles.' "[19]

The *Philadelphia Inquirer* hailed the new alliance of "residents and cops" as "partners against crime." It described the effectiveness of foot patrols and satellite stations (community policing) in helping citizens and overcoming police-citizen animosity and pointed out that these advances had not come easily. As ten-year police veteran Thomas Bray said:

> We were pessimistic and apprehensive . . . but at the same time we were eager because we knew it was going to be a challenge. . . . Initially community residents were suspicious. . . . Unfounded rumors spread of the existence of a jail cell in the mini-station. Little by little, however, things changed. Children, lured to the mini-station by games . . . returned to their homes talking not of jail cells but of the friendly officers. . . . Slowly, adults began to trickle in to meet the officers. . . . The trickle grew to a steady flow . . . as the officers proved adept at contacting city and state agencies to help residents with housing problems and other troubles.[20]

Not only are the citizens actually safer, they feel safer. One resident observed, referring to Officers Brian Grievous and Martin Derbyshire, "I always feel better when I see those two guys." Another said, "They are really doing a good job. Before they came, it was like a revolution out there. . . . Now it's calmed down. You can really see the difference."[21]

Several officers described their renewed eagerness to go to work, their kinship with the citizens, and their satisfaction at "making a difference." Such progress shows that police-citizen efforts at improvement do not have to be adversarial and that even in departments where some police are corrupt or brutal, others are committed to high standards of faithful service.

These advances in Philadelphia do not imply that everything has been done or that the future is entirely rosy. They have to be sustained and refined by assiduous leadership over many years to come. Genuine reform never becomes secure by short-term progress. And police reform was not without its critics within the Philadelphia Police Department. A spokesman for the police union, Rick Costello, accused the panels of "writing their own report card," since they were appointed by the commissioner, and dismissed their reports as "long on rhetoric."

These criticisms were part of an internal struggle over new merit standards for promotion. Since merit promotion had been undermined by favoritism in the past, according to Costello, he asked, "Unless they can assure us that favoritism won't come back, how can we support it?"[22] The answer is for command personnel to establish rigorous criteria of merit and procedures for their application. Beyond this, only a growing record of conscientious judgment by command personnel within the standards has a chance to earn respect.

As Philadelphia shows, police-citizen cooperation is especially important where citizens in poverty have been ravaged by street criminals. Barriers of secrecy are most likely to be penetrated by activities that join police and citizens in the common purposes that improve their daily lives. Temptations to corruption might be reduced for officers who find fulfillment in their work every day with citizens whose faces and names mean something positive rather than negative to them.

Will greater police responsiveness and neighborhood policing reduce corruption? Not necessarily. Close association between police and the citizens can be a force for good and a cause of corruption. Where the cooperation is for the public good, officers being rotated to new stations introduce their incoming colleagues to the community in hope of perpetuating good working relations and worthwhile projects. But where the cooperation serves illicit purposes, police may continue traditions of corruption and pass them along. Rotation is imperative to prevent bad habits from persisting unheeded.

No working relation between police and public, and no form of decentralization by itself, changes the need for close supervision of personnel by command and for performance in accord with departmental policy. Problems of favoritism, nonenforcement, bribery, and so on, can be made worse rather than better by close association with members of the public. In Philadelphia as elsewhere, the issues of long-range improvement of services and reduction of corrupt activities remain in the balance.

Review and Advisory Boards

Experience in such programs has not established the rightful place of civilian boards in addressing problems of corruption. But it does suggest that citizen attention is wisely engaged in cooperation with police, rather than being isolated with corruption as its only object. If citizens address *only* corruption, they are likely to be kept outside the barriers, but if they come with a cooperative attitude to a broader appreciation of policing, they can gain insight and trust.

This is an uphill path. As Chief Robert C. Wadman, of the Omaha Police Department, and Chief Robert K. Olson, of the Corpus Christi Police Department, write, "The commitment to past police practice is strongly felt and defended not only by police, but often by a public. . . . The same public . . . still reacts negatively to major changes in their police."[23] But if police teach citizens that "Neighborhood Watch groups, Senior Citizen Alert programs, and Career Criminal operations"[24] can increase safety and improve personal life, then bonds may develop that make citizen criticisms a bit more welcome. Most of us take criticism better when it is constructive. Wadman and Olson conclude that "the police should develop liaison with any and every organization in the community that is interested in enhancing the positive aspects of neighborhood life. . . . We must organize and encourage citizens to take an active part in their own well-being."[25]

Whatever the extent of citizen engagement, the chief or commissioner must in the end exercise authority in implementing anticorruption policy. Departmental committees, ethics committees, and civilian review may all be useful, but command must ultimately take the responsibility for problems of corruption. Command personnel should not have to stand alone, however, in combating corruption.

Two problems limit the effectiveness of civilian review boards. First, they are often composed of representatives of many segments of society, without regard for understanding of law enforcement or institutional administration. Second, their members sometimes have political ambitions and betray confidences to the media when it is to their advantage. Working with already functioning citizen groups may be more useful in maintaining communication and improving services.

Many police administrators in major cities rely on civilian advisory boards, task forces, and blue ribbon commissions. A police chief has much in common with business and other high-ranking executives, who also face problems of fraud, misconduct, union negotiation, budget, and discipline, so their experience can be instructive.

A task force or advisory board can give counsel on difficult issues. People in such positions generally respect confidentiality, especially with regard to the media, and can significantly expand the resources available to chiefs and commissioners without compromising their authority.

7
Leadership and the Character of a Department

This reminds me of a conversation which I once had with the Hon. Frederick Douglass. At one time Mr. Douglass was travelling in the state of Pennsylvania, and was forced, on account of his colour, to ride in the baggage car, in spite of the fact that he had paid the same price for his passage that the other passengers had paid. When some of the white passengers went into the baggage car to console Mr. Douglass, and one of them said to him: "I am sorry, Mr. Douglass, that you have been degraded in this manner," Mr. Douglass straightened himself up on the box upon which he was sitting, and replied: "They cannot degrade Frederick Douglass. The soul that is within me no man can degrade. I am not the one that is being degraded on account of this treatment, but those who are inflicting it upon me."

BOOKER T. WASHINGTON[1]

Booker T. Washington and Frederick Douglass were heirs to the very old and wise moral insight that inflicting wrongs is worse than suffering them. This moral tradition does not suggest that a person should willingly suffer avoidable wrongs or should behave as though helpless. No self-respecting person will tolerate abuse when he can decently prevent it; the point is rather that if a person must choose between suffering and doing wrong (that is, if there is no alternative), suffering is better. The tradition does not imply that individuals should never use force in defense of themselves or others or in prevention of crimes and injustices. It is not a pacifist tradition. Many of its advocates—such as Socrates—were respected combat soldiers.

To find out where one stands on the matter, a person need only ask: "Would I rather be in Frederick Douglass's shoes or in the shoes of the people who discriminated against him?" Or, if this question seems to ignore the complexities of Douglass's times, a person can take a timeless—and therefore contemporary—example: If I had to choose between perjuring myself and having someone commit perjury against me, which would I choose? Few people want to be in either position; but if these are the only choices, which will it be?

No question of conviction in public life is more fundamental than this one. A police department whose members are not committed to this moral tradition is vulnerable to two corrosive flaws. First, officers who are more determined to avoid suffering wrongs than inflicting them may act preemptively—Do unto others before they do unto you! They may use force precipitously, act with prejudice toward suspects and others, and behave vengefully toward anyone they believe disrespectful. Second, officers who view suffering wrong as shameful may be unsettled by abuse that is best ignored; if it undermines their self-respect, it can make them cynical and subject to burnout. Public life requires a thick skin and an awareness that a person's honor is not besmirched by the misconduct of others.

The department's leadership should convey in word and deed its commitment to the Douglass lesson. Since mistreatment and failures and disappointments cannot be entirely prevented in police work, this lesson is irreplaceable. Perpetrators may go undetected or escape punishment, and wickedness may appear unjustly rewarded, as when a drug dealer amasses immense profits and lives out his life in luxury and comfort. Police who prefer doing wrong to suffering it may use wrongful means to get at a suspect or known perpetrator. The Prince of the City, the Buddy Boys, and other cases show how dangerous and self-destructive this temptation can be, and how yielding to it can breed disaster. Police must learn what is genuinely intolerable to do and to suffer.

Realistic Expectations

Policing unavoidably includes a significant level of failure. No society—and certainly no constitutional republic that pays heed to civil rights and liberties—can prevent all crime or apprehend all perpetrators. Command personnel must promote a realistic sense of what counts as success, what counts as failure, and how to live with both.

All of us want to succeed, but we often do not grasp what success is. Someone may believe that an internal affairs investigation succeeds only if it discloses wrongdoing, but its purpose is to discover the truth. If an investigation proves an accused person innocent, the investigation has succeeded.

People who succeed can fail at success. A basketball star is a considerable success, but not if the wealth and status of stardom lead to drugs and self-destruction. Similarly, those who become police officers in a department with serious recruiting and training standards have achieved a significant success. When they abuse authority and power, however, and do not live up to the trust of their office, they fail at success. Success can destroy a person whose character is not up to it.

So, too, with failure. Those who cannot live with the disappointments and failures of their job will be consumed by resentment, disgust, self-pity, and contempt for themselves and others. If they work diligently to reduce crime in a neighborhood and discover that the resources available are inadequate, they face partial failure and can respond in a variety of ways: by giving up; by becoming contemptuous of political leaders and police command personnel for having foolish expectations; by becoming indifferent to their own ideals; by resorting to more ruthless means of enforcing the law; by becoming corrupt themselves; and so on.

Or, they can adjust their expectations to the challenge, learn what the circumstances, the law, and departmental policies allow, and go on with endurance. If the expectations of politicians and police leaders are foolish, the officers' disregard may be warranted, but succeeding despite failure means enduring, with expectations that are in conformity with the facts.

Good character and wisdom allow a measure of equanimity in the presence of failure, and the lack of these qualities is a principal cause of burnout. A department should therefore recruit and sustain candidates who have achieved some moral and intellectual strength and teach them truthfully the hazards posed by both success and failure.

Burnout

Hillary Robinette, a supervisory special agent of the FBI, writes in *Burnout in Blue*:

> To elevate burnout to the lexicon of clinical terms, as if it were some new malevolent strain of Asian flu, is to deny the reality of human process. Lance Morrow is accurate when he says that the term "burnout" denies the human experience of "the ups and downs—even the really awful downs— to which all men and women, in all history, have been subject."[2]

101

Burnout is not a cause, but a description of failure. Clinical studies treat burnout as "the debilitating malaise that affects people in the helping professions . . . like police officers, who initially have high expectations of personal contribution" but whose expectations, either of themselves or their work, go basically unsatisfied.[3] As Morrow and Robinette point out, low times, sometimes of extended duration, are part of every human life. Although other accounts refer to it as a debilitating malaise, some people clearly have the fortitude to persist through terrible lows, without being debilitated by them. No one should be blamed for being so ground down by circumstances that counseling or medical treatment is needed. But those who consistently conduct themselves badly because they feel low show a failure of intellect or of character. In the same way depression will inevitably come to many officers, but only those who do something about it reflect the character needed for police work.

Police officers may lack the self-knowledge to see that they have chosen the wrong line of work, or they may lack the resolve either to give it their best or to change to another kind of work. Or they may lose fortitude in the face of tedium, departmental shortcomings, the unavoidable inefficiency of government that respects both law and liberty, and the impossibility of completely succeeding at the police mission.

Work should contribute to meaning in life and help overcome feelings of pointlessness, as love, friendship, religious devotion, and avocational accomplishments do. But when a person's work seems futile, life itself may be cast into the balance. The only remedy is to pursue something else.

The challenge for departmental leadership is to try to prevent false expectations—and to find recruits whose backgrounds show fortitude. It can try to build channels of information to reveal problems in the streets that may be addressed by changes of policy, of resources, of personnel, and so on. And it can refuse to treat burnout as a given in policing.

This task should be an abiding priority of a department, reflected in programs of peer counseling and in routine sessions of patrol and command personnel, with mutual candor and trustworthiness and without fear of reprisal. Since police work places stress on personnel at all levels, leadership should work to reduce its effects. Ways to increase the durability of departmental personnel include good diet, healthy exercise, brief sabbaticals, assignment rotation, and confidential support services, including such professional counseling as its budget will permit. Baltimore

County and other departments are making progress in these areas.

When work is tedious and its purposes are blunted by persistent poverty, ignorance, helplessness, crime, and violence, some will stop thinking of success in terms of the institutional mission and purposes. Success is then reduced to matters within the departments: salary increases, promotions, approval from peers, and the like. As the emoluments of office cease to be marks of success and are transformed into success itself, the approval of peers becomes more important than performance that merits respect. If a person has given up on the work itself, then life inside the department becomes the antidote to futility.

This dangerous confusion is the most debilitating feature of life in a subculture that looks only inward. It can be squarely opposed by proven departmental respect for performance in the job—respect for merit. Since meritorious performance can take many forms in police work, each department must make its expectations clear and reward its best personnel.

Most command officers understand how difficult this is, given the power of unions, the faults of civil service, and the pressure of external political, legislative, judicial, and social agendas, especially in the tension between merit policies and affirmative action programs.

Merit and Affirmative Action

On Christmas Day 1987, Loyal Garner, a thirty-four year old black man from Florien, Louisiana, was arrested in Hemphill, Texas, for suspicion of driving while intoxicated. Two days after being beaten in jail, he died. A week later Hemphill's police chief and two deputy sheriffs were indicted on charges of violating his civil rights, and two months after that, they were indicted for murder.

In January 1988, a white candidate for sheriff of Sabine County, where Hemphill is located, said: "I don't know if you can blame the Loyal Garner death on there being no black law enforcement officials here. . . . It's hard for me to say whether it was a racial incident. But the time has come for blacks to be represented on the force. That's the least we can do."[4] The county never had a black deputy sheriff.

The philosopher Tom L. Beauchamp wrote eight years earlier that "it is unrealistic to believe . . . that in contemporary society discriminating practices *can* be eradicated by legal measures which do not permit reverse discrimination."[5] Although he insisted that

103

"all discrimination, including reverse discrimination, is prima facie immoral," he also asked, "What government policies are permissible and required in order to bring about a society where equal treatment is the rule rather than the exception?"[6] To establish a society where equal treatment is the rule, he concluded, "we ought to relax our . . . reservations against allowing any discriminatory practices whatever."[7] We ought to recognize that equal treatment in the short-run is not an absolute duty, because past and present discrimination against minorities should be remedied. Affirmative action can provide the remedy.

By contrast, the philosopher William T. Blackstone argued in 1975 against affirmative action policies: "Such policies are simply self-destructive. In place of the ideal of equality and distributive justice based on relevant criteria, we would be left with the special pleading of self-interested power groups . . . who gear criteria for the distribution of goods, services, and opportunities to their special needs and situations. . . . Such policies would be those of special privilege, not the appeal to objective criteria which apply to all."[8]

On the one hand, it is argued, in a racially and ethnically diverse country the needs of the citizens can be met and their rights upheld only if their police departments represent the minorities. On the other hand, some argue that job opportunities and advancement should be based on past accomplishments and current performance irrespective of race or ethnic background.

The first position says, in effect, that institutions of power and authority cannot be fair if major portions of the citizenry are unrepresented. The second says that such institutions cannot be fair if they deprive the best qualified individuals of opportunity so that others may be represented. A complicating factor is the racial and ethnic discrimination that has denied equal opportunity in the past. Given our history, what is fair now?

In some situations, the tension largely eliminates itself. If the best candidates for deputy sheriff in Sabine County are black, then the community can achieve black representation by hiring them and thereby respecting both conceptions of fairness. But the tension in law and policy in America since 1970 has arisen partly from the fact that these conditions are not always satisfied.

Title VII. In 1970, Title VII of the Civil Rights Act established that it is:

[U]nlawful employment practice for an employer (1) to fail or refuse to hire or to discharge any individual, or otherwise to discriminate against any individual with respect to his compensation, terms, conditions, or privileges of employment because of such individual's race, color, religion, sex, or national origin; or (2) to limit, segregate, or classify his employees or applicants for employment in any way which would deprive any individual of employment opportunities or otherwise adversely affect his status as an employee, because of such individual's race, color, religion, sex, or national origin.[9]

The legislation seemed straightforward: no one shall be deprived of opportunity on grounds of race, color, religion, sex, or national origin. Discrimination on these grounds is unjust and wrong, because these features of a person are separate from considerations of merit. Support of this law is natural for anyone opposed to bigotry and respectful of individual merit. The law stood in the tradition of the Constitution and the Fourteenth Amendment by guaranteeing rights to individuals—not to groups.

One response was that the legislation was fair in giving everyone at last an even chance. But others denied that it was fair to give even chances: since some groups had been discriminated against for generations, fairness required that their past wrongs be redressed.

In 1978, Jesse Jackson asserted, "Equality can be measured. It can be turned into numbers."[10] Jackson stood with those who believed that if an ethnic group is not proportionately represented in, say, a police department, the group has suffered discrimination. Equality could then be turned into numbers by adopting policies that lead to proportionate representation. William J. Bennett and Terry Eastland wrote in *Counting by Race:* "By the middle 1970s, the idea of numerical equality . . . requiring no specific findings of discrimination . . . came to be, through the bureaucratic implementation of executive orders, government policy."[11]

Since proportionate representation could not be quickly achieved by equality of individual opportunity and selection by merit alone, it was to be achieved in practice by preferential treatment of groups that suffered discrimination. If the short-term goal was proprotionality of representation, then the measures must include preference by race, sex, ethnicity, and so on.

On its face, preferential treatment by race seems to run counter to Title VII, but advocates of equality by numbers argue that it does not. The philosophy professor Carl Cohen explains that al-

105

though preferential treatment "does of course distinguish by race, and does, admittedly, give favor by race," its proponents claim that it "does not 'discriminate' by race in the bad sense that the law condemns." Although some programs may adversely affect white workers, in this view they "are nevertheless justified by pressing societal needs" that make clear "what interpretation of the law is required by justice."[12]

This position was taken by Congressman Andrew Young of Georgia in 1974, when he said that affirmative action "is perhaps an individual injustice. But it might be necessary in order to overcome an historic group injustice or series of group injustices."[13] Professor Thomas Nagel argued that discrimination is warranted if it is "clearly contributing to the eradication of great social evils."[14] The same interpretation of justice and the law has been accepted in a number of judicial decisions. Despite assurances in Congress that the intention of Title VII was not to force racial balance or quotas on employers, events have often turned out otherwise.

When the bill was being debated one of the sponsors, Congressman Emanuel Celler of New York, said that under the law, "the court could not order that any preference be given to any particular race, religion or other group, but would be limited to ordering an end to discrimination." He added, "It is likewise not true that the Equal Employment Opportunity Commission [established by Title VII] would have power to rectify existing 'racial or religious imbalance' in employment by requiring the hiring of certain people . . . because they are of a given race or religion."[15] Congressman John Lindsay of New York said, "This legislation . . . does not impose quotas or any special privileges of seniority or acceptance. There is nothing whatever in the bill about racial balance."[16] Senators Richard Clark and Clifford Case of New Jersey also said: "Any deliberate attempt to maintain a racial balance . . . would involve a violation of Title VII because maintaining such a balance would require an employer to hire or refuse to hire on the basis of race. It must be emphasized that discrimination is prohibited as to any individual."[17]

Nonetheless, in the 1979 case of *United Steelworkers of America, AFL-CIO-CLC* v. *Brian F. Weber, et al.*, the Supreme Court, by a vote of 5 to 2, upheld the preferential treatment of racial groups. Justice Brennan, writing for the majority, held that to promote racial balance an employer might have to "trammel the interests of the white employees."[18]

As the result of such rulings, Harvey C. Mansfield, a professor of government at Harvard, says that we and our institutions are now forced to accept an "immoral moralism," the principal tenet of which is that the end of racial balance justifies means that ride roughshod over individuals and their right to equal treatment under the law. He holds that proponents of affirmative action quotas "try to redefine merit. It no longer means the best, or the best available; it is made to mean acceptable, or beyond a certain minimum. Sometimes 'merit' is defined as what society needs."[19] "Affirmative action is obviously a way of helping people who are considered insufficiently capable of helping themselves. But just as obviously, this fact cannot be admitted. Or, if it is admitted in general . . . it must be denied in all particular cases."[20] Mansfield concludes that, in practice, we now have "government by consent decree" rather than "government by consent."[21]

In some police departments, consent decrees have required hiring of minorities by quota and promotion by quota—including promotion of patrolmen to the rank of captain, skipping intermediate ranks. Minority members are sometimes promoted ahead of others with better test scores and field performance.

Individuals, Groups, and Rights. Is affirmative action a rightful means of redressing injustice or a wrongful form of "reverse discrimination"? No decent person can tolerate what happened to Loyal Garner or look on the history of racial discrimination with complacency, but are racially preferential schemes the answer to past discrimination? As Supreme Court Justice William O. Douglas wrote in 1974 in his dissent in *De Funis* v. *Odegaard*, "There is no constitutional right for any race to be preferred. . . . There is no superior person by constitutional standards." A person "who is white is entitled to no advantage by reason of that fact; nor is he subject to any disability no matter his race or color. Whatever his race, he has a constitutional right to have his application considered on its individual merits in a racially neutral manner." Douglas, who was concerned for the quality of public service as well as the rights of individuals, added, "Minorities in our midst who are to serve actively in our public affairs should be chosen on talent and character alone, not on cultural orientation or leanings."[22]

Although institutions refer to themselves in employment advertisements and on their stationery as "Affirmative Action/Equal Opportunity" employers, they can in no way adopt preferential hiring and stand for equality except by claiming that past discrimination against a group makes current discrimination in its favor "equal." Institutions that claim to be both types of employer may be trying to ignore hard questions, like those that follow.

How shall we think about history? The economist Thomas Sowell offers this perspective:

> The past is a great unchangeable fact. *Nothing* is going to undo its sufferings and injustices, whatever their magnitude. Statistical categories and historic labels may seem real to those inspired by words, but only living flesh-and-blood people can feel joy or pain. Neither the sins nor the suffering of those now dead are within our power to change.[23]

We can redress the wrongs suffered by those who are dead only by honoring them in our behavior and testaments. To have real regard for what befell them is to behave now so they will not have suffered—or died—in vain. The decency of individuals, as well as of families and of countries, depends on a sense of history and of the importance of what has gone before. Admitting that past evils cannot be undone does not reduce those evils to insignificance.

On this principle, Mahatma Gandhi advised a repentant Hindu who had orphaned a Muslim child in a religiously inspired military action to adopt the child and raise him as a Muslim. Lyndon Johnson and others advocated affirmative action by pointing out that two runners are not fairly matched when one has had every advantage in training and opportunity and the other has been deprived. History matters.

Throughout history, savage bigotry over race, sex, or religion has always been directed against individual human beings. We should seek to redress the specific injustices suffered by those now living and to avoid visiting injustice on anyone. To treat each individual with the regard so often denied in the past, our laws and policies must be directed not to generalities of historical discrimination but rather to the specific effects of discrimination within institutions that are identifiable now. If an institution has discriminated against specific employees or candidates for employment on grounds of race, and other identifiable individuals have benefited, however unintentionally, the wrong should be remedied. Those who have suffered discrimination deserve redress.

How should we think about representation of groups within institutions? When a group is underrepresented, is discrimination necessarily the cause? What does "underrepresentation" mean?

If specific discrimination against individuals can be redressed, but not general discrimination, we must question speculation about what "would have been" if our history had not included prejudice and favoritism. Can we say with confidence that except for discrimination, the proportion of any ethnic group in a given field would equal the proportion of that group in the general population?

Many factors besides discrimination influence people in their choice of a career and in achieving high positions. A group with a median age substantially lower than another will probably include fewer in high positions. We cannot be sure, therefore, that under-representation in any occupation reflects discrimination. Only the facts of specific cases can prove discrimination. If a group seems underrepresented, we must define what we mean precisely.

In policing, the main appeal has been to community needs: if 60 percent of the population is Puerto Rican, for example, then 60 percent of the police force should be Puerto Rican, so that police who understand the culture, the language, and so on, can respond to calls. This appeal is not to "what would have been" but to how the police mission can be best fulfilled. Perhaps the benchmark ought to be, not the number of people, but the number of calls for police services. If Puerto Ricans constitute 60 percent of the population but make 75 percent of the calls for police, then 75 percent of the personnel ought to be Puerto Rican.

These suggestions have been buttressed by the argument that minority youngsters need role models in positions of authority who are of the same race, ethnic group, or sex. Such exposure to minority doctors, lawyers, police, business executives, and so on will encourage aspiration and high expectations, proponents say. If so, however, the police and the other role models must be good at their work. No one gains from exposing children to incompetence or from offering minorities worse services. Thus, arguments based on community needs are driven back to considerations of individual merit, rather than preferential hiring of minorities at the expense of individual competence.

The Rev. Martin Luther King, Jr., focused on the essential point in his famous speech in August 1963: "I have a dream that my four little children will one day live in a nation where they will not be judged by the color of their skin, but by the content of their character." Clearly, a role model must have good character. Human beings are not so different because of race or ethnicity or gender that they cannot admire, emulate, serve, and learn from those outside their own closed group. Counterexamples can be found throughout history and in our own lives. Boys learn from their mothers and sisters, as daughters do from their fathers and brothers; many people who are not black have learned from and emulated Frederick Douglass, Martin Luther King, Jr., and Sojourner Truth. The Rev. Dr. King testified to his own indebtedness to Socrates, Thoreau, and Gandhi, just as many others of various minority groups have admired and emulated Eleanor Roosevelt.

Because we are not culturally impenetrable to each other, our ideas of excellence in character and other accomplishments are not utterly idiosyncratic by race, ethnicity, or gender. Thomas Short, associate professor of philosophy at Kenyon College, writes: "The dogma of cultural separateness . . . incorporates the double lie that American minorities have a culture essentially different from that of other Americans and that Western civilization . . . exclude[s] women and minorities."[24]

Since history—and experience—teach otherwise, children deserve to learn as much. Ideals are shared across lines of race and gender: parents of all backgrounds do not want their children to grow into bigots, cowards, drug addicts, and the like. Students of history understand the contributions of women and minorities to our own and other countries.

How should we think about rights? The Declaration of Rights, adopted by the Continental Congress on October 14, 1774, declares that individual inhabitants of the English Colonies in North America have rights to life, liberty, and property, and that their ancestors were always entitled to the rights, liberties, and immunities of free and natural-born subjects of England. The Declaration of Independence similarly emphasizes individual rights, and the Articles of Confederation entitle individuals to "all privileges and immunities of free citizens." When the U.S. Constitution refers to the rights of the people, it clearly means each person. The First Amendment prohibits abridgement of the right of the people to assemble peaceably; the Third Amendment prohibits quartering of soldiers in anyone's house "without the consent of the owner"; the Fifth Amendment specifies that no person shall be "deprived of life, liberty, or property without due process of law"; and the Fourteenth Amendment says that no state "shall deny to any person within its jurisdiction the equal protection of the laws." In *Shelley v. Kraemer,* the Supreme Court explained:

> The rights created by the first section of the Fourteenth Amendment are, by its terms, guaranteed to the individual. The rights established are personal rights. . . . Equal protec-

tion of the laws is not advanced through indiscriminate imposition of inequalities. . . . Whatever else the framers sought to achieve, it is clear that the matter of primary concern was the establishment of equality in the enjoyment of basic civil and political rights and the preservation of those rights from discriminatory action on considerations of race or color.[25]

This tradition implies, as Carl Cohen writes, that "individuals have rights, not races. . . . Rights do not and cannot inhere in skin-color groups." He adds, "It is true, of course, that many persons have been cruelly deprived of rights simply because of their blackness. Whatsoever the remedy all such persons deserve, it is deserved by those injured and because of their injury; nothing is deserved because of the color of one's skin. . . . [T]he sacrifice of fundamental individual rights cannot be justified by the desire to advance the well-being of any ethnic group."[26]

On these grounds, we have a right to redress of injuries, not if we belong to a certain race or ethnic group, but only if we can show that our own rights have been violated—either by direct action or by policies that have adversely affected equal opportunity now. This is true for every individual, regardless of race, ethnicity, or sex. Otherwise individuals who have suffered no injury for which any one is identifiably responsible would be entitled to benefits at the expense of others who have done no wrong. Inflicting a wrong on innocent people in this way—in the name of social justice—underlies the resentment toward preferential employment and promotion.

But what of an institution that has in the past discriminated against candidates or employees who are no longer interested parties? Does it owe special consideration to present candidates because of its past wrongs against others? Do the rights of individuals who have suffered wrongs transfer to others? Do institutions that have committed wrongs in the past now owe preferential treatment to other individuals?

The argument offered above suggests that the answer is no. Because institutions always owe all of us equal treatment, injustice is an affront to us all. Those who have specifically suffered it gain a right to special treatment, but no one else does.

Even those who consider America a racist society oppose preferential hiring and admission to college. According to a Media General–Associated Press national poll of 1,223 adults, conducted in 1988, 53 percent of whites said that "American society is racist overall, as did 68 percent of blacks." Yet 79 percent opposed preferential hiring, and 76 percent opposed preferential admission to schools; "large majorities of whites were opposed, and blacks were split evenly on the questions."[27]

In the words of Joseph Califano, the former secretary of Health, Education and Welfare and assistant for domestic affairs to President Johnson, affirmative action was an acceptable policy to the majority of Americans "only as a temporary expedient to speed blacks' entry into the social and economic mainstream. . . . Affirmative action has pried open some important doors for blacks, but it was never conceived as a permanent program and its time is running out. . . . More imaginative efforts to target talented blacks and open white networks to them can help ease the tension created by the across-the-board affirmative action programs that anger many whites and lead some blacks to question their own sense of achievement."[28]

What are the effects of racial and ethnic quotas, of "favor by race"? In a police department, comradeship is basic to performance. Since commonality of purpose and ideals must transcend race, ethnicity, and sex, police departments emphasize what their members share. Los Angeles Police Department brochures, for example, say "Our cops only come in one color: Blue." Preferential treatment at the expense of those who have done no wrong can undermine comradeship and fragment a department. Resentment over matters as important as compensation and rank can have dangerous results.

Racial tension in police departments has many causes. I have never seen a department in which officers of one race feared that others of different races would fail to assist them in time of need— racial differences seem to stop there. But mistrust and lack of confidence may be revealed in unexpected ways. Some white officers hand dirty money to one another but pass it to black officers in unmarked envelopes delivered surreptitiously so that they cannot identify the white carrier. Racial tension is a problem that calls for forthright leadership, probity, mutual confidence, and trust.

Much more than bare justice is required for people to live and work well together. Mutual respect, not merely in general, but for specific individual accomplishments is basic. When individual performance is undervalued, professional standards are bound to decline.

The worst consequences of preferential treatment may be suffered by those who receive preference. As Charles Murray, a senior research fellow at the Manhattan Institute for Policy Research, has written, such a person "has to put up with the knowledge that many of his coworkers believe he was hired because of his race; and he has to put up with the suspicion in his own mind that they might be right."[29] If this suspicion gnaws at those who were hired preferentially, they may conclude (perhaps accurately) that others expect low performance of them, and they may reject high standards of performance and become progressively more isolated, even from colleagues who are not racially prejudiced. They may fail to live up to the rightful ideals of policing.

Recent Judicial Rulings. Under Section 1608.4, the Title VII Civil Rights Act of 1964 was amended in 1985 to read that reasonable affirmative action plans "may include goals and timetables . . . which recognize the race, sex, or national origin of applicants or employees . . . regardless of whether the persons benefited were themselves the victims of prior policies or procedures which produced the adverse impact or disparate treatment or which perpetuated past discrimination."

How this will be interpreted over time is as uncertain as the interpretation of Title VII was in 1970. Prior to this legislation, the courts had held, as in *Janoviak* v. *Corporate City of South Bend*, that "race-conscious programs do not, as a matter of law, violate either Title VII or the Equal Protection Clause of the Fourteenth Amendment." In this case, the Seventh Circuit Court held, however, that statistical preference in employment by race could not be based solely on a "finding that a disparity existed between the percentage of minorities in the community and the percentage of minorities in the [police and fire] departments." The court rejected a two-to-one hiring plan designed to reach equivalent proportions and insisted that such a plan be warranted on evidence of past discrimination.[30] The case has been appealed to the Supreme Court and *certiorari* has been granted.

In *Williams* v. *City of New Orleans* the Fifth Circuit Court held that Title VII does not prohibit promotion quotas and does not require that only specific victims of prior discrimination may benefit from such programs. Although the court rejected a consent decree that required promotion of black and white officers in equal numbers until half the police at all ranks were blacks, it did so because it found the plan unfair to other minorities. Judge Thomas Gee cautioned in a separate opinion that quotas "are desperate measures, inherently invidious as calculated denials of the rights of one citizen in order to enhance those of another—both on the frank grounds of race." He described them as "a last resort . . . if ever appropriate."[31]

Quotas have frequently been upheld since. In 1987, in *United States* v. *Paradise,* the Supreme Court affirmed a court order "imposing an interim one-black-for-one-white promotion requirement for state troopers if qualified black candidates are available" on the Alabama Department of Public Safety.[32] Later in the year, in *Johnson* v. *Transportation Agency, Santa Clara, California,* the Supreme Court held that the "county agency did not violate Title VII by taking a female employee's sex into account and promoting her over a male employee with higher test scores." The Court held that the promotion was in accord with an affirmative action plan designed to remedy "underrepresentation of women and minorities in traditionally segregated job categories, and did not *unnecessarily* trammel the rights of male employees or create an *absolute* bar to their advancement [emphasis added]."[33]

As elsewhere, the idea of what is necessary is complicated by the question of the conditions and constitutionality of specific plans. In *United States* v. *Paradise,* the Court insisted that applicants be qualified. In *Wygant* v. *Jackson Board of Education* in 1986, the Supreme Court held that preferential plans (as in protection against layoffs) must show prior discrimination by the employer and not just a history of societal discrimination.[34]

The matter of qualifications was tested in *Davis* v. *City of Dallas* in 1985 by the Fifth Circuit Court, which held that the police department could legally require that candidates have forty-five semester hours of college credit with a C average; that no one would be eligible for candidacy who had been convicted of more than three hazardous traffic offenses in the past year; and that recent or excessive marijuana use were prohibitive of candidacy. These standards were held to be job related, and therefore legitimate, even if they reduced minority hiring. Citing earlier cases, the court was "unwilling" to require the city to "lower . . . its preemployment standards for such a job."[35] Denying the plausibility of requiring empirical proof of job-relatedness, the court relied largely on expert testimony. The job-relatedness of college education is probably not settled, and other court-recognized standards for employment may decline precipitously if marijuana is ever legalized.

Largeness of Spirit. Since the law is a living thing that grows, evolves, and changes, these rulings are neither comprehensive nor final. Litigation will continue, consent decrees will be entered and challenged, and few rulings will satisfy everyone—in terms either of principles or of methods and results. Because issues are complex, reasonable people will disagree about them. Scholars on opposite sides of affirmative action show sympathy for the concerns of their opponents although they do not always do so in other legal and ethical disagreements.

When people of good will are defeated they should try to find in themselves the largeness of spirit to make the best of things. They owe it to themselves and their professions to live as decently as they know how with rulings they believe to be wrong.

When worthy persons are not promoted while someone else is promoted because of race, they can wallow in resentment and bitterness, or they can remind themselves that they chose to be police officers—and the best they could be. If they allow adversity to undermine their convictions and aspirations, they become their own worst enemy. No one should willingly be defeated by circumstance.

One reaction to this view has been, that's easy for you to say—you are not the one who has been passed over by reverse discrimination, and you don't have to live with incompetent supervisors who have rank only because of race. Some add that it is unfair and unrealistic to expect people whose hopes have been dashed by affirmative action quotas not to be bitter.

Although all of us sometimes have to put up with incompetent supervisors, most of those set back by affirmative action will resent it. The issue is what to do about it. The task for the leadership is to ask everyone to try to make the best of the circumstances, to exercise self-control, to promote respect for fairness, and to oppose prejudice and its effects.

One important step is to minimize surprises about departmental policies and relevant laws and court rulings. When recruits are in training, the department should inform them of its methods of performance evaluation, of its goals for inclusion of minority members in the various ranks, and of binding consent decrees and related obligations. If persons with higher performance evaluations can be passed over while others are promoted because of quotas, the recruits should be told in the beginning so that expectations about merit and hard work will not be dashed later. The disgruntlement that may result from hearing the truth in the beginning is preferable to later resentment against department leaders and policies.

The leadership should be intolerant of bigotry in all its forms, whether it is displayed by members of minority groups or by others. The case of Donald Rochan of the FBI illustrates behavior that should not be tolerated. Rochan, a black agent who joined the FBI in 1981, accused colleagues in Omaha of harassment; the *Washington Post* reported that "the face of an ape was pasted over a picture of his son in a family photograph on his desk. The message 'Don't come' was scrawled on invitations to office parties. A photograph of a black man who had been beaten was placed in his mail slot."[36] After he was transferred to Chicago in 1984, Rochan "received unsigned, typewritten letters threatening him with death and mutilation. . . . He received two letters requesting payment for death, dismemberment, and burial insurance that he had not purchased."[37]

The mistreatment was not denied by Rochan's FBI supervisors. According to remarks attributed to his Omaha supervisor, the incidents were "pranks," which were "healthy" marks of "esprit de corps" in the field office.[38] When an FBI agent in Chicago was proved to have forged the insurance documents, "he was simply suspended for fourteen days, and his colleagues chipped in to pay his salary."[39]

In the FBI, office personnel traditionally pay the salary of colleagues who are suspended or whose sick leave benefits are exhausted before they return to work. Although these are healthy signs of esprit de corps, the treatment of Rochan—no matter the reasons—is not. The leadership must insist upon this distinction and refuse absolutely to tolerate prejudice against others because of race or sex.

Racism and other forms of bigotry are often disclosed in the feel of a place. An institution may have an atmosphere of insidious bigotry that could never be proved in litigation. All levels of personnel ought to be alert to this, but the leadership should pay special heed, especially to subtle forms of bigotry, since the temptation to pass them off is likely to be greater.

Routine references to women by obscene anatomical terms or to minorities by racially derogatory epithets are signs of such an atmosphere even when it is denied. Casual acceptance of such behavior by ourselves and others is not harmless. We should put ourselves in the place of others and ask how we would feel in such an atmosphere in our own institution. We can preorder a Kosher meal on an airline and see whether any change occurs in other passengers when the attendant delivers it. We can call a realtor and identify ourselves as black or hispanic or pretend to be illiterate and ask for assistance with a government form. We can ask how we would feel if our own daughter worked in the atmosphere where we do.

Departmental planning should focus on recruitment, selection, and promotion plans that minimize the likelihood of incompetence at any rank. The adverse effects both of racial preference in hiring and of past discrimination may be limited if good candidates of all backgrounds are selected and every candidate is demonstrably qualified and motivated to do well. Those unjustly passed over are more likely to be magnanimous if they know that the promotions went to individuals who deserved them. High standards for recruiting, selection, and advancement may be the most important measures for combating internal friction over affirmative action or other discrimination. The courts have recognized that they are indispensable to faithful public service.

Recruiting, Selection, and Promotion

Between January and August 1988, more than twenty Detroit police officers were charged "with felonies ranging from assault and armed robbery to murder." At least one hundred others were "under investigation for ties to the drug underworld." Police officials denied that the corruption was systemic: "The department didn't commit those crimes. . . . People did, who happened to be wearing badges." One Wayne County prosecutor said that the department "needs to revise its recruiting standards very carefully."[40]

People do not just "happen" to wear the badge. They wear badges because they were hired by a police department, which is responsible for its employment and training policies and practices. What should be its criteria for recruitment and selection? David C. Couper, police chief of Madison, Wisconsin, answers that the skills and intelligence required for policing should be central, and not race and sex or size and strength. He adds:

> Selection criteria must be demonstrably work-related. . . .
> Screening procedures for applicants should be structured to
> eliminate people who are clearly unsuited—psychologically,
> intellectually, physically, or morally—to do police work. . . .
> But more important than eliminating unqualified applicants
> is identifying, through testing, medical and psychiatric examinations, personal interviews, and background investigations, the candidates with the necessary sensitivity,
> compassion, integrity, maturity, stability, intelligence, and

117

ability to handle the complexity and stress involved in police work.[41]

As Couper points out, these standards are perfectly consistent with hiring minorities, whose representation in policing demonstrates to "minority communities that police authority is legitimate and should not be antagonistic." He adds, "Women should be assigned to all fields according to their talents and skills." Couper appeals to research that shows women officers to be "particularly effective at defusing violent situations" and "less likely to use unnecessary force than men officers."[42] Good judgment and restraint are not, however, a function of sex or race; they are achievements of individuals, who should be assessed as such by a department.

Whether or not a department has been guilty of discrimination or has to hire more minority officers in order to provide good services, it can avoid errors in recruiting, especially if it does not make past residence in a specific locale a requirement. It is easier to teach police about an area and its residents than to make good police from unqualified applicants. The Standards Manual of the Law Agency Accreditation Program, which favors affirmative action, recommends the following: (1) The department should advertise broadly for candidates and need not restrict recruiting to the area of its own jurisdiction. (2) The department should have trained personnel conduct a written background investigation of every eligible candidate, including verification of credentials, "a criminal record check, and verification of at least three personal references." In some cases, polygraphs may be used as "an investigative tool." (3) The department should have trained personnel conduct an oral interview of each candidate, and also test "general health, physical fitness and agility, emotional stability, and psychological fitness." (4) The department should require of all candidates a six-month probationary period and completion of entry-level training.[43]

Although a one-year probationary period for entry-level positions may be better, these procedures are effective if the standards and criteria are genuinely job related and are applied uniformly. To fill positions, a department should never forsake procedures and standards or lower its qualifications. Serious problems of unfitness of the kind encountered in Miami, Detroit, and New York may be prevented at the outset or addressed early in candidacy.

Police executives and federal law enforcement officials have asked how the use of polygraphs can be justified, since such tests are not admissible in court and some candidates for employment object to them. One answer is that a background investigation (or a departmental investigation of possible corruption or misconduct) is not a trial. A defendant in a trial is compelled to be a defendant, but a candidate for employment can terminate his candidacy if he does not wish to be examined, and an officer under investigation can resign. Therefore the standards of a trial need not be treated as binding elsewhere.

The Employee Polygraph Protection Act enacted in 1988 does not apply to federal, state, or local government agencies. Although it specifies that private employers "are generally prohibited from requiring or requesting any employee or job applicant to take a lie detector test," it specifically "permits polygraph tests to be administered in the private sector, to certain prospective employees of security service firms (armored car, alarm, and guard), and of pharmaceutical manufacturers, distributors, and dispensers."[44] Thus, even in the private sector polygraph tests are legitimate if security and narcotics are involved.

Since rehabilitation and discipline are more difficult and expensive the longer a person is employed, supervisors should be alert to signs of trouble during training and probationary periods. If stress is a problem in police work, it can also be an asset in training, which should be sufficiently realistic, and therefore stressful, to discourage less dedicated and less able candidates. Rigorous training identifies people who are at their best when things are at their worst, the sort a police department needs.

Many departments maintain high standards while increasing the proportion of minority employees, without creating double standards for candidacy or promotion. In some, standards for candidacy and for performance evaluation are more rigorous now than they were even a few years ago, and the leadership remains stable without a rapid turnover of chiefs. As the chief of one such department observed, "Making progress takes courage and commitment to training. Getting the best people depends on widespread recruitment; state certification requirements help, and you can't live with double standards inside." He added, "It also takes a good bit of luck." Another emphasized that "skip" promotions are always a bad idea and that achieving proportionate representation of minorities is pointless if standards are compromised.

A comprehensive recruiting plan, developed in 1987 by the Personnel Department of the Police and Fire Selection Division in

Los Angeles, contains many good ideas. Noting that the challenge "is to find previously untapped recruitment sources," the plan stresses

(1) mobilization of community resources, including the City Council, Mayor, community-based organizations, citizens, and LAPD personnel at all levels to reach qualified prospective female and minority candidates;

(2) establishment of a recruitment cadre of police officers to discuss careers at school career days, job fairs, church events, and athletic competitions;

(3) advertising on radio and television programs recorded in Spanish and Asian languages and whose audiences include bilingual members of ethnic communities;

(4) expansion of the recruitment program to include testing on more college campuses and military bases;

(5) greater LAPD involvement in activities of children and young adults in Boy Scouts, Girl Scouts, YMCA, YWCA, and ROTC, and expansion of departmental youth activity programs such as DARE (Drug Abuse Resistance Education);

(6) increased cooperation with magazines and newspapers to encourage feature stories about police and departmental career programs; and

(7) scholarships to students majoring in Administration of Justice.[45]

The program is expensive, and therefore prohibitive for some departments, but some of the activities may be implemented locally without great cost even by small departments.

The New York City Police Department is experimenting with a police cadet corps, an effort to recruit college graduates. During the last two years of college, the city provides cadets with educational loans of $3,000, which are forgiven after two years of police service; students who do not choose police work must repay the loans at 3 percent interest. For two summers the cadets work full time as observers with the Community Patrol Officers Program, and are paid seven dollars an hour; they also work three days a month during their college years. Some cadets seem more interested in the loans and jobs than in police careers, but others express enthusiasm about becoming police:

> CPOP is a fabulous program. We attended community board meetings, tenant association meetings, block parties. Sometimes we talk to crime victims and tell them about

compensation that's available to them. . . . We also escorted senior citizens to the bank. . . . Now, there's no question that I will [become a police officer].[46]

Ordway P. Burden, president of the Law Enforcement Assistance Foundation, writes that the NYPD believes "that college graduates may bring greater sensitivity to the officer's job."[47] He recalls a 1965 study in Los Angeles by B. E. Sanderson, which found that college graduates "did significantly better in the police academy, had fewer sick days and injured-on-duty days off, were less likely to be disciplined, and were much more likely to be promoted."[48]

Although the program is a worthwhile experiment that will no doubt bear some favorable results, college-educated people should not be assumed to have better character than others, to be more resistant to stress, or to have better work habits. Some of the most notorious businessmen and officials in history have received fine educations. And as their professors know, many college students do not work very hard. Police departments everywhere have benefited at all ranks from the excellence of personnel whose formal education does not include college. A member of the Police Cadet Advisory Council said: "It's an open question . . . because whatever correlations are found between college education and performance . . . you're stuck with not being able to determine whether it's the college education that makes the difference . . . or the mix of personality, ambition, and talent that leads people to get a college education."[49]

According to some police officials, many current recruits—regardless of their educational level—display troublesome characteristics that seem related to influences of the 1960s on their families. Some are undisciplined and have difficulty adapting to a police academy; some who are college graduates cannot read at the eighth-grade level; and some object to working nights and weekends. Some believe naively that they will rid the streets of crime, while others seem interested only in compensation and financial security, and not performance.

Some of these characteristics are partly a function of youth, whatever the social and familial influences of our times may be. Few of us have always been as self-disciplined, adaptable, skilled, realistic, or concerned about performance as we should have been. Some commentators infer that police should bring in older recruits, at least in their mid-twenties. While this may deal with part of a department's recruiting problems, it risks having more officers retire immediately after they complete twenty years of service, so that they can undertake second careers, as has happened in some federal agencies. Most important, all efforts to draw fine applicants to police work have to be combined with rigorous training and high performance standards.

8

Illegal Narcotics—
Moral Issues and Public Policy

Every reflecting man becomes daily more alarmed at our situation.

JAMES MADISON[1]

Corruption of public officials by narcotics traffickers has become a subject of widespread concern among law enforcement agencies. Exposure of corrupt police has led many to suspect that the problems within law enforcement run deep. The Justice Department awarded $375,000 to the International Association of Chiefs of Police to prepare a manual for command personnel on preventing and reducing such corruption.

As the public became more alarmed about drug use and increases in drug-related murders and other crimes, the media, a few scholars, and a handful of public officials sought to persuade the Congress that legalization of narcotics should be debated. Most law enforcement executives have remained convinced that narcotics should not be legalized; many are developing more and better ways of combating the problems, using high technology to gather and use information and establishing procedures for greater accountability of their own personnel.

The moral issues raised in this public policy debate are perplexing. Should police executives speak out, write editorials, and bring their knowledge and experience to the attention of the public and the makers of law and policy? Is legalizing dangerous and destructive substances moral, or is banning narcotics an immoral infringement of our freedom? How can we get a handle on the moral arguments in these public policy issues? Command officers have to answer the question I have heard put by officers about urban areas blighted by crack dealers and users: *"What are we going to do?"*

I have encouraged police leaders to speak publicly on policy issues and to set aside fears of being considered self-serving—of alarming the public in order to increase their own budgets. Just as many of them informed public attitudes and legislation on the sale of cheap handguns, they ought to help increase an understanding of narcotics issues.

To show how to move through the moral terrain of public policy arguments, a summary of the competing arguments in the case of narcotics follows, together with an analysis of them. Since public policy debates often resemble one another, this analysis has application to other disputes, such as those over easy and legal purchase of Saturday night specials.

The analysis may therefore be useful to police even if the current legalization controversy is short-lived.

Morality and Public Policy

In analyzing a policy dispute, the areas of agreement should be identified first. In this case, everyone agrees that no amount of diligence or expenditure on the supply and demand sides of narcotics can eliminate drug use. The issue is control of a problem, not eradication.

Furthermore, everyone wants policies and laws that promote public safety, reduce crime and corruption, respect individual liberties, limit profits to dealers, safeguard children, encourage productive adult lives, discourage criminal careers, and lower the levels of demand. All agree that greater emphasis on education, prevention, and treatment is imperative.

The issue—like most other public policy arguments—can be approached on four fronts: a set of policy and legislative recommendations can be offered, and it can be addressed by three kinds of arguments: assessments of the success and failure of current policies and laws; appeals to moral principles; and predictions of consequences. First, then, let us look at the basic proposals and arguments of the competing positions.

Arguments *for* Legalization of Narcotics

Proposals by Advocates. According to advocates of narcotics legalization, possession and use of many illegal drugs should be decriminalized, so that the government can sell or distribute them to addicts and other adult users, at low prices. Different substances are to be subject to different forms of government regulation: low-intensity coca chewing gum might be marketed like other gum; high-intensity coca beverages would be sold in the same way as alcohol; and cocaine products, by contrast, could be purchased only with a prescription.

User taxes on some substances, like those on alcohol and tobacco, would generate income for drug treatment, rehabilitation, and education programs. Advocates of decriminalization propose the elimination not of all regulation and control by law, but rather of the profits in illegal drug dealing. The new laws and policies would undercut the market.

Assessment of Current Policies by Advocates. Proponents of legalization argue that current efforts to reduce supply and demand have failed. Although confiscation and arrest rates may be up, supplies of drugs have not been curtailed, nor have profits. Street crime is growing worse, as the demand in some sectors grows. Large sums of money—roughly $10 billion a year—are being poured into law enforcement efforts that fail, while inadequate funds are available for prevention and education.

The supply side of drug traffic cannot be controlled by the military, police, and other agencies, they say, because the flow of people and vehicles in and out of the United States is too massive. So many nations have climates favorable to cultivation of drug crops that international policies against production can never work for long. Within the United States, police sweeps have limited effectiveness against sellers and buyers of drugs who either avoid the sweeps or are freed soon after arrest. Some suburbanites now go to ghettos to buy drugs in inexpensive old cars, which would constitute a small loss if confiscated.

In sum, the flow of narcotics cannot be controlled by enforcement agencies.

Appeals to Moral Principles by Advocates. Advocates of legalization argue that the efforts of the criminal justice system to reduce drug supply—and demand—threaten basic moral principles of our heritage. Government is obliged not to interfere in the lives of competent adults, they say, except when their behavior adversely affects others. Since the sale and purchase of drugs do not involve victims or complainants in the way a robbery does, for example, illegal trafficking must be detected by undercover investigations that endanger agents, officers, and informants. Such investigations, they say, involve deception and rough treatment of rights to privacy. Furthermore, drug testing to determine compliance with the law or to assess liability in accidents also jeopardizes rights to privacy. In addition, crimes without victims to report them invari-

125

ably encourage citizens to become informants, as children in totalitarian countries are encouraged to betray their families. All this leads to erosion of civil liberties, to distrust among citizens, to the breakdown of families, and to a weakening of the social fabric.

Some proponents insist that illegal narcotics are not as dangerous as the media and some public officials say and that prohibition of drugs—as opposed to alcohol and tobacco—is therefore prejudiced. Except for drugs that pose a high danger of chronic dependency for all users, drug use is not a problem, though drug abuse is. Many people, the argument runs, live productive and healthy lives while using drugs, although others may have problems with drugs. Sometimes the problems are connected to larger patterns of recklessness, aggressiveness, social isolation, low achievement, and bad habits in general. Social policy should therefore focus resources on controlling the supply of the most dangerous drugs, and on educating the public on behavior generally.

Proponents also argue that the effects of efforts to control supply by criminal laws are immoral. Successful reduction of the supply drives up street prices, thereby increasing crime and dealers' profits. High profits in turn enable subsequent corruption of criminal justice and other officials.

Prediction of Consequences by Advocates. Advocates predict, first, that legalization would immediately reduce criminal justice expenditures by several billion dollars, thereby freeing resources for expanded drug treatment, prevention, and education. Second, governmental control of sales and taxation would provide further revenues. Third, because drug prices would be controlled, the number of crimes committed by addicts to pay for their habits would drop. Fourth, drug dealers would be largely forced out of business by legalization, thereby reducing crimes of violence among them and their victimization of users. Fifth, elimination of the enormous illegal profits would reduce susceptibility of law enforcement and other public officials to corruption. Sixth, police would have more time to prevent and solve crimes against life and property, and our prisons could hold more of the most dangerous criminals. Finally, though estimates of drug use and abuse after legalization are tentative, proponents doubt that drug use would increase significantly. Some proponents doubt especially that the use either of highly dangerous drugs or of shared needles that would increase the spread of AIDS would rise.

Proponents of legalization point to experiments with decriminalization of marijuana in California, Michigan, and other states. Studies indicate that prohibition of marijuana was a negligible deterrent and that use increased only slightly after sanctions were eased.[2] Many advocates liken current drug laws to those that prohibited alcohol in the United States from 1919 to 1933; they point to the failure of Prohibition and blame the rise of organized crime on it. We are making the same mistake again, they say; legalization can alleviate the worst consequences of that error.

Arguments *against* Legalization

Legislative and Policy Proposals by Opponents. Those who support criminal laws against narcotics favor international measures against the supply: military intervention to eradicate crops in countries that grow them, or funding of local military and law enforcement efforts; economic and diplomatic pressure; increased resources for interdiction at sea and in the air; and greater control of our land borders.

They also advocate expanded law enforcement inside the United States: profile arrests, nationally computerized tracking of the movements of known and suspected dealers; zero-tolerance of illegal narcotics, with confiscation of property, arrest, prosecution, and heavy fines for possession; and the death penalty for drug-related murder. They also propose increased emphasis on the rest of the demand side, with more accessible programs in drug abuse prevention, treatment, and education.

Assessment of Current Policies by Opponents. Despite the gravity of the problems, opponents of legalization say, the success of present policies can be seen in the increased arrests and punishment of major traffickers, in the seizure in 1987 of more than $500 million from traffickers, in the rising street prices in some areas, and in the apparent reductions in demand among some groups. Through the use of forfeiture funds, the technological capacity of law enforcement is expanding to deal with the flow of narcotics and the movement of dealers. Diligent patience is called for, therefore, rather than precipitous experiments with legalization.

According to many in law enforcement and public policy forums, Title 21 of the U.S. Code [Section 881 (A) (7)] can be applied more widely and effectively to obstruct supply. This law, as Houston Chief of Police Lee Brown explains, "provides for the forfeiture of real property that has been used to commit or to facilitate the commission of drug law violations."[3] It can be used to obstruct the operation of crack houses as long as the owner is notified that the property is subject to forfeiture.

Many acknowledge that local law enforcement by itself cannot control the supply but often only inconveniences the dealers, while stepping up arrests of users. Although organized crime units can infiltrate and "sting" drug operations, these forms of pressure, even with international interdiction, cannot eradicate the supply or the demand. Yet all of them are held to be necessary parts of a comprehensive effort that—even if it succeeds—will result in continuing drug use by some.

In Seattle, local law enforcement cooperates with federal agencies so that suspects arrested for drug and gun violations that carry modest state penalties are turned over to federal authorities, who apply federal drug possession and weapons laws that carry substantial mandatory sentences. Such cooperation, together with surveillance of airports, train stations, and bus depots leading to profile arrests, has slowed the incursion of Los Angeles–based gangs in Seattle. The federal penalties can persuade suspects to become informants.[4] Although the traffickers take counter-measures, including different patterns of dress for traveling, coop-eration among law enforcement and other agencies is essential to success.

Appeals to Moral Principles by Opponents. Because drug use adversely affects families and the broader society, opponents say, government has a rightful interest in prohibition. A government that supplies dangerous substances, they add, not only suggests approval of them but gains enough power over those who are addicted to threaten their civil liberties. Many opponents see profound differences between the normal effects of alcohol and tobacco and those of cocaine, crack, PCP, and "double-strength" marijuana (sinsemilla and high THC marijuana cultivated by hy-droponics using dissolved inorganic materials). Opponents of le-galization add that drug testing for accident liability would be necessary even if narcotics were legalized, just as it is for alcohol abuse. The law and the courts safeguard against wrongful inva-sion of privacy and illegal investigative techniques. Proper selec-tion, supervision, education, and discipline of criminal justice personnel, they argue, are the best responses to the issue of public corruption.

Prediction of Consequences by Opponents. According to those who view experiments with the legalization of heroin and meth-adone as reckless, it has never dramatically reduced illegal traffick-ing in England or the United States.[5] Unless the government legalizes the purchase of every drug in whatever quantity and potency every user wishes, illegal trafficking will be largely un-touched—particularly in drugs with the most dangerous and bi-zarre effects such as cocaine, crack, PCP, and LSD. Government could not conscionably legalize a drug such as cocaine, which addicts use in binges that result in depression, paranoia, and violence. If cocaine were sold by prescription, users would buy quantities exceeding the prescription from illegal traffickers. Events in the Bahamas suggest that reduced prices lead to more widespread use: in 1982, no one sought treatment for cocaine-related problems in Nassau's only psychiatric clinic, but in 1984, after the price of cocaine had dropped by 80 percent, 300 people did so.[6]

Even if drugs were available at lower prices through govern-ment regulation, opponents argue, addicts would still commit crimes for money to buy them and pay other living expenses. Thus law enforcement would still be forced to deal with illegal traffick-ing and related crimes.

Opponents of legalization point to emphatic differences be-tween the Prohibition of the 1920s and our present situation. Custom, habit, and public opinion favored legalization of alcohol, but, according to polls of both teenagers and adults, they oppose drug use and legalization. After thousands of years in which wine, beer, and hard liquor were accepted, Prohibition was opposed by such a weight of public desire that it was bound to fail. The current issue of drugs, however, remains in the balance. Legalization would disarm parents in their opposition to drugs; impair the efforts of businesses, schools, the military, and other institutions to become drug-free; and send a confusing signal to the young that might tip the balance toward widespread dependence on debilitating narcotics. Moreover, the end of Prohibition did not end organized crime but signalled more clearly its beginning. If drug dealers lost that enterprise, they would more likely engage in extortion, robbery, burglary, murder-for-hire, and the like than become law-abiding citizens.

Antilegalization arguments include the warning that experi-ments of this sort are extremely difficult to reverse. They conclude that the likelihood of adverse consequences is too great to risk.

Analyzing the Arguments

Disagreements over policies often stem from implicit differences about what counts as success and failure. In this case, certain facts are cited by both sides: that drug-related violence is increasing in some areas; that large amounts of money are spent on enforcement; that many dealers make high profits; that public corruption is often bought by narcotics money; that seizures and confiscations are on the rise; and so on. The disagreement is over how these should be understood and weighed.

Increases in seizures of money and drugs are a sign of progress against specific dealers, but they ought to be measured against the availability and price of drugs as well. If dealers are put out of business and incarcerated, then success is achieved in the apprehension and conviction of lawbreakers. If that has no effect on the volume of drug traffic, however, some goals of narcotics laws are not achieved. Since we have never had a comprehensive and cooperative supply-side program that included all appropriate agencies in cooperation with expanded demand-side programs, how much it could accomplish remains to be seen. The conclusion that we cannot control the supply of drugs is therefore untimely.

Disagreements can arise when different moral principles are considered of higher relevance or priority. One side in a dispute might consider justice paramount, another public safety. But in this case, the disagreements arise over matters of fact—and their bearing on the application of principles. Both sides are concerned for public safety, civil liberties, and so on; but they disagree about how dangerous various narcotics are, how far the rights of "competent" adults should go, and how adequate the legal safeguards of civil liberties are in the face of undercover investigations and the like.

My experience indicates that use of narcotics—even marijuana—is not healthy or harmless. Although people who use such narcotics may in some sense lead productive lives, it does not follow that they are unharmed by them. Students who use marijuana may get good grades, but their stamina, will power, and judgment are often diminished, and their sense of restraint and of self-respect is sometimes impaired. Clearly, narcotics like crack are immensely destructive, both of individuals and of entire communities. Addicts describe the drug as deadly; it kills individuals, and it ruins whole neighborhoods.

After a series of riots, Liberty City in Dade County, Florida, made progress in the early 1980s when widespread civic determination led to new investments by businesses and renewed concentration on schools. Some residents saw a promising future until the incursion of crack reversed much of the progress. In a few years Liberty City became a stagnant place as businesses closed and the sale and use of drugs became a dominant feature twenty-four hours a day.

Unfortunately, powdered cocaine and crack have become the drugs of choice among many users. The streets of our inner cities at night reveal the patterns of user dependency: "hits" or dosages are repeated until the money, but not the desire, is gone. Young prostitutes take a hit of crack, turn a trick, take a hit, and so on, hoping to end the night with enough money for a hamburger and more crack. Because so many users are not adults, the concern of legalization advocates for the rights of adults is irrelevant.

More experience in the streets or more exposure to white-collar crime among narcotics users might settle some disagreements about the real dangers of narcotics but not about the rights of competent adults. As our laws concerning seat belts, motorcycle helmets, and social security taxes show, we do not entirely accept the argument that adults ought to be able to do what they please as long as they do not harm others. Although the legitimacy of such laws may be challenged, dependence on drugs clearly undermines a person's competence. Given that addiction almost always harms the family and others, the argument that laws against narcotics infringe on rightful freedoms remains unpersuasive.

Are the law and the rulings of courts inadequate to defense of civil liberties, privacy, and so on? To suppose that vigilant pursuit of narcotics traffickers must erode civil liberties implies a distrust of police, prosecutors, and judges, and of the criminal justice system itself. To make a legitimate case against a suspect, police and prosecutors must overcome significant restraints and undertake rigorous procedures.

Because prediction in social matters can seldom approach exactness, disagreements over consequences often remain unsettled in public policy disputes. Conscientious and honest use of statistics and historical precedents is not necessarily conclusive. Crucial questions for both sides of the debate are: How much do we risk by this policy? What exactly do we risk? How much do we lose if the optimistic predictions do not come true and the pessimistic ones do?

The fundamental prediction at issue is whether legalization of narcotics will undercut profits and thereby reduce the black market and with it street crime, public corruption, and other adverse effects. How any of this would result from legalization is unclear. If narcotics dealers were indisposed to other illegal activities, we might infer that they would go straight when deprived of the profits in drugs, but we have no reason to think this. And we do have reason to doubt that legalization would destroy profits or reduce criminal activity.

First, legalization of drugs spawns its own variety of crime,

131

like those that have become associated with drugs that can now be prescribed by a physician. Criminal diversion of Valium, Percodan, and other prescription drugs is a huge criminal enterprise, involving bribery, extortion, theft, hijacking, and counterfeiting.

Second, many in the narcotics traffic have little education and few skills to offer in the legitimate job market. They are as likely to pursue other criminal careers as to go straight. The major traffickers, accustomed to the profits of narcotics, are even more likely to behave as their predecessors in organized crime did when Prohibition was repealed. They entered other areas of crime, including loan-sharking, murder-for-hire, weapons smuggling, extortion, gambling, and prostitution.

Third, some traffickers might attempt to thwart legal sales, by hijacking deliveries, underselling the government, using clever marketing schemes for high-potency drugs, investing more resources in marketing to children, corrupting public employees, and fomenting rumors that government drugs sterilize people, cause AIDS, or induce impotency. Some might continue to use violence for such purposes, since many drug dealers are criminals by habit and disposition.

Fourth, the markets in crack and other extremely dangerous—but preferred—drugs would be untouched by legalization. Criminal violence surrounds the marketing of these drugs, and legalization of other drugs offers no promise of its reduction whatsoever.

Both sides favor the reduction of traffic and profits on the supply side by expanding programs on the demand side. But even here, disagreements persist. Some officials doubt that the government or corporations can produce narcotics as cheaply as the cartels can. If drug production had to be subsidized by government revenues, they would yield nothing for demand-side programs. The costs of dealing with alcohol abuse and its effects in America alone exceed $100 billion a year—at least twice the estimated amount spent on all drug-related problems. Would legalization therefore result in any financial gain? Without much greater evidence of gain from legalization, even this rationale is too uncertain for such an "experiment."

The analysis remains incomplete without an assessment of the promise of expanded programs on the demand side, which bears on the extent of the risk of legalization.

Demand Reduction

The National Drug Policy Board, established in 1987, reports that drug education programs are having an effect on both attitudes toward drugs and drug demand. In July 1988 the board's *Progress Report* reported that "only 54 percent of high school seniors in 1986 believed 'occasional' use of cocaine put one at 'great risk.' In 1987, this figure was 67 percent. During the same period, 'past month' use of cocaine by high school seniors dropped from 6.2 percent to 4.3 percent."[7] From February 1987 to March 1988, the Media-Advertising Partnership for a Drug Free America conducted two surveys involving 14,000 people—children aged nine to twelve, teenagers, college students, and adults. "While the study found an increase in anti-drug attitudes in all groups, it was most pronounced among college students."[8]

Clearly, prevention and educational programs need to be expanded in schools, churches, businesses, the military, and youth organizations. Guides to family instruction about drugs are now available (through *Reader's Digest*, for example). The attitudes and behavior of adults and younger peers are especially important, because people are not necessarily constrained merely by learning how dangerous a form of behavior is. Drugs promise intense pleasure, and they often deliver on the promise. Even a person who knows the risks and understands that drug profits go to murderous drug traffickers may be too weak to resist the temptation. Persons of bad, weak, or unformed character may not have what it takes to "Just Say No." And bad judgment is possible for people who know that drugs are dangerous, just as corruption is possible for public officials who know that it is wrong and hazardous.

A reduction of demand throughout society probably cannot be achieved merely through education about the dangers of drugs. Many of those in school who have heard speakers tell horror stories about their ordeals from experiments with drugs are now asking for speakers who have never used drugs. Tired of stories of failure and recovery, they want to hear from people whose lives have never gone off-track with drugs and are fruitful and productive. Exemplars of virtue can be every bit as compelling and informative as reformed failures.

Education and prevention programs hold their greatest promise for those reached by other forms of education, but they will not reach adults who naively believe they are exempt from the perils of addiction—the cocky and self-indulgent college-educated suburbanites who frequent ghettos to buy drugs. With youths deprived of a good family, school, or neighborhood, and without church influences and examples, programs are difficult to implement.

The columnist George Will argues that "not all Americans are equally open to teaching and there will be a class bias in the results of any policy that emphasizes teaching. . . . Drug abuse is disproportionately an inner-city problem. This will become increasingly so as public information campaigns become more effective at modifying the public's behavior."[9] Although Will is correct that drug abuse is disproportionately present in inner cities, many advantaged youths and adults also depend on drugs for emotional or physical pleasure. At lunch hour or immediately after any work day, office workers can be seen visiting the inner city to buy drugs. Many have clearly convinced themselves, "It won't happen to me," and others probably will be similarly reckless in the future.

Many ghetto youths are extraordinarily ignorant of the dangers of their behavior. I have talked with teenage prostitutes who cannot read or write and who either are completely unaware of AIDS or believe that only homosexuals can be afflicted with the disease or transmit it. Many of these youths act as if they have nothing to lose in using drugs. The information that drugs debilitate and kill does not influence them because of the brutality they face every day. No quick or easy solutions can work with schoolage and even younger children who prowl the streets day and night completely deprived of adult love and instruction, while their parents turn tricks or lie insensate on filthy blankets in crack houses.

Because of such facts, the demand side of narcotics cannot be viewed as an isolated problem. It is intertwined with problems in education at every level and with economic and social problems in families, schools, neighborhoods, corporations, and other institutions.

Such broad and complex social issues require resources far beyond any that might be gained from a reduction in law enforcement on the supply and demand sides. Furthermore, because of the disproportionate levels of drug abuse in our inner cities, legalization of narcotics could hurt the already-disadvantaged most of all. Finally, some narcotics cannot be legalized because a single dose can addict a person virtually for life, despite repeated treatment; demand-side reductions will have to be combined with supply-side pressures.

Conclusion

The supply side may become manageable if more and more of the public resolutely oppose drug trafficking and use at home, on the job, and in the exercise of civic authority and civil liberty, and if peer pressure grows against purchase and use of drugs. If public opposition to narcotics becomes powerful enough, specific locales and neighborhoods have a good chance of improvement. We might witness effects resembling those of the campaign against smoking.

But this issue promises to remain forever in the balance. With each new generation, all the learning must be acquired anew and all the habits of good character must be formed again by diligent practice and healthy instruction. The ability to bear the responsibilities of public and private life must be nurtured afresh, and opportunities for the fulfillment of worthy aspiration in school and at work must be provided for all. The question of drugs is inseparable from the question of whether we have the character and will to give the best of ourselves to successor generations for their sake. If not, the country's resources will be exhausted in efforts to save the citizens from themselves, whether or not narcotics are legalized.

Police can improve conditions in the neighborhoods worst plagued by narcotics, but only briefly. Saturation policing works but has few lasting effects. Much broader civilian follow-up is required to achieve stability, including more individuals, and facilities to provide drug treatment, counseling, tutoring in school, family assistance, and so on. Legalization seems unlikely to set the stage for such follow-up. Certainly in the crack zones it would be irrelevant.

The arguments for the two positions suggest that legalization invites grave risks and offers few benefits. Therefore, I conclude that the public policy debate should be settled against the legalization of narcotics that are now illegal.

An important consideration in this conclusion is that legalization of gambling in Atlantic City and Las Vegas has been accompanied by increases, not reductions, in crime. In Atlantic City, where gambling has been legalized and taxed since 1977, Ovid Demaris reports that violent crimes in this "South Bronx by the Sea" have

> doubled, tripled, and quadrupled. Pacific Avenue, only a block away from the Boardwalk, is crawling with hookers, pimps, pickpockets, drug pushers, car strippers, and thieves. Loansharks are having a field day, and muggers attack people in broad daylight. . . . Slumlords . . . are burning down their buildings to collect the insurance. . . . Hotel rooms are broken into, guests assaulted, purses and wallets snatched, cars in the subterranean garages rifled. . . . Gambling is a game of fantasy . . . that involves

135

greed and political corruption and organized crime and murder.[10]

Public officials, as I know from experience, privately lament the levels of public corruption.

Where off-track betting and state-run lotteries have been established, illegal bookies and numbers runners do enormous business, largely because they allow betting on credit and do not report bettor winnings for taxation. Many law enforcement officials believe that levels of criminal activity become worse where gambling has been legalized. Whether for gambling or narcotics, one law enforcement colleague observes, "Any system of legalization will require some set of rules, and there will be big money to be made in breaking those rules."

Advocates say that narcotics legalization is not a capitulation to drug traffickers but a means of destroying their profits, not a statement that drug use is perfectly all right but an expression of willingness to let people decide for themselves. Granting that advocates do not intend to capitulate to dealers, I believe that their recommendations would have little effect on black market profits, because we could not legalize every drug in the amount desired by every prospective purchaser.

I am not willing to see children raised in a climate where our opposition to dangerous narcotics is unsupported by criminal laws. Respect for liberty is not the same as legalized tolerance of socially destructive intemperance. Neither is government service to the public the same as producing and marketing substances that destroy the ability of citizens to govern themselves.

Some legalization advocates, who spurn such arguments, regard moral considerations as emotional and their own views as pragmatic. But morality should not be denigrated by those who profess a concern for civil rights and liberties and for the safety of police and other citizens. In any case, they are not being pragmatic if they forsake morality in policy making, or if, in education and elsewhere, they ignore the cultivation of self-control and good judgment. Neither is it pragmatic to suppose that with legalization the drug dealers will quietly go away: the determination of ruthless people, who declare war on everyone who trifles with them, should not be underestimated. The streets, and their predators, are much meaner than most legalization proponents understand.

Many police officers recognize that their efforts and sacrifices in combating narcotics cannot completely solve any problem. The wisest among them also understand that their mission is not to reform society single-handed but to do their best to enforce the law, keep the peace, and safeguard the public, with patience, honesty, courage, and fortitude, even when things are at their worst. Their good example is critically needed now.

9
The Fundamentals of Character and Training

Only thought can determine what course of action is best on any occasion; excellence of character has the sole but important role of making the agent willing to do what reason determines is the best course of action.

J. O. URMSON[1]

In the training of police, four misleading views about ethics are best cleared away early.

First, if asked, many respond roughly this way: Whenever I hear the word "morals," I think of sex, and whenever I hear "ethics," I think of money.

Second, many believe that realism—in belief, judgment, and action—and idealism are somehow incompatible. Some say that a realist is a person who cares only about "the facts," and an idealist is a pie-in-the-sky unrealist, a person who is naive about "the way things really are."

Third, many believe that people concerned about ethics tend to be holier-than-thou goody-goodies, who disdain every pleasure, and purse-lipped prudes, who are, underneath it all, deeply unhappy.

Fourth, to a surprising number of people, including ethics teachers, the principal or sole subject matter of ethics is the treatment of moral problems, rather than the formation of habits of good character.

Both teachers and students in the academy program should be alert to these misleading views. They can be addressed without extensive theoretical baggage and with stories of police in action.

Sex and Money

That people think of morality and ethics in terms of sex and money is not surprising. Ethics scandals in government and business

138

involve money, and morals scandals in the popular media usually involve sex. Sex and money get high billing because they titillate readers and viewers and because they are sources of great temptation.

They are not the causes of scandalous behavior, however, only two of many occasions for it. Sexual attraction and wealth are also occasions for much good and for behavior that is entirely honorable. The causes of bad conduct, by contrast, are character faults, bad judgment, and, infrequently, complex and even tragic circumstances.

Many philosophers, following the lead of Socrates, Plato, and Aristotle in ethics, have stressed the question: What is a person of good character? Answers to this question go far beyond matters of sex and money. Discussion of specific kinds of virtue—courage, for example—in the lives of police suggests that real examples that are not academically tedious are better than hypothetical ones.

Courage may be understood by contrasting it both to an excess and a deficiency—specifically, to recklessness and cowardice—which are deviations from true courage. A courageous person feels, judges, and acts differently from a reckless person or a coward. These differences are appreciable to beginners and suggest analogies to other aspects of good character.

Most experienced police officers can describe what courage requires in specific instances and can distinguish it from recklessness and cowardice. For example, courageous officers understand that a domestic violence call poses dangers to everyone involved, including police. They will respond as quickly as they can, with such information about the situation and the parties as can be gathered from the dispatcher on the way and from bystanders at the scene. They are not likely to enter without adequate backup—indeed, department policies may disallow entering alone. They will carry the proper tools, including a radio and a nightstick. Since any combatant in a domestic fight may turn on the police, the officers will not ignore the risks; their purpose is to prevent the violence from continuing or growing worse.

By contrast, I have occasionally seen an officer who would rush into a scene, uninformed, without backup, and without nightstick or radio. Even if the motive is to end the violence as quickly as possible, such conduct is reckless and can lead to avoidable injuries that can end a police career.

Although outright physical cowardice is rare among the police known to me, I did witness one command officer who went to great lengths to avoid responding to domestic violence calls and gun calls. On his way to them, he would make sudden stops to break up harmless groups of idlers, radioing in that they were "hinky" and that "something was going down." Later he would try to save face by insisting that he was delayed by other problems, but his excuses wore thin. He had little credibility with his colleagues, who never counted on him for backup.

Neither sex nor money figures in any direct way in these illustrations. They highlight the moral importance of everyday conduct, as seen in realistic cases as opposed to hypothetical ones. Experience shows that courage is integral to the police function, with relevance to a range of specific issues, from the kind of colleagues an officer can depend on to the idea of aspiring to the best. Similar points about courage, recklessness, and cowardice can be made about high-speed pursuit, for example, and the handling of misguided peer pressure.

Robert Wadman, chief of police in Omaha, and his coauthors Monroe J. Paxman and Marion T. Bentley, describe the following case in *Law Enforcement Supervision: A Case Study Approach:*

> Chad Wilson has owned the Ranchero Steak House for the past twenty years. Formerly a reserve deputy in the county, he has always enjoyed the friendship of police officers. Wilson has arranged a table in his restaurant so police officers can come in and eat and not be bothered by other customers. For the past ten years Wilson has made it a practice to allow the uniformed officers working in his area to eat anything they want for "free." He states, "The police don't get paid enough, and I want them to have a good meal. They need a place where they can take a break and not be hassled by the public."
>
> Officer Harlow is working the night shift in an area several miles from the Ranchero Steak House. At approximately 2:30 a.m., he observes a vehicle weaving slightly and stops the car to see if the driver is under the influence. As he approaches the driver's side of the car, he smells a strong alcoholic beverage. He asks the driver to step out of the car. The driver identifies himself as Chad Wilson and starts naming officers on the department who are his close friends.
>
> Officer Harlow is a new police officer with approximately eight months on the job. He conducts a field test and determines that Mr. Wilson is under the influence of alcohol. After making this determination, he places Mr. Wilson in his police car and transports him to jail.
>
> At the jail, one of the officers who eats regularly at the Ranchero Steak House sees Mr. Wilson in custody. This officer makes several comments about the quality of the arrest and states to Officer Harlow, "You have a lot to learn.

This guy isn't drunk, and has been a friend of the department for years."

Officer Harlow is concerned about the situation and two days later comes to you as his supervisor and states, "I arrested one of the best contacts of the department and guys are sure letting me know it."[2]

Officer Harlow might have let Chad Wilson go when he learned who his friends were, an act that would have shown reckless disregard for the safety of other citizens—and for Wilson himself. Or later, because of peer pressure, he could have canceled the citation, or failed to show up in court, or asked the prosecutor to dismiss the charges—all actions that suggest cowardice and some of which might constitute obstruction of justice. Instead, Wadman, Paxman, and Bentley explain what actually happened:

> Officer Harlow was put under extreme pressure to drop the case prior to trial. He refused to do so because it was a violation of department orders. Mr. Wilson became upset with the department and discontinued the free meals to officers. Many of the officers who had enjoyed the meals at the Ranchero Steak House continued to make sarcastic comments to Officer Harlow. No supervisory action of any consequence was ever taken in the matter, and Officer Harlow, after several months, was accepted as a good officer by his peers.[3]

In this case, money or money's worth is involved, but it is not as central as the character of the officer. This was reflected in his attitude toward violations of law and of departmental orders, and in his courage in the face of peer pressure, just as the character of his peers was reflected in their treatment of him.

Realism and Idealism

The idea that realism and idealism are somehow opposed to each other—as though realism meant cynicism and idealism meant naiveté—needs to be corrected as well. This error suggests that ethics and morality are separate from real police work. Analysis of the actual experiences of officers will help make the correction:

> On a Saturday night, I was with two uniformed officers on patrol in an inner-city area. While we were waiting for detectives to arrive for investigation of a TV store armed robbery, an emergency call came about a shooting at a nearby address. The officers hurried to the home, where a woman in her early twenties stood screaming on the front porch. Two men were found in an upstairs bedroom, one pistol-

whipped, the other shot in the wrist. Other officers and command personnel arrived, the two men were taken by ambulance to the hospital, the house was searched revealing ammunition and traces of drugs and no other people.

One of the partners questioned the woman on the porch; it was about eight feet wide, screened on top with paneling to about waist level. The doorway was in the middle of the front of the house. Three steps led to it. Suddenly, the officer shouted to his partner, "There's somebody in the house!" pushed the woman into a chair, drew his sidearm and started into the house. As he did so, a command officer stepped hesitantly up nearly into the doorway onto the porch. The partner shoved him aside, saying, "Get the hell out of the way! My partner may need that door," made it onto the porch, preventing the woman from moving, and once the first officer had a protected position inside, followed him into the house.

A suspect was later apprehended, having fled through a basement window after successfully concealing himself in a cranny near the basement ceiling.

In his action, the second officer exhibited realism—awareness of facts, sensibility to potential danger, knowledge of how to safeguard his partner. He also showed regard for ideals—loyalty, personal responsibility, and courage. He was a realistic idealist, bringing respect for the facts and regard for standards and ideals into the union required for competent judgment, action, and life.

This combination of realism and idealism is required for the responsible exercise of command as well. A chief recently faced a situation in which eight hostages were taken by a gunman with a history of drug use and hospitalization. Police negotiated with him for twenty-four hours, securing release of seven hostages. Although they had several opportunities to shoot the gunman, the department persisted in negotiations, trying to save the remaining hostage and the perpetrator. When the hostage-taker demanded materials to build a time machine, the department provided all the specific items he requested.

Finally, however, after the gunman threatened to detonate a bomb, a police sniper shot and killed him. Patient negotiation had shown courage and respect for all the lives involved—high ideals in any setting—but when negotiations held no prospect of a better outcome, decisive action was realistic.

If realism and idealism are not joined in deliberations about what to do, our thinking may become useless or futile. When officers begin police work, they need to know that high ideals do not mean naiveté. When told by experienced police not to be naive, they should see that this is good advice—unless it is taken to mean that they should stop taking their ideals seriously. Losing sight of this profound difference encourages cynicism, not realism.

Morality and Happiness

Those who think that morality runs against happiness, that it means forgoing every enjoyment, should be reminded that philosophers—and parents and teachers—encourage good character because they believe that decent people are better and happier than others. People who act reasonably rather than impulsively, and honorably rather than deviously, are better off for doing so. But many mistakenly believe that what is right will make them unhappy and what is wrong will make them happy. The Buddy Boys knew that they were doing wrong, rationalized that others profit from wrongdoing, and believed that the profits of drug dealing would make them happier. How wrong they were could be seen in their grinding awareness that they corrupted—and then betrayed—friends on the force in their desire to spare themselves the consequences of wrongdoing. Countless lives are ruined by misjudgments about happiness and by failures to understand the deep fulfillment that comes with peace of mind.

Everyday experience teaches us that a person can know the right way to behave and not follow it. At times we all know what is right but do not do it. Sometimes we are weak willed, or we believe that doing right will interfere with our happiness, or we deceive ourselves for a while about what is right. Ashamed afterward, most of us who are honest with ourselves can admit not only that we should have known better but that we did know better.

Sometimes, of course, duty and happiness may be in conflict, as when a police officer imperils—and loses—his life. An officer who discloses the wrongdoing of a corrupt partner and is made an outcast by others may be made terribly unhappy.

But serious character faults cannot make anyone happy. Fair and decent people are far happier than cowards or unjust people who fear those they have wronged. People who cannot be trusted never enjoy the trustworthy companions who contribute so much to our lives.

The novelist Robertson Davies once said that happiness is like a cat. If you chase after it, the cat will never warm up to you. But if you go about your business, you will often find the cat rubbing up against your legs. Likewise, if you chase after happiness, it is likely to elude you. But if you pay attention to doing your best at work and in private life, happiness more often comes to you. In this respect, happiness is like fun—if we go out in order to have fun, we are unlikely to have a good time, because having fun is not a specific activity. If we go out with friends, however, and bowl our best while encouraging them, we are much more likely to have fun.

Happiness consists to a large degree in being able to offer ourselves as the very best people we can be to our colleagues, friends, and family; to this extent, morality, character excellence, and happiness are indivisible. When we understand this, we are unlikely to indulge moral shortcomings in ourselves that we can identify and prevent.

Moral Problems

Some police academy courses and in-service programs reduce the study of ethics to deliberation about moral problems. By ignoring the nature of basic character, this method may obscure the fundamentals of good and bad judgment in unproblematic situations.

Emphasis on character and the kinds of habits that form a good second nature is crucial. Only people who have acquired enough virtue to be ashamed of wrongdoing can appreciate the force of questions about right and wrong actions. What should we do? is a question for people who care to do what is right, but not for others. For them, ethics is only an academic pursuit, a matter of intellectual gymnastics. Education in ethics for police is not intended for that.

Good practical judgment means being able to tell what justice, courage, temperance, and other aspects of character excellence require in specific circumstances. It amounts to acting on an occasion with consideration for the right persons, in the right degree, in the right way, at the right time, for the right reason. Right action is conduct in accord with what reason requires in that case. Sometimes, of course, deciding what is right is terribly difficult, but often it is not.

Most of what matters in moral life does not involve difficult questions. Our lives are not filled with situations of the sort popular in ethics courses, such as what to do when not everyone can fit into the only available lifeboat. Giving such hypothetical problems the central place in ethics is highly misleading. Complicated hypothetical questions may refine our thinking, but only after we have

144

given due importance to commonplace morality. We should not obscure the importance of the ordinary by preoccupying ourselves, our colleagues, or police recruits with the extraordinary.

Habits

Good character consists of good habits that are within our power to form, and most of us have formed some admirable habits. John Stuart Mill wrote that "a character is a completely fashioned will." Normal individuals can fashion their will by the daily behavior they make habitual. "The great thing . . . in all education," the philosopher William James observed, is to make habitual, as early as possible, "as many useful actions as we can, and guard against the growing into ways that are likely to be disadvantageous to us."[4]

Police academy students can see that officers who respond to domestic violence calls should not sit in their cruisers agonizing over whether to take their nightstick and radio. They find them in their hands or on their belts because habit has put them where they belong. In the same way habit safeguards officers from neglecting the possibility of danger posed by every combatant in a domestic battle.

The role of habit in character underscores the importance of learning by experience. Provided with opportunities to repeat actions, learners can see right and wrong ways to behave. With our support and encouragement, they can form the right habits. As we work with more mature students, we should make clear how much they can do for themselves in the same way.

When we teach youngsters to ride a bike by running alongside to give support, we enable them to feel and to learn by practice to correct a fall by turning the handlebars to that same side. When we teach marksmanship, we teach students by practice to raise or lower their aim in a crosswind, depending on the direction of the wind in relation to the rotation of the rifle bullet. When we teach billiards, students learn by practice that a lateral spin, or English, on a cue ball will "throw" an object ball in the direction of the spin and cause the cue ball to drift the opposite way. We encourage repeated practice to establish the right habits in all these activities.

By keeping a careful eye for the interests and curiosity of our students, we can teach them the reasons that specific habits may be trusted to work. We thereby encourage the habit of listening to reason, instead of acting on impulse or supposing that they can become good at anything without diligent practice. The more students grasp the connections between good habits and reason, the more they can do for themselves. They may be trusted with discretion, according to their ability to apply reason to novel situations and in that way become good police officers. Good professionals understand the standards of their profession, sustain those standards by habit, and know how to use reason to make necessary decisions. For policing to become fully a profession, it should settle for no less.

Such training and education presuppose that careful background investigations have established that candidates are already disposed toward right action. Emphasis on the formation of good habits can scarcely be overdone. As William James observed, "Could the young but realize how soon they will become mere walking bundles of habits, they would give more heed to their conduct while in the plastic state." By our actions "we are spinning our own fates, good or evil."[5] James added that because habits are formed by what we actually do each day, each student who learns to work diligently and well can "with perfect certainty count on waking up some fine morning, to find himself one of the competent ones of his generation."

Particularly appropriate to police work is James's insight that the formation of powerful and reliable habits "alone prevents the hardest . . . walks of life from being deserted," just as it "keeps the fisherman and the deck-hand at sea through the winter." Knowledge that the formation of good habits will serve them whatever their walk of life encourages the young. Ignorance of this fundamental fact of human life has probably, as James concluded, "engendered more discouragement and faint-heartedness in youths embarking on arduous careers than all other causes put together."

Cultivation of habit and good judgment is very different from mere shrewdness and cunning. A shrewd intelligence that enables its possessor to do wrong with impunity is only a servant of the passions, however excessive or depraved they may be. A developed capacity to understand the reasons for behaving courageously is, by contrast, a guide to control of such feelings as overconfidence and fear. This is wisdom, which serves to govern a life, not to gratify desires slavishly.

Youngsters who live in homes where family members tell each other the truth learn by experience that trust makes a household warm and intimate. Even if children sometimes lie because they can find no other weapon to defend themselves, they learn how it feels to keep company with people whose love for each other is expressed in truthfulness. When habits of right action are formed, they help a person to want to achieve good character. Anyone exposed to human beings who behave courageously, for example, can recognize, "That is the kind of person I want to be."

For this reason some police training has to be done by drills. They are essential, for instance, to the development of good judgment and reliable action in the use of force, including deadly force. Drills conducted in simulated conditions disclose personal weaknesses that must be overcome, and strengths and talents that can be refined. They contribute to self-knowledge that makes an officer better able to use force rightly.

Also imperative are consideration and discussion of fairness, of inordinate force, and of the differences (and similarities) between a fast gun and a wise, just, courageous gun. Lectures, readings, writings, stories, testimonies of senior officers, explanations of departmental policies and the reasons for them, discussions of examples from the history of the department, careful criticism by teachers, and conscientious field training are all necessary to enable an officer to grasp the reasons for behaving in particular ways that make the judicious and wise use of force fully second nature—and that enable the officer to behave as quickly as the circumstances require without being precipitous.

Police training and instruction need, therefore, to include exercises for the formation of habits that make up such aspects of good character as courage, justice, temperance, and compassion. The formation of good habits is sometimes undertaken as well by initiative and by outspoken resolve—for example, when those who want to break a habit of intemperance say to their loved ones, "I will not do that any more." In this way resolve is distinguished from the mere good intentions that pave the road to hell.

Current Fashion in Ethics Education

Many "ethics educators," according to Lawrence W. Sherman of the Crime Control Institute, "reject the idea of making people moral as naive and unrealistic."[6] Surely, it is entirely true that no one can make another person moral. The will to do the right thing for the right reasons is, finally, up to each person; no one can acquire it for anyone else or force it upon another.

Each person must succeed or fail in this as an individual, but no one can achieve good character entirely alone. Excellent habits and excellent reasoning do not arise in a vacuum. Ethics education seeks to make people worthy to bear the public trust. It must provide them the opportunities to make the best of themselves.

Sherman, and many others, say that "teaching the reasoning process for arriving at moral decisions"[7] is the fundamental purpose of education in ethics. For this reason, Sherman—with other members of the 1978 Police Foundation's National Advisory Commission on Higher Education for Police Officers—stresses that "every police education program should include in its required curriculum a thorough consideration of value choices and ethical dilemmas of police work."[8]

Their position resembles the view of the Institute of Society, Ethics, and the Life Sciences at Hastings-on-Hudson: "The primary purpose of courses in ethics ought to be to provide students with those concepts and analytical skills that will enable them to grapple with broad ethical theory in attempting to resolve both personal and professional dilemmas, as well as to reflect on the moral issues facing the larger society."[9] The Hastings Center identifies five basic goals: "stimulating the moral imagination, recognizing ethical issues, developing analytical skills, eliciting a sense of moral obligation and personal responsibility, and tolerating— and resisting—disagreement and ambiguity." To these, Sherman adds "understanding the morality of coercion, integrating technical and moral competence, and becoming familiar with the full range of moral issues specific to criminology and criminal justice."[10]

All this sounds well-intentioned enough, but is it realistic and theoretically and practically sound?

With respect to realism, I doubt that any program of instruction can acquaint students with the "full range of moral issues specific to criminology and criminal justice." The curriculum would have to be vast. Even "understanding the morality of coercion" takes a great deal of work. Immanuel Kant says in *The Metaphysical Elements of Justice* that coercion "is a hindrance or opposition to freedom. Consequently, if a certain use of freedom is itself a hindrance to freedom . . . then the use of coercion to counteract it . . . is just. It follows by the law of contradiction that justice [a right] is united with the authorization to use coercion against anyone who violates justice [or a right]."[11] Analyses of this sort are difficult, even for advanced students. In police training, it is enough to see that justice may require the forfeiture of the rights of those who aggressively violate the rights of others.

The same point holds for "grappling with broad ethical theory in attempting to resolve both personal and professional 'dilemmas.' " Even those educated in such theory seldom decide what is right or how to behave by grappling with broad ethical theory. Even if police academies or undergraduate courses could be sufficiently deep and thorough to make anyone a scholar of broad ethical theory, such scholars are not necessarily persons of good character. Instruction in ethics for police has to be more specific, precise, and respectful of time limits.

Undertaking a "thorough consideration of value choices and ethical dilemmas of police work" amounts to presenting students with problematic cases and asking what should be done. A teacher can show students "the reasoning process for arriving at moral decisions," but that process is pointless for a person who lacks the character to listen to reason or who simply does not give a damn about behaving rightly. It may help weak-willed persons to avoid rationalization and self-deception, but only if they want it to. Only those already decent enough to care what is good and right can have a moral problem about what is good or right.

Few common moral failings and failures stem from inept reasoning about dilemmas. Many more arise from moral indifference, disregard for other people, weakness of will, and bad or self-indulgent habits. Otherwise, every philosopher who is good at moral reasoning, and every student of ethics, would be a person of excellent character. This is simply not the case.

Much of what is done in ethics instruction with value choices and ethical dilemmas is question-begging or misleading, and some of it discourages rather than promotes character excellence. The philosopher Matthew Lipman describes the futility of basing ethics education on dilemmas:

> Dilemmas are constructed by arbitrarily ruling out meaningful options and by limiting those that remain to those that contradict either one another or themselves. In laboratory settings, the technique is employed to determine how subjects will behave if their reasoning powers are neutralized and they are left to their instinctual or emotional devices. In a classroom, such a technique, if unaccompanied by the exploration of rational alternatives, can be of little educational value.[12]

Much more valuable is the study of specific situations with seasoned officers to learn how to bring one's best habits wisely to bear.

149

"Value" Choices and "Ethical Dilemmas"

Lawrence W. Sherman focuses on decision making about problems and dilemmas because he believes that the "primary question of normative ethics" is, "How should we discover what is morally right, what we ought to do?" Sherman rejects values clarification, values inquiry and analysis, and moral development techniques as irrelevant to ethics education. He is convinced that a vague treatment of ethics throughout the curriculum gives no assurance that this question will be treated explicitly. "If ethics is to be taken seriously," he says, "teaching it as a separate course seems to be the only viable option."[13]

Sherman is quite right to insist that moral instruction must not be a vague part of the curriculum, but if it is offered as a course, the rest of the curriculum must be consistent in its regard for moral standards. Otherwise, the course will be isolated, and it will be treated as an aside by the students.

Sherman is also right to reject values clarification and similar methods of moral instruction. Such methods are intended to enable people to discover what they already consider good and right, not to ask what we ought to consider good and right. They reduce the inquiry to questions of what individuals happen to like or want—a far different matter from what is worthy of our aspiration and respect.

Thus, by discovering that they enjoy seeing discrimination against a certain race or sex or religion, they "clarify" their values. Many values clarification strategies explicitly teach students that ethics and morality consist of no more than this. They teach that no value is better than any other—that everything is a matter of personal taste. In this view, the ideal is for those who like, for instance, racial discrimination or "kiddie porn" to discover that they like it. And since no form of character or conduct is better or worse than any other, this discovery concludes the educational program in ethics.

By contrast, true ethics is in part about justice, and justice is incompatible with bigotry; it is in part about temperance, and temperance and justice are both incompatible with sexual exploitation of anyone, let alone children. Accordingly, values clarification cannot compose an ethics curriculum. It may help people discover that they like things they shouldn't, but ethically, it has no other purpose.

The place of dilemmas in the ethical education of police is suggested by the place of dilemmas in moral life generally. A moral dilemma is, by definition, a choice between two mutually exclusive courses of action, each of which has a serious claim to being morally right. In order to be torn between two arguably right but mutually exclusive actions, a person must already care about doing what is right.

Because a dilemma may be genuinely unresolvable, a person may be perfectly right in following either course of action. For example, a father who has important reasons for spending Father's Day with his father and other important ones for spending the day with his own children—and who cannot be with both—is faced with a dilemma. If he judges the reasons for each course to be equal, he cannot resolve the issue by further reasoning. Sometimes, the proper response is to recognize that more reasoning is futile and simply to do one thing or the other. Since endless effort to try to find—or fabricate—an overriding reason can be a fault, persisting in pointless deliberation is not a mark of character excellence for police or anyone else.

We should not assume that character excellence and decent behavior are based on skill at resolving dilemmas. A tremendous intellectual skill at diagnosing the elements of moral issues may be used only to maintain appearances and have no other effect on behavior.

Equally important, teaching police that moral life is one hard decision after another is both false and misleading. If that were the case, everyone who tried to be moral would burn out and grow weary of moral deliberation in a very short time. Moral decency and habits of character excellence in daily life are for the most part not fraught with problems of decision.

For twenty-five months during the Nazi occupation in World War II, the family of Anne Frank was hidden in the secret annex of a Dutch home in Amsterdam. Asked in 1987 how he and his wife found the courage to hide and feed the Franks—Jews in a city controlled by those who wanted to murder them—Jan Gies said, simply and eloquently, "It's not like one day you wake up and say to yourself, 'Let's be brave today.'"

Indeed it is not. It is not a matter of painful deliberation but of character and therefore of habit. I do not mean to deny that we must learn to reason conscientiously in hard moral cases. But moral seriousness in daily life requires a firmer foundation than the habit of reasoning. Jan Gies and his wife did not reason through a dilemma, nor did they struggle toward some grueling decision about the relative advantages of courage and cowardice. They behaved as decent and courageous people behave. Given

151

their conception of decency, they even deny (without false modesty, I might add) that they were heroic. I think they were heroic, but I know no heroes who make a big point of it. They seem to know intuitively what Emerson said about a dinner guest who celebrated his own virtues: "The louder he talked of his honor, the faster we counted our spoons."

To take another instance, on February 22, 1988, four motorists stopped on a highway to help an Ohio trooper struggling with a man who was trying to take his gun. If no one had stopped, the outcome could have been tragic. One of the citizens who went to help, Jeff Stroud, a sales representative for a manufacturing firm, said later, that he stopped "just because it seemed the right thing to do."[14]

Three conclusions can be drawn from these illustrations. First, good character exhibited in morally important acts frequently involves no difficult decision. Second, knowing how to make a decision is not itself a motive for decency. Third, those who are motivated to behave decently cannot necessarily explain how reliable decisions are made. We must address the issue of motivation and the fact that the normal circumstances of daily life do not require so many hard decisions. Only in this context can we fruitfully raise the levels of knowledge about how to deliberate in hard cases.

Many educators who wrongly treat dilemmas as the heart of moral life also wrongly elevate questions of choice to the status of moral dilemmas. This obliterates the distinction between temptations toward wrongdoing and conflicts between morally arguable courses of action.

I have encountered the following type of case in discussions with city government officials, businessmen and women, and police.

> You are a deputy police chief in a mid-Atlantic city where you have worked for eleven years. You accept an offer to become chief in a Western city within thirty days, but soon learn that your wife is pregnant. You decide that you do not want to move far and accept instead a chief's position in a nearby town. You then tell the Western city manager you have decided not to come because of the baby. You point out that you gave him no acceptance in writing.

The question is what you should do when faced with the supposed dilemma of wanting to change plans after you accepted an offer.

As this hypothetical case is cast, is it a moral dilemma? It presents a tension between duty and desire, not between two obligatory courses of action. The case might be made into a moral dilemma if the facts were changed: if you and your wife have had great difficulty conceiving, if your wife's health is frail, if she needs to be near the doctors you have worked with for several years, and so on. Then the main question would be, Why did you accept a job so far away in the first place?

To see that the case as offered poses no dilemma, we can put ourselves in the place of the city manager. What would we say if we received such a call from a man who had accepted our offer to be police chief? My response would be to say I was glad to learn of his wishes and say goodbye. I would then tell my colleagues that we had misjudged the man, that he was immature or dishonorable or both, and that we were fortunate to learn it before he could take office. He is immature because he cannot plan his personal life to accommodate perfectly normal events, let alone plan the future of a police department. He is dishonorable because he breaks commitments when they interfere with his desires. And he implies that his word counts for nothing unless he gives it in writing. Imagine telling a child that you could break a promise because it was not in writing. Few of us want our sons and daughters to grow up that way.

The case illegitimately elevates a tension between duty and desire to the status of a dilemma. But even if this were a genuine dilemma rather than a problem for reflection, the exercise would still miss the point about many of the elements of moral life. Therefore, it cannot be the essence of education in ethics and morals.

Individual and Departmental Character

The purpose of developing moral habits is to learn from experience that it is better to be courageous than to be reckless or cowardly, better to be just than unjust, temperate than intemperate, charitable and compassionate than otherwise. And the purpose of developing intellectual competence is to learn that it is better to be wise than foolish, to reason well than badly, to be capable rather than inept.

With such a background, police can apply what they have learned to narcotics, drug enforcement, and drug use; to use of force; to racism, both among the public and inside law enforcement; to dealing with the ravages of poverty or with cynicism and corruption; to personal problems with alcohol, gluttony, and physical indolence; to preparing reports, serving warrants, and testifying in court; and to deception in undercover investigations and to the use of informants.

Some circumstances in police work call especially for justice and compassion. New officers, for example, are often assigned to ghettos or projects in inner cities, where they tend to be confrontational, especially with suspects. Newcomers may not realize that in any public meeting with police, citizen pride and "face" may be at stake. When officers are confrontational, citizens may see no way but violence to maintain self-respect or the respect of their peers. Learned in the streets, this lesson can be harsh or even deadly. A better way to learn it is from instruction in justice and compassion—and in listening to reason.

Justice is a complicated idea that cannot be contrasted to some simple excess or character deficiency. J. O. Urmson says that a just person is one who is "impartial, without fear or favor, even-tempered and . . . clear-headed; in a word . . . of generally good character."[15] We could stress that justice is incompatible with prejudice, or with indifference to the rights of others, or with cheating, or with greed or selfishness. Sometimes we say those who obey the law are just, but what is lawful is not always identical to what is just. If we contrast justice to forms of excess and deficiency, we might say that a person could be excessive in giving too much weight to the rights of others and deficient in giving too little weight to his own.[16] But sometimes we contrast the just person with one who is vengeful or takes the law into his own hands, doing on his own initiative what he judges the law ought to do. We also contrast being just with being tolerant of abuses of other people so long as we are not abused. Cicero made this point when he criticized his fellow citizens for believing they did enough for their country by managing to avoid being killed by its political factions.

To the extent that these various ideas of justice overlap or share a common thread, they suggest that just persons do not play favorites and avoid exceeding their own authority or treating people in ways they do not deserve. They feel as indignant at the unfair treatment of others as of themselves. To decide whether to approve certain conduct, they may—as a matter of fairness—ask whether they would be willing for everyone to behave that way. In all this, a person of just character gives consideration to others—equal initial consideration, subsequently weighted by relevant facts. And even this relatively dispassionate regard for the rights and interests of others links justice to compassion.

A compassionate person is one who tries to understand how things look and feel to others. To be just in daily life, we must try to grasp the point of view of others, because their perception is an irreplaceable element in the overall facts. To decide what to do, just persons try to take into account how their conduct seems to others and how their actions affect them.

In the novel *To Kill A Mockingbird*, Atticus Finch, a lawyer in a small Southern town who is defending a black man falsely accused of attacking a white woman, expresses this to his six-year-old daughter, Scout.

> "If you can learn a simple trick, Scout, you'll get along a lot better with all kinds of folks. You never really understand a person until you consider things from his point of view—"
> "Sir?"
> "—until you climb into his skin and walk around in it."[17]

Police officers on the streets have to want to do this and to learn to ask, How would I feel if I were the other person? Without being able to "climb into the skin" of others, officers will be thwarted by differences of race, ethnic background, economic circumstances, and sex. With justice and compassion, they have a far better chance to enforce the law and keep the peace without unnecessary—and self-endangering—confrontations. Although they must not compromise their judgment or integrity, officers have to see things even from the point of view of informants to work effectively with them.

Instruction of this sort should show newcomers that exposing their partners to the hazards of unnecessary confrontation is unfair and foolish. As one officer said to me of another, "When he gets into this 'macho' crap in the projects, it's not just his ass on the line. It's mine, and every other cop who comes in here."

Questions of justice and compassion naturally lead academy students to questions about departmental treatment of the police themselves and the rationale for specific policies. How does the department conduct its review of shootings by officers? How do seasoned officers review cases of accidental discharge of a weapon in a struggle with a suspect? What are the department's policies about recruitment, appointment, retention, promotion, and discipline? Where does it stand on affirmative action and on merit? Does it hold that "if you wear a badge, you are supposed to be a cut above your environment"? How has it responded to the situation described by another law enforcement official:

155

Holding to a higher standard for police becomes more difficult each year as our nation has changed into one dealing
with self-gratification, recreational use of drugs, and deterioration of home, family, and church associations. Continually, when it is necessary to discipline somebody for an
infraction of rules, you do not find the support of the local
government or the state labor board who hear grievances
concerning these matters. More and more we are being told
by others that a police officer is no longer different from any
other worker.

What does the department expect of its members—who, unlike
many workers, take an oath of office and say they are members of
a profession? In all these respects, why are the department's
policies what they are?

A police officer is authorized to make decisions about the lives
of others, an enormous power the rest do not have. Such power
should be exercised only by those whose public and private behavior befits authority. A person who is hung over or weakened by
other intemperance is more prone to errors of poor concentration,
inattention to detail, and so on. The public cannot allow those who
have special powers to indulge in excesses allowed others. The
rights of police arise from their institutional mission.

Academy recruits should deal with such matters at the initiative of the department rather than wait for experience to tempt
them toward cynicism. Morals apply not only to how the officer
behaves, but also to how the department behaves. Nothing lowers
morale or undermines command personnel's concern for moral
standards as much as discrimination and favoritism within a department. Injustice within it is ruinous to justice everywhere else.

What of compassion for the families of officers subject to
disciplinary action? One way to address this is to call departmental
requirements to the attention of all personnel. This places responsibility for adverse consequences squarely on them—and appeals
to their own compassion for their families as a motive to refrain
from conduct that could hurt them. Police candidates should learn
that the consequences of misconduct may discredit fellow officers,
endanger other police, disgrace the badge, and jeopardize the
happiness of loved ones. No command officer can safeguard
everyone else from a particular officer's wrongdoing. Officers can
do so only by their own conduct.

Candid instruction about justice and compassion necessarily
includes telling newcomers that as police they will be subjected to
injustice, contempt, lack of respect, and abuse by some citizens. In

some urban areas, an enormous network is involved in drug sales, all mobilized to prevent police effectiveness. In areas I have seen, when a police vehicle enters, three cars pull out in front of it and four or five behind, with their lights on and their radios blasting, to warn the dealers and buyers and to prevent free movement by police. Each car is occupied by two armed dealers, to intimidate and control the police. For two police officers in a vehicle to try to contend with this potentially lethal abuse would be reckless. Some dealers are also users, with a total disregard for life and a proclivity to violence. The wise and courageous alternative is to implement policies that thwart the dealers—such as using police in force, arresting buyers as well as sellers, and impounding vehicles—without needlessly jeopardizing the police or the general public. Provision must be made for immediate processing of arrests, or the drain on resources will be self-defeating.

To see such steps in progress is the best antidote to becoming resentful over injustice. A proper police response can forestall the frustration of officers and ill-advised or vengeful behavior in the streets. A department must show them they are not alone, because the streets can, over time, tax the reserves of good will, hopefulness, and compassion of most officers.

Former police detective Dorothy Uhnak describes in *Policewoman* a lecture to her academy class by a veteran command officer:

> Tomorrow, you will all graduate from the Police Academy. . . . But you don't know this city. . . . You don't know it because you haven't seen it, but you are going to see it now with policeman's eyes. . . . There is dirt and corruption and moral disease and agony and tragedy, and you are going to be a part of it. . . . You are going to touch and handle the living flesh and the dying blood. . . . You will deal with the vilest and the lowest and the most depraved forms of humanity . . . and what shocks you now will become merely routine. . . .
>
> This is not a job, it is a whole way of life, and if you decide to live it, you will have to live it twenty-four hours a day for as long as you are a police officer. [18]

Though true, this counsel should not be taken to mean that officers' lives must be directed solely to their job. Treated as a twenty-four-hour-a-day responsibility, the job can destroy the recreation and relaxation everyone needs. If the job obscures everything else, it invites an exaggerated sense of self-importance, a prescription for burnout.

The study of being an honorable person applies to private as well as public life. Someone who does not form habits of justice and compassion is unlikely to forge a durable marriage. And someone who does not fear drug habits or excesses of alcohol or food or a deficiency of physical stamina is unlikely to maintain the mental and physical conditioning needed to face each day, at home or at work.

10
Deliberation and Moral Problems in Training

There is no more contemptible type of human character than that of the nerveless sentimentalist and dreamer, who spends his life in a weltering sea of sensibility and emotion, but who never does a manly concrete deed. . . . There is no more miserable human being than one in whom nothing is habitual but indecision.

WILLIAM JAMES[1]

As officers develop good character by forging good habits, they learn to address hard questions productively. Deliberation about complex issues of right and wrong—or of which of several right actions should take precedence—becomes natural for a person of habitual moral seriousness. Responsible people learn to deliberate well and to be decisive and timely without being arbitrary or impulsive.

Officers also need a sense of which situations require no more than their habitual conduct and which ones call for careful—even if fast—decisions. Not every situation calls for deliberation. Officers who make everything a problem of deliberation are like the man the philosopher Brand Blanshard wrote about, "who is so anxious to cover all contingencies with insurance that he exhausts his income on it, and has nothing left to live on."[2] No reasonable person reasons consciously about every action. We waste ourselves, as Blanshard also observed, "in incessant deliberating over what should be matters of mere habit." The rational person "instead of perpetually questioning his habit and so check-mating his will, like the unhappy centipede that began to consider how it ran, will make habit his ally, turning over to it the larger part of his life so that he may bring his intelligence to bear freely on the rest."

We no more need to spend our first waking moments each day thinking about whether to behave honestly toward family and friends than we need to deliberate whether to brush our teeth.

Thinking, as a philosopher observed, "is like cavalry; it should be used only on special occasions."

The habit of deciding with care when circumstances require is, like other habits, acquired by practice. The rest of this chapter describes practical questions raised by police that offer opportunities to practice deliberation.

Moral Deliberation

Although they do not normally need to deliberate about whether to tell the truth, in discussions of ethics many police raise questions about honesty. On the one hand, they do not want to betray the truth by deceiving others in order to manipulate them for personal profit or to conceal their own failings. On the other, they do not suppose that being honest means spilling every piece of confidential information. Honorable people are neither deficient in truth telling by lying nor excessive by gossiping.

Honesty as a form of character excellence was described by Theodore Roosevelt in his 1904 Memorial Day tribute to those who fought at Gettysburg:

> The lessons they taught us are lessons as applicable in our everyday lives now as in the rare times of great stress. The men who made this field forever memorable did so because they combined the power of fealty to a lofty ideal with the power of showing that fealty in hard, practical, common-sense fashion. They stood for the life of effort, not the life of ease. They had that love of country, that love of justice, that love of their fellowmen without which power and resourceful efficiency but make a man a danger to his fellows. . . . Exactly as in time of war, courage is the cardinal virtue of the soldier, so in time of peace honesty, using the word in its deepest and broadest significance, is the essential basic virtue, without which all else avails nothing.

Clearly, honesty is directly connected to the courage of our convictions, to fairness or justice, and to compassion or fundamental respect for others. But do not situations arise that allow exceptions to the general principle of truthfulness? Samuel Johnson replied this way, as his biographer, James Boswell, reported:

> We talked of the question . . . whether it was allowable at any time to depart from *Truth?*
> JOHNSON: "The general rule is that Truth should never be violated, because it is of the utmost importance to the com-

fort of life, that we should have a full security by mutual faith; and occasional inconveniences should be willingly suffered that we may preserve it. There must, however, be some exceptions. If, for instance, a murderer should ask you which way a man is gone, you may tell him what is not true, because you are under a previous obligation not to betray a man to a murderer."[3]

The lie Johnson calls legitimate involves a question initiated by a murderer. How does this apply to police work?

Such questions are pointless for anyone who has not established basic habits of honesty. But a person who aspires to behave honorably in both routine and difficult situations will take questions of honesty seriously. He can ask, What would an honorable person be likely to do in this situation? How would that conclusion be reached? What principles and possible consequences would be taken into account? And what should I do?

Police have presented various situations to me as problematic. Let us examine some of them with this question in mind: What would honorable persons (and hence honorable police officers) do?

Question 1. News reporters ask in an interview for information about an investigation that is confidential. Should police lie to protect confidentiality?

Question 2. Political superiors interfere in matters of police promotion and transfer. Should a command officer lie to them about what can legally be done to prevent them from manipulating the department?

Question 3. Adversarial relations between management and union threaten police performance. Should police lie to each other to gain advantage for one side or another?

Question 4. Political figures in a city vastly exaggerate what police can and should do for the public. Should police leaders remain silent for the sake of political survival?

Question 5. A suspect confesses to a number of crimes in addition to the one he is charged with. Police know it is unlikely that he committed all the others. Should they treat the confessions as true and clear the crimes to improve the record of the department?

Question 6. The truth about a series of crimes may panic the public or encourage it to take the law into its own hands. What should the police do?

Question 7. Routine burglaries are unlikely to be investigated, and homicides committed by strangers are extremely difficult to prevent or solve. Should police tell the truth, which may outrage the victims and the public?

Question 8. Several people suspected of committing a crime together are in custody. Should police lie to them individually in order to secure confessions?

In deliberating about such questions, honorable persons will consider truth telling obligatory in normal circumstances and will not lie for the sake of exploiting others. Nor will they lie simply to relieve short-term pressures. They reject opportunities for gain that betray duty and will not take advantage of their position at the expense of those who rely on them. What, then, might be included in classroom discussion as the sort of thing to be considered in these specific cases?

1. *Lying to the media.* Reporters asking for sensitive information about an investigation or a victim have no right to it; the police have a duty to safeguard confidentiality. Police must not be deceived by media protestations that "the public has a right to know." The media have neither the duty nor the authority to decide what the police should reveal and hence what the public may rightly know. Honorable persons will not break confidence, but they may preserve the truth by saying, "That is confidential" or "I am not at liberty to discuss the matter."

Such a reply might, however, suggest that the police have the information in question and it might endanger an investigation by tipping a suspect. "No comment" might therefore be a better reply. In any case, only fools lie to people whose trust they need, as police need the future trust of the media. Prudence and morality join together against deliberate deceit. The answer to the question of when to lie to the media, according to most high administrative officers, is Never. Even if journalists use police-band radios as a way of ambulance chasing and interfere with investigations, police should not lie to them. If they break the law in pursuit of stories, police may enforce the law.

These points hold even though police cooperation does not always result in complete media cooperation with police. In early 1988, a magazine in Charles Town, West Virginia, ran an article on drug sales in the county with emphasis on a Jamaican crack connection. ABC News then sent a crew to film street sales of crack. Law enforcement officials feared that if the film were broadcast, the suspects would go into hiding. U.S. Attorney William Kolibash told the Associated Press, "that he had offered to let the crew tape from unmarked police vehicles, but that he had asked the network not to broadcast the footage until the suspects were arrested." He added that ABC officials "refused to hold off," and so the police raid had to be moved up several weeks. Police arrested only twenty-six of the forty people for whom they had warrants; one officer was shot in the foot, and two were injured in a car crash. ABC officials later insisted that the police "offered to move the date, they volunteered to do that."[4]

Police officials who conducted the raid confirm that they did not want to change their timetable—having invested several months in the investigation. But they appreciated the problem facing ABC; the network needed to gather footage for an already scheduled national broadcast on narcotics in America. Except for the scheduling problems, mutual cooperation was very good, with ABC filming the day before the raid from police vans, and other television stations filming during the raid itself. The police set up a press conference at the command post that continued during the raid. Police spokesmen assure me that the change in timetable had nothing whatever to do with any officer injuries.

The cooperation of police with the media and their candor about their plans were both admirable and prudent. Open communication averted potentially worse consequences. If ABC had run the footage without prior police knowledge, the investigation would have been completely wasted, or if the television show and the arrests overlapped, the police and the suspects would have been placed in graver danger. And the media coverage may have alerted viewers to the seriousness of illegal narcotics trafficking in the United States.

2. *Lying to political superiors who try to manipulate departmental affairs.* If a mayor wants a crony in the police department promoted or transferred to a choice assignment, honorable police are unlikely to protect institutional autonomy through lies. Lies are a frail and temporary protection, too easily discovered in matters of this kind to be of much use. They also threaten to undermine trust and to invite reprisal. A conscientious person takes into account probable and possible long-term consequences, not just short-term.

A police executive appointed by a mayor has a twofold duty—to act in accordance with legitimate policies of the administration, and to make clear when the mayor is overstepping his bounds. If this was not clarified when the job was offered, it should be when the problem surfaces. To do less is to invite progressively worse problems—that cannot be solved by deceit.

To this, the reply may be, But if I tell him to back off, he will fire me. A command officer who has lost authority over personnel assignments, however, has already been undermined in his ability to serve the public.

3. *Lying to union or management adversaries.* Where management-union relations are adversarial, morale at all levels suffers. The principal task of command—and of union—officers is to find areas of common purpose where trust may be built. Honorable people use imagination in such matters. For example, one urban police commissioner discovered soon after his appointment in the mid-1980s that when officers were killed in the line of duty, their families had to pay funeral expenses. Horrified, he informed the mayor that this practice would be ended immediately and that, if necessary, discretionary funds would be used until proper budgetary arrangements were made and an official policy formulated. Facing departmental tension over compensation, he did not pander to the fashionable but frequently false generalization that all police are underpaid. Instead, he appointed an independent task force to review compensation matters and, on the strength of their report, announced publicly that police in his city were underpaid in comparison with other police in similar cities. By taking such initiatives, which he believed obligatory, he took a step toward improved management-union relations and mutual trust.

Although such a step can do little without reciprocity, it is a mark of conscientious leadership and far superior to the deceit that clouds such issues in many cities. Mistrust undermines common purposes and commitment to mission within institutions. Even if representatives of different groups must hold in confidence the terms they would accept, they need not lie.

4. *Remaining silent in order to survive in office.* When politicians spout public nonsense about what police can and should do, silence is not a lie, but it is the deliberate toleration of falsehood, possibly at the expense of the public. According to the police executives I know, if you allow politicians to create unrealistic expectations, those expectations will come back to haunt you. You will be subject to unanswerable criticism, possibly at the price of your job. They advocate forthrightness—either in cautioning political superiors that they are on the wrong track or in publicly denying their claims if no other method is effective. Police executives have a duty to subordinates to promote public understanding of the police mission and its limits. Silent toleration of political nonsense is a betrayal of these personnel, a basic failure of leadership. Many patrol personnel in my experience care more that their superiors defend them from unwarranted criticism and safeguard them from unrealistic expectations than they do about any-

thing anyone else says. Here, honesty by command officers takes courage, but the moral issue is not complex.

5. *Clearing crimes by acceptance of confessions believed to be false.* This is an obviously dishonest means of manipulating political and public opinion. It closes the files on crimes by perpetrators who may remain at large. It may bury information useful in other investigations and prosecutions, thereby endangering the public. Certainly, it falsifies departmental data on accomplishment and makes a mockery of accountability.

In addition, dishonestly clearing crimes leads to false and unrealistic expectations among citizens about what officers can accomplish. Such deceit is an attack on the credibility of future officers. No officer who cares about them would falsify clearance rates at such a price.

6. *Lying to avoid panicking the public or encouraging vigilantism.* As in dealing with the media, the main question is whether judicious responses and regard for confidentiality serve the public interest. Honorable people in positions of responsibility do not assume that obligations to tell the truth entail obligations to tell the whole truth to the press or the public. Whether a lie is really necessary to protect the public from itself is a question likely to arise rarely and only in extreme cases. But if the fear of public panic or riot is genuine, then concern for public safety may legitimately override concern for honesty about a specific issue. Normally, if some morally overriding reason such as public safety obliges a person to lie, then it also requires an explanation or apology for the deception later, after the crisis has passed. The possible consequences of such an admission deserve consideration in the initial decision.

7. *Lying to avoid enraging or depressing victims of crimes.* Experienced police know, and newcomers soon learn, that crime victims feel violated—their homes, their bodies, or their freedom and security have been invaded. They want hope that their losses will be restored and the perpetrators punished. In many cases, both hopes will be disappointed. In my experience, good police listen patiently, express sympathy, take careful reports, and pass on information that may be useful to other police, but they do not make false promises or hold out false hopes. They may not explain that limits of personnel, time, and money prohibit investigation of many crimes, but they do not lie about this either. To force the truth on the victim would be cruel, and to lie would raise false hopes that will turn to cynicism.

8. *Lying to suspects to secure confessions.* In investigations, po-

lice sometimes tell suspects that they have been implicated in a confession, even if they have not been. The fear and distrust of the suspects are manipulated by deceit. This practice is highly questionable because even innocent suspects may have records that make them less than credible, and they may therefore feel that they cannot afford to stand on their genuine innocence. They may feel that lying is the only way of safeguarding their deepest interests and thus may confess to crimes and suffer punishments unjustly, while allowing the actual perpetrators to go undetected.

Police, however, have no overriding duty to sustain by their honesty a successful criminal conspiracy of silence. We sometimes agree to bargain for a lesser offense or grant immunity in order to break up such conspiracies—in hope of safeguarding the public. A consideration of relevant details is needed to determine whether an alternative is better than deceit: how dangerous are the suspects known to be, and so on? Thus, I would ask for more details of the specific case and a review of possible alternatives to deceit.

Identifying Genuine Moral Problems

Obviously, such issues should be treated more thoroughly in police training, addressing questions and objections. But these general themes suggest the considerations that are relevant. And when personnel who are rising in rank understand how much is not morally problematic, they can identify real moral problems and distinguish them from other kinds of choices.

Let us take an extended example of the difference. First, a question of choice that does not involve a decision about conflicting moral goods: Would an honorable person whose duty includes enforcement of drug laws use drugs whose possession, sale, and purchase are illegal? The use of such illegal drugs violates the law the officer is sworn to uphold. Furthermore, use of drugs impairs human capacities, including strength and judgment. Finally, violating the laws the officers are sworn to uphold may generate feelings of hypocrisy in themselves and make them lax in enforcing those laws. Honorable persons do not force themselves into living a lie, because this is the most profound violation of the truth, not covered by any exceptions of the sort Samuel Johnson described.

Not every police officer who learns this will refrain from the use of drugs, because moral instruction cannot make people moral. But such instruction at least forewarns officers what they are letting themselves in for. This knowledge cannot entirely protect them from doing evil, but it does protect them from being deceived that what they do is not evil—for it is demonstrably a betrayal of duty and a self-inflicted harm. There is no dilemma—only a potential tension between temperance and duty on the one hand and desire for drug-induced delusion or euphoria on the other.

A moral choice does have to be made about working undercover, say, in narcotics. Undercover work is by nature deceptive; it is the adoption of a false persona for the purpose of gathering admissible evidence against suspected criminals whose covertness seldom provides obvious evidence. Undercover work requires being able to "get inside the skin" of others; as Malachi L. Harney and John C. Cross observe in *The Narcotic Officer's Notebook*, "Generally, the more readily the undercover man comprehends crime from the criminal's standpoint, the better. After all, he is now a figure in the world of crime, or so he pretends."[5] But the more successful undercover investigators are, the greater the trust narcotics traffickers will have in them, and the greater the capacity to exploit that trust. Although experienced undercover agents caution against being "too friendly with the suspect's wife or women friends," they do acknowledge that "an exception might extend to small courtesies to the suspect's mother or children."[6] Thus, undercover work may involve deception of innocent members of a private family.

Critics of undercover investigations argue that they are of questionable value and that they risk entrapment, misconduct by informants, psychological or moral damage to the agent and to the victims of deception, violations of civil liberties and democratic ideals, and erosion of trust within society. But even they generally agree that "certain types of crimes can be detected only by using deception and employing informants."[7] From the array of arguments on moral grounds for and against undercover investigations and use of informants in law enforcement, students should be aware of the following arguments.

Malachi L. Harney and John C. Cross served as undercover investigators for the Treasury Department and as superintendent and assistant superintendent, respectively, of the Illinois Division of Narcotics Control. They observe that the use of informants and undercover agents is necessary to solve crimes where the evidence is otherwise invisible, and to prevent planned crimes:

- From the dawn of history, internal law and order has had to depend in greater or less measure on the informer.

- No modern policeman who properly uses informers needs to be apologetic about them. The apology should come from the officer who fails to use this device to protect his community.
- The citizen has a right and a duty to inform the government of violations of its laws. The fact that he recognizes this most readily only when his own person or property or his loved ones are involved does not invalidate the principle.
- The easily demonstrated fact is that the big cases usually are made by informers *and* undercover officers.[8]

Judge Learned Hand said, "Courts have countenanced the use of informers from time immemorial." Former Assistant Attorney General of the United States William F. Tompkins added, *"What our critics fail to, or will not recognize, is that those who are engaged in a criminal enterprise have no right to be free from such surveillances. . . .* It is not a question of informing on one's fellows, but of protecting society from those who would do us harm by their original conduct."[9]

Irwin B. Nathan, the Department of Justice lawyer in charge of the ABSCAM prosecutions, endorses this view:

> Detractors of ABSCAM attempt to portray an image of high-level Justice Department officials engaged in a crusade against selected public officials or seeking to test the honesty or morality of randomly chosen politicians. The truth of the matter, as shown by the evidence developed in eight public trials, is far different. At critical junctures in the investigation, high-level officials in the Criminal Division and the FBI were faced with essentially only one simple choice: either ignore serious allegations of corruption by refusing to allow contacts with those represented to be ready and willing to engage in criminal conduct, or authorize FBI operatives to pursue the leads they had developed during their investigation, up to and including meeting and offering bribes to public officials identified by proven criminals. It would have been scandalous to have refused to explore fully these serious allegations.[10]

Nathan adds that every person indicted or convicted in ABSCAM could have rejected bribes. In addition to this personal safeguard, access to appellate courts by defendants ensures that undercover operations are not unconstrained political attacks on targeted individuals.

Sissela Bok argues against undercover investigations and use of informers: "Deceit and violence—these are the two forms of deliberate assault on human beings. Both can coerce people into acting against their will. Most harm that can befall victims through violence can come to them also through deceit. But deceit controls more subtly, for it works on belief as well as action."[11]

Sanford Levinson of the University of Texas College of Law adds that undercover deception is a con game:

- Willingness on occasion . . . to identify with the con artist depends partly on dehumanizing the victim and being willing to ignore the implications of legitimating the con. Yet in all con games—no matter what the context—both victim and artist are diminished by the encounter. And in the case of the undercover agent . . . we lack both an ethical norm and a public policy that takes account of the damage done to the agent, the victim, and society.
- We are entitled to the belief that persons who present themselves to us will not actively be wishing us ill and using the encounter as a means of furthering their malevolence toward us.
- Neither warrant nor reasonableness seems necessary prior to a decision by a police department to attempt the infiltration of the life of a suspected criminal.[12]

Levinson fears as well that use of undercover investigations and informers undermines trust in society—among the citizens and between citizens and government.

These types of pro and con considerations should enable police to see, as Harvard professor Mark H. Moore observes, that "Law enforcement in a free society must strike a deliberate balance between protecting individual rights to privacy (especially from government-sponsored surveillance) and society's interest in detecting criminal offenses and punishing offenders."[13] They also suggest the complexity of crime prevention and deterrence and of morally acceptable means to these worthwhile purposes.

Once exposed to such arguments, police students can ask, Would an honorable person work undercover, engage in systematic deception of suspects, and use informers? The obvious reply is that many honorable people have gone undercover, often at considerable personal risk, to gather evidence unobtainable otherwise. Many have used their wits rather than weapons and, by staring down threats and bluffs, preserved their false personas over long periods. They have waited out long delays designed to test their trustworthiness, without being able to communicate with any other law enforcement personnel.

Two measures of their honorability are their resolve not to

169

commit any crimes of entrapment and their attitudes toward informants. Harney and Cross, both very successful and experienced undercover agents, insist that the most important fact about entrapment is that it is immoral:

> In all his contact with underworld suspects the undercover man must avoid "entrapment," which is a good legal defense for the suspect and, more important, is . . . morally wrong and indefensible. A criminal in the unconscionable narcotic traffic . . . may be given an opportunity to complete a sale of contraband to the officer for the purpose of exposing evidence and it is the right and duty of the officer to afford him the opportunity, when advisable in obtaining evidence. But no officer, by word or deed, should lure into a wrongful act a person who, on his own initiative, had no intent to commit a crime. Brutal frankness should suggest that if anyone is to "do time" under these circumstances it should be the officer.[14]

They are equally straightforward about the treatment of informants:

> Obtaining and managing informers is a fine police art. . . . Important in this area is the reputation of the law enforcement agency and the individual officer for integrity, fair dealing, and intelligent police operation. In many cases the informer takes a considerable personal risk. Like any of the rest of us, in danger he would want to be in the hands of competent people. The officer should be completely fair with the informer. He should not misrepresent nor hold out false promises. . . . He should not humiliate or degrade him. He should see that the full powers of all police agencies having jurisdiction are invoked if the informer is harmed or threatened.[15]

This approach shows that the issues are not simple and that responsible advocates of undercover operations do not believe they are free of moral restraints, or of standards of decency.

Serious discussion should be welcomed on whether the various statements of proponents and critics are true. For example, does being deceptive toward a narcotics dealer diminish the agent? I do not see how, nor do I understand why deception should be by its nature coercive. Neither should deception and violence be lumped together as affronts to human decency. The movement of police away from brutality and toward more sophisticated investigations is a mark of professionalism and civility.

Good undercover work bears no resemblance to the deception of Shakespeare's character Iago, who convinces Othello that his wife is unfaithful. He takes advantage of Othello's free and open nature, which "thinks men honest that but seem to be so, and will as tenderly be led by th' nose as asses are."[16]

A jealous, vengeful man, Iago employs deceit to gratify his own passion to destroy two people. In such a person, one sees how deception and violence can be kindred instruments of evil, but not everyone who uses deception is as vile as Iago.

Some undercover operations go badly awry, as illustrated in Lawrence Lindeman's "Underground Agent." After eighteen months working undercover with the Hell's Angels motorcycle gang and obtaining numerous arrests of high-level narcotics traffickers, a California police officer could not recover control of his life. He abused drugs and alcohol and was finally imprisoned for bank robbery.

Vanderick Desper, an exemplary police officer, in Montgomery County, Pennsylvania, also went undercover and became a drug addict. His experience raises questions of how long officers should remain undercover at a stretch, what they should be told never to do, and what sorts of supervision they should be guaranteed. Desper's downfall came from using drugs to win the confidence of dealers, a practice he describes as "not infrequent among narcotics officers." When he went back to work, after treatment for addiction, he says, "I was treated like I had leprosy. . . . Nobody helped me. They let me down. They let me and my family suffer. It was hypocritical."[17]

Such examples illuminate the absolute necessity of departmental policy that refuses to compromise an officer for the sake of an investigation or to allow the use of drugs undercover except when threatened with death. Since many dealers do not use drugs, their confidence might be won by saying, "I don't put that in my body," or "I am a businessman, not a user." If not, the investigation should be sacrificed, not the officer.

The fundamental principle of undercover work and informant use is that the police officer must be in control, not the informer or the dealers. Because dealers and informers are in the business of selling things, officers must learn to use their advantage as buyers to control events.

At the same time, many informers are con men and women who must be kept at a certain distance. Moreover, most of us do not have an entirely clean conscience and tend to resent informers, so care must be taken against prejudice toward them. Some informants are courageous in facing hard decisions and taking severe risks. Clean officers who work as informants in external investigations of narcotics corruption in police departments run great risks and merit our respect. Former Mafia enforcers who wear wires in racketeering and murder investigations also risk their lives.

Not every way of being in control is either decent or productive. Jonathan Rubinstein, the author of *City Police*, tells of an officer who intended to turn a waitress at a lunch counter into an informant:

> She thinks I don't know she's hustlin' the truckdrivers. She'll find out tomorrow. I don't care if she makes a few bucks on her back, but she is gonna tell me what I want to know.[18]

This attitude may coerce an informant in the short run but will generate neither trustworthiness nor reliability. If the woman tells others, the officer may find difficulty in getting information on the street. Arrogance of power limits its own effectiveness.

The lesson to be learned is that one genuine good can conflict with another. Honesty and lawfulness in government officials and respect for privacy and friendship can be brought by circumstances into conflict with other goods, such as conviction of the guilty, protection of the public, and prevention of crime. These conflicts are no trivial matter. The importance of the values in conflict must be recognized to appreciate the need for restraint, limits, and accountability, all of which are crucial for undercover investigations to be legitimate.

As the sociologist Gary T. Marx says of undercover operations,

> paradoxically, no matter what action is taken, there are moral costs. There are clear costs whenever the government uses deceit. . . . But not to use the tactics can have costs, too. . . . The danger of automatically applied technical, bureaucratic, or occupational subcultural formulas lies in their potential for generating the self-deluding and morally numbing conclusion that a cost-free solution is possible.[19]

At least some of these costs are paid by the undercover agents themselves. Those who go undercover voluntarily sacrifice the opportunity for wholeness that consists of being the same person in public and private. They engage in practices as part of a public persona that they reject in their private lives and their normal professional lives. Their undercover deception may not coerce, but it is intended to disarm and when successful may render those deceived easier to coerce.

The acceptance of extremely dangerous responsibilities, however, tends not to diminish but to ennoble us. We owe undercover officers of good character a special debt of gratitude that may increase if their duties require them to engage in authorized law-breaking. And we owe them our assurance while undercover that they are not alone, that being out of sight does not take them out of mind. They must have colleagues and superiors with whom they can be the same person in public and private.

Identifying Relevant Reasons for Decisions

As Lon L. Fuller observes in *The Morality of Law,* "Even if a man is answerable only to his own conscience, he will answer more responsibly if he is compelled to articulate the principles on which he acts."[20] A police officer should learn to ask, Is there a moral problem here, or is the problem answered by departmental regulations and policies, or by the law? Or is the answer morally obvious? If not, on what reasons is the issue to be decided? What principles and consequences should be taken into account?

Here are some cases that have been raised with me that invite these questions; I have suggested the lines of reasoning and the resources of the department to be used in facing these problematic situations. Since problems like these have been deliberated for centuries in law enforcement without arriving at any simple all-purpose solutions, readers should not expect to find them either in this book or in their discussions with fellow officers. To arrive at a solution, more of the specific circumstances of each case would have to be known than can be conveyed here. Some approaches, however, are clearly more fruitful than others. By considering the situations that follow, together with the suggested approaches to a solution, officers can improve their ability to address similar difficulties they will encounter on the job.

- While driving a new patrol car, you become suspicious of its speedometer. A check confirms that at fifty-five mph, by the gauge, your speedometer reading is 25 percent above your actual speed. What should you do about the traffic citations for speeding that you have issued while driving that car? Why?

Officers should ask whether they would defend the citations in court while admitting that their equipment for speed detection was malfunctioning. Would they consider it fair to receive a ticket from an officer working with defective equipment—especially if the violation were borderline? Should some corrective measure be

173

taken—such as a formal letter of remission and apology to unfairly cited motorists? These questions suggest consideration of possible consequences, and call for the application of principles of consistency and justice.

- You are a team with Officer X, who drinks heavily or plays around with women on duty, or uses his position as an officer to take economic advantage of retailers and others, or accepts bribes from inefficient towing services with city contracts, or accepts bribes from criminal elements. What should you do in each case?

What other information, if any, do you need to deliberate responsibly? What principles should you apply in reaching a decision? Consider the following observation of Aristotle:

> Suppose . . . I have made a friend of a man in the belief that he is a person of good character, and he turns out—or one gets that impression—to be a scoundrel. Am I to go on treating him as a friend? Surely that is out of the question. . . . Should we then . . . break off the friendship on the spot? Not, I suggest, invariably but only when the friend is incurably bad. So long as he is capable of redemption our duty is to give him our support.[21]

The department's policies on conduct becoming an officer are clear for such misconduct. Is this counsel affected by that fact or by your being police officers who must bear the public trust?

These approaches recall police to the nature of their mission and the kinds of conduct that impair its fulfillment. Normally, they lead to discussion of what it means to be compromised by bribes, sexual favors, and the like. They may be supplemented by stories or questions that disclose the potential consequences of such forms of misconduct.

At the same time, the questions provide an opportunity to discuss loyalty to friends—loyalty that does not allow you to stand idly by when your friend's career and happiness are at risk. The department's resources for helping officers with problems, such as peer counseling and medical care, can be examined. These resources also expand the alternatives available to their colleagues. How to report corruption, whom to approach, and how to follow up may then be discussed.

Questions of this kind lead to discussion of conflicting standards and ideals within police departments. Tell the truth, but maintain silence about other officers. Don't get involved, but be compassionate. Be faithful to your partner, but don't tolerate misbehavior. In many departments, such standards stand in a kind of rough and informal hierarchy: confidentiality, even secrecy, between partners is more binding than silence about other officers; maintaining silence is more important than disclosing minor infractions but less important than disclosing major misconduct; and so on.

Such practices and unwritten codes of conduct suggest an underlying sense that in order to live and work effectively together, we must have some measure of give, some willingness to compromise. Compromise is not by its nature wrong, but some compromises are wrongful. The challenge is to discern which compromises are decent and which are not.

In this case, pleasure and profit on one side conflict with responsible behavior on the other. The pleasures of alcohol, sex, and extra money are the motives for misconduct. The behavior is wrong on its face, it is dangerous to self and partner, it is likely to grow worse, and it is a betrayal of the citizenry. Toleration of it is clearly unacceptable. Compromising with such forms of wrongdoing has no justification: it does not contribute to reliable partnership, dependable friendship, or good work. Given that it must stop, the questions become: What should I do to stop it? And what should I do about what has already happened? The first question is one of proportionality and of means sufficient to the purpose. The second may be the harder, and for that reason, one should learn what can be done to stop such behavior as soon as it becomes known.

- Circumstances make it clear that enforcing the curfew in a city park can lead to violence, possibly on a wide scale. As the officer called to the scene by local residents who want the curfew enforced, what should you do?

An officer should learn beforehand not to tackle this kind of situation alone. Enforcement requires backup and a commitment of forces that may disrupt normal police services. If many arrests are contemplated, both jail and court officials may have to be warned. Accordingly, the situation calls for a command decision to risk a confrontation or to work with community groups to avoid one. Thus, the main questions about consequences involve the risk of taking steps that will lead to an uncontrolled situation. Such steps should be authorized and planned by command.

- Does a citizen who has made unique contributions to the community deserve special treatment when he is found to be driving while intoxicated? How should you treat a complaint against an apparently upstanding citizen by a complainant whose character is questionable?

Both questions invite discussion of the relevance of the given facts. Is the community service of the drunk driver relevant? Does the good citizen pose less of a risk to others—and to himself—when driving drunk than anyone else does? Is it fair to give special consideration? How does the department routinely treat first offenses? Are you serving the interests of the good citizen by overlooking his dangerous behavior?

In the second instance, is the character of the two individuals relevant? Is the complaint sufficiently implausible so that resources would be wasted pursuing it? Do the circumstances of the complaint suggest anything about the complainant's motives? Does the complainant waffle about having to testify in court?

By taking the inquiry in these directions, the discussion can emphasize that fear of the consequences of enforcing the law with a powerful citizen is no justification for failure of enforcement. Once, when the question of drunk driving was put to me in class, I learned that the violator was a powerful political figure who had influence on the police department's budget. After some officers criticized the inexperienced officer who had arrested him, we discussed the contempt the person might feel for police who were afraid to apply the law. Suspicion of their integrity in other matters might result.

- While investigating what is obviously the suicide of a young boy, you learn from his distraught mother that the boy's father has always been hard on him, and she thinks the boy always viewed his younger brother as the favorite. The father fears this, too, and is suffering massive feelings of guilt. Continuing your investigation, you discover a note written by the dead boy. It says, "I have been a bother to you ever since Tommy was born. I no longer wish to be an embarrassment to you." You fear for the emotional well-being of the parents. What should you do with the note?

This is an issue of officer discretion. What do departmental policies allow? Within those limits, is there any obligation to disclose the note to the parents? If the officer has a right not to disclose it, should he exercise the right? The note must be made known to the medical examiner, of course, but what would be the point of disclosure to the parents?

The boy clearly intended his parents to see the note. It is his last testament, his last words to them. Normally, we honor the last wishes of the deceased, and our respect for their wishes has to be balanced against the consequences for the living. My sense is that the police should intrude on the relation between the boy and his parents with great caution. My own experience with student suicide suggests that at some point the parents should be made aware of the note.

- While working a stakeout, you discover $9,000 in a paper bag in a garbage can. Since you are utterly alone, no one would know if you kept the money. What should you do?

   Suppose, as actually happened, you turn in the money, which is reclaimed by an elderly man. He dumps the money on the desk, counts it, looks at you, and says, "You son of a bitch, it's a good thing it's all here." What should you do?

Here, departmental policies and the requirements of honesty are obvious. The main point is to remind inexperienced officers of the folly of expecting gratitude from every citizen for a job well done. Good officers do their duty because it is their duty, without expecting a reward. A story of this kind tends to generate both laughter and cynicism. The humor may be drawn upon as an antidote to the bitterness. The discussion of ethical issues should not be humorless.

- You and your partner stop a car that has been driven erratically through a red light. The intoxicated driver produces a license from another state and offers money to each of you. As you take him downtown, he increases his offer. After you cite him for DWI, do you also charge him with attempted bribery? Suppose the police are corrupt in his hometown where traffic violations are settled by passing money to them under the table. Does this make a difference?

This case provides opportunity to discuss actions people commit while incapacitated. Sometimes we treat drunkenness as an excuse for conduct we would not otherwise tolerate. By contrast, Aristotle described Athenian law that holds a man who commits wrong actions while drunk doubly responsible and calls for double punishment, because he has brought the incapacity on himself.

   The case also raises the question of the standards accepted elsewhere. When speeders say that drivers can go ten miles per hour over the speed limit in their home state, should you let them do so here as well? Obviously not. How is attempted bribery different? Or is the drunken driving citation enough?

- In addition to your regular duties as a police officer, you work in security at a local department store, where you see an old woman conceal several items of children's clothing. After apprehending her, you learn that her pension and social security benefits are insufficient to buy gifts for her grandchildren. What should you do? What factors go into the decision?

This problem can be used to highlight knowledge of local agencies that assist the poor. Where can the woman find inexpensive or free clothing and toys for her grandchildren? If the stolen items are returned, the merchant will probably decline to press charges, so the issue is whether the woman's circumstances can be improved.

- After working morals for some time, you have learned that certain gambling rooms in the city "have the blessing"—that is, political and administrative pressure is exerted on the police to refrain from inspection or arrests. To your knowledge, no police are on the pad; you conclude that political contributions are made to get this favorable treatment. Since you do close other gambling operations, you begin to feel like the agent of these interests. You realize you can do virtually nothing about this policy by yourself. What should you do? Why?

  What are the differences between the duties of a patrol officer and a command officer in such a case? If the problem is reported and the command officers do nothing, is a patrol officer obligated to take further steps? If IAD has been informed and does not act, should the officer then forget it? Should a chief who learns of the matter treat it as trivial compared with direct bribery?

Truthful accounts of past efforts of the department are needed here to ensure that an officer is never put in this lonely situation. If the department routinely allows such betrayals of its own officers, it is in a condition of moral disgrace. The increased levels of responsibility that attend increased authority can be discussed here, together with accounts of the usefulness of external agencies, such as the FBI. The emotionally charged issues of informing should be addressed, and with them the need for courage in the performance of duty.

The only way for a department to come clean in such a case is to reverse the administrative pressure. This fact invites discussion of honorable and dishonorable compromise with political interests.

- On a snowy December morning you are called to assist the court bailiff in an eviction of a family of nine, who insist they have not been notified. All procedures required by the court have, however, been satisified, and the family is six months behind in rent. The property owner and the bailiff are insistent on eviction, even though the family has no place to go or to put the furniture. What can you do? What should you do? Do you want other facts?

Again, the issue is the officer's knowledge of available alternatives and services in the community. Caution in estimating the possible reactions of desperate people can also be discussed.

- As a captain, you are visited one morning by the wife of one of your officers, a good officer who does his work properly. She complains of his carousing, seeing another woman, spending money recklessly, and striking her during quarrels, and she wants you to talk with him. You know that locker room gossip supports her charges, but his private behavior appears not to affect his professional performance. Is his private life any of your business? What should you do?

Because problems in private life are often relevant to professional performance, a command officer may want to look into the officer's performance at work more carefully. Once the wife approached him, the matter was no longer private. If she does not want to press charges for assault, the issue becomes what counseling programs are available within the department. A confidential talk with the officer, or a request to a friend, priest, or other intermediary to encourage him to seek counseling inside or outside the department may be useful. An expression of concern that his problems may otherwise grow worse and end in disciplinary action would be appropriate. Given the extent to which marital problems affect police, a department should be prepared to address such matters.

- While off duty, you attend a meeting in your neighborhood of Little League Baseball managers, coaches, and umpires for the new season. You recognize a man introduced as a coach as someone who was taken downtown in connection with a sexual assault of a young boy. The man was released for lack of evidence—the boy was not sure he was the man. As a citizen and a police officer, what should you do?

Here departmental policies and the code of ethics on confidentiality may be reviewed. Although the man must be presumed innocent, he may have a record of convictions for sex offenses. Would that be part of the public record, and could it legitimately be brought to the attention of other league officials? How about a record of other arrests without conviction?

Can respect for confidentiality and presumption of innocence be squared with concern for the safety of the children? The conflict between these ideals may not yield any entirely satisfactory solution. The officer can review profiles of sex offenders and discuss the case confidentially with a departmental psychologist. That should result in a better judgment of the levels of risk and of possible actions.

- As the investigating detective in a serious felony case, you discover excellent physical evidence that a particular suspect is guilty. But you also discover information that, if made available to the defense, would increase the chances of acquittal. What are your obligations, and to whom?

This question suggests the wisdom of including a prosecuting attorney in some sessions. Like defense lawyers, prosecutors do not like surprises at trial or in plea bargaining. The question will probably be raised whether the defense could acquire the information for itself. Perhaps more important, the information may make the prosecutor doubt that the suspect should be held for trial. Laws about the rights of the defense to information disclosed by the investigation should be explained.

- After the brutal murder of your partner, who was very close to you, you frequently stop his wife for driving while intoxicated. She leaves her children untended and is becoming generally unstable in her grief. What should you do?

The initial question is why this has been allowed to become frequent before the problem is addressed. Does the department make provision for support and assistance to such spouses? If so, have they been called into play—or can they be? Clearly, the situation is likely to grow worse without intervention. The children could lose their mother to an accident or to imprisonment for an accident lethal to others. A friend cannot allow this to continue.

The officer may seek advice within the department, from service agencies, and from groups that provide support in the face of grief and substance abuse and dependency.

- You are called to an average-income home by neighbors because of the sustained crying of a baby. Finding the house a shambles and four young children who have been beaten, you also learn that the father is away, and the mother is a heavy drinker. The eldest child, who ran the household, has just run off with her boy friend. As you are making arrangements for the children with a children's home, the mother returns drunk and threatens to kill herself if you take the children. What are your options? What should you do? Does the fact that the household is "average income" make a difference?

The income is not relevant, but the nature of the neighborhood may be. In some ethnic areas, after neighbors call for assistance and learn of a problem, they say to police, "No report, no report," meaning that they will address the problem themselves. They are often more effective than the overburdened social service agencies. To decide what to do, officers have to know their beat and the sources of assistance that operate formally and informally within it.

Clearly, the children cannot be left to a mother who is not in control of her own life. Whether they must be moved—and whether the mother should be taken to a detoxification center or hospital—must be decided. If so, the mother's threats should be told to the medical personnel.

In general, a desperate person's threats should not deter an officer from safeguarding others. The mother cannot be allowed to determine the resolution of the problem.

- As a patrol officer with years of experience, you have come to know and trust (at least in certain contexts) several informants and have promised to keep their identities secret. One day you are ordered within the department to divulge the identity of an informant. What should you do?

Did you have a right to make the promise? Do you have a right—or a duty—to keep it? What are the department's policies about informants and about auditing officer-informant contacts and payments? Is command supervision of informant contacts standard practice? Should it be? If you have knowingly made a promise in violation of departmental practice in order to persuade the informant to cooperate, what are your subsequent duties?

Such questions may be used to introduce further consideration of obedience to orders. Suppose a superior gives an order you believe to be unwise or immoral, or in violation of policy. How should you proceed? Suppose, for instance, that undercover narcotics officers are told, off the record, to make themselves credible to dealers by using drugs.

The inquiry may show that some disagreements are trivial and that obedience to an order is both right and obligatory, while other disagreements over principle must be faced. Compromise may be possible, but it is not likely to be easy. Such distinctions show that some compromises are decent and some are wrong. They also reveal that a person who repudiates a colleague over a trifle makes a serious error, just as an officer who compromises everything does.

- During an arrest of five suspects by you and three other officers, one of the officers is verbally abused by a suspect being escorted to a shield car. You do not see what else happens, except that the officer strikes the suspect on the arm with his nightstick. In his report, the officer does not mention that but says he bruised his arm entering the vehicle. When internal affairs later asks you about the suspect's complaint that the officer struck him, you know the allegation is true, but, for all you know, the officer may have been justified in striking him. What should you do? What if the record of this officer is outstanding?

A case like this can be used to show the importance of explicit expectations between partners. Although new partners would be unfriendly to announce in advance everything they will and will not tolerate, they owe it to themselves and each other to make known any expectations that could not be taken for granted—for instance, not covering for a partner who brutalizes prisoners. Beyond this, officers should deal forthrightly with each case as it comes up. When their perception of an incident differs, or one has clearly omitted or concealed facts, the two had better sort out their duties to the public, the department, and each other. Although these conversations may be difficult, they are preferable to the development of habits that cause conflict or the erosion of standards.

In this case, the officer might feel obliged to encourage the other officer to tell the rest of the story to IAD. Or the two officers might "stonewall" IAD and agree not to get into such a situation again. Although this course is clearly wrong with respect to the past, its long-term consequences might be good if their resolve is more than just words. Discussion of this fact can disclose that in moral deliberation, we are concerned for principles—such as that of honesty—and not only with consequences.

In many police departments, officers feel a strong sense of responsibility to a suspect in handcuffs. They understand the officer quoted by William Ker Muir: "When you've handcuffed a guy, you are taking care of his welfare and his rights, and you have to look out for them and not treat him as if he were in the ordinary situation where he can look out for himself."[22] Partners ought to have this much, at least, clear between them from the beginning.

Finally, if a partner behaves badly, an officer can request a change. One officer who was exposed to the small-time corruption of a partner on his first day as a street cop opted for another partner. He was given one and went on to become one of the great police administrators and investigators of our time.

- Investigating a homicide, you become suspicious of the story told by the daughter and son-in-law of the victim. As you question the son-in-law, you point out the inconsistencies in his story, although you do not know what happened or who committed the crime, nor do you have reason to suspect that the son-in-law was involved. Nervously, he assures you that he didn't do it, but he knows who did. He volunteers to tell what happened if you promise him immunity and promise to keep secret his identity as the informant. What should you do?

Officers cannot guarantee immunity and in well-run departments have no right to conceal the identity of an informant from specific supervisors. Once the son-in-law has gone this far, an effective interrogator can probably elicit the information, either by encouraging words or by reminders about legal penalties for concealing evidence and obstructing justice.

- You and your partner, and possibly other units, are called to a family disturbance in which a sixteen-year-old girl has badly hurt her mother with a knife. Since investigation reveals that the daughter was not defending herself, the extent of the injuries makes her action felonious. Moreover, she has been in repeated fights at home and at school, though not charged previously, and she has been under psychiatric treatment for over six months.

Both the girl's mother and the psychiatrist hired by the

family object strongly to your charging the girl or involving juvenile court. The mother refuses consent for a second medical opinion. What are your alternatives? Which should you choose?

In this case like others, the officer would show good judgment by using the department's resources, a police psychiatrist for example. Obviously, judgment will have to be exercised as well in assessing the credibility of the mother and the family's doctor. Since the girl has proved that she is dangerous, should other considerations weigh as heavily as this one? Should you consult school officials?

Although it seems hazardous to allow the girl to go on without intervention, the normal procedures of the local juvenile court must be considered. Will the girl simply be released to the custody of her mother?

- As a uniformed patrol officer, you have found the information given you by a voluntary informant reliable and instrumental to making cases against drug dealers. Later you learn that his motives have been self-serving. He is a dealer seeking to eliminate competition. What should you do? What other information do you want, if any, in order to decide?

When this issue was raised in class, I was a little surprised that the officer had not suspected from the first that the informant was a dealer. Many of the best police tell informants that they will be arrested and prosecuted if they commit any secret crimes regardless of their informant status. In practice, this is no idle threat.

Several questions apply to this issue: What is departmental policy on criminal activity by informants and on their previously concealed criminal actions? How serious are their crimes? If an informant is credible because he deals drugs, should he continue in that activity—but with the knowledge of the police? If the informant deliberately deceives the officer, should he be arrested and prosecuted? Police experienced with informants can offer guidance on such questions, especially on police control of the informant and the risks of tolerating deception by the informant.

- Working an office where complaints are received, you often get calls from intoxicated people reporting auto theft. Many of these complaints turn out to be untrue—the caller has misplaced the car, loaned it out, or abandoned it after an accident or it was repossessed or towed for illegal parking. Theft reports cost time and effort, and so does removing them from the records. Should one have a policy about responding to such calls? If so, what? If not, how should one decide what to do?

This situation encourages discussion of discretion and policy as well as of limitations of available resources. No priority should be given to complainants who are obviously intoxicated or cannot say where a car was left. If they call after sobering up, they can be referred to the impound lot or elsewhere, and their complaints can be handled normally. If departmental policy says otherwise, then its rationale should be discussed.

- You work a district that has habitual drunkards. Arresting them is costly and time consuming; it leaves your district unprotected; and it does no apparent good, because they are frequently back in the street soon after. But if left alone, they often do not care for themselves and bother others. What should you do? Has some other agency obligations on this score?

Attention to local details is imperative here. In some districts, lack of funds has closed "detox" centers, jails are overflowing, and hospital services are unavailable. There is no place to take the helpless wino. In others, police and related services are well enough staffed to help take public drunkards off the streets.

The issue of the realism of departmental policies may be raised, and the procedures for review of policy discussed. In addition, any population of homeless or others who need help harbors a criminal element that preys on them. Even if homeless alcoholics cannot be taken off the streets, they can be protected by police who are alert to crimes perpetrated against them and who seek to apprehend the perpetrators. Departmental preparations to protect the helpless as severe weather approaches should also be raised.

- As a police officer, you have become thoroughly competent during several years of work, including patrol in several districts. Currently, you are assigned to the narcotics undercover unit; you have managed to get very near the top levels of a major drug-distributing organization.

  Accompanied by several members of the organization, you are on your way to a big drug transaction. Stopped at an intersection, you see two men violently, perhaps murderously, pistol whipping the owner of a local carry-out store as they rob it. The episode is noticed by your companions as well. What should you do? Why?

Many such questions can be answered by departmental policies and regulations or by moral principles that can be straightforwardly applied. The real usefulness of institutional policies and of well-established habits and clear principles is to show that such issues do not have to be approached alone or without guidance. Still, cases such as this one are likely to generate disagreement over the relevance and relative weight of reasons adduced.

In the case of the undercover officer who witnesses a life-threatening crime in progress, some police officers held in classroom discussion that:

> officers should give priority to undercover assignments because: (a) they are assigned to them; (b) all the normal duties of police service are suspended for undercover officers, as they are for wartime spies; (c) a lot of money may have been spent on the undercover investigation that would be wasted if the cover were blown; and (d) in the circumstances described, the officer's life would be placed at risk just by trying to get out of the car to aid the victim.

One officer asked, "Suppose the victim of the beating were a police officer—would you go to his aid?" All who had given priority to the undercover assignment earlier replied that they would; if the victim were a police officer, the undercover assignment no longer came first. He then asked why the life of the officer mattered more than the life of the citizen.

A command officer in the class wrote this reply to the statement that the undercover assignment took priority.

> Whether the officer in question is assigned to an undercover role or any other role imaginable, I cannot conceive of a situation where he would be justified in allowing someone to be killed because he failed to act. I agree that one cannot be expected to do what is not possible, but the officer involved would be hard pressed to satisfy his superiors that his action or lack of action was the only way to go. When any officer feels his assignment is more important than life itself, that officer's values have been misplaced. Police Division procedures are clear on this point as well as the law. If police procedures and the law as applied to criminal matters are not enough, the officer would be guilty of malfeasance, misfeasance, or nonfeasance in office.

Another officer expressed a similar opinion:

> This officer is, in my opinion, morally, legally, and professionally obliged to take whatever action is reasonably pos-

sible to prevent the death or serious injury to this victim regardless of his assignment at the time. The fact that he would, in all probability, blow his cover is certainly a consideration, but the life of a citizen is by any measure more important than the successful conclusion of a drug case. Another undercover agent or informant or some other operation might allow for the arrest of these individuals at some later date, but if that victim dies from these injuries, that cannot be corrected.

Both officers appealed to the section of the police manual that says the police department should protect all persons within its jurisdiction from criminal attack.

By such discussion, officers can see how reasons outweigh one another in arriving at sound decisions. The situations should be not only realistic but drawn from the actual experience of police if possible. Everyone should be forthcoming about what actually happened and where things went right or wrong. And everyone should understand that deliberation among colleagues who disagree is not a contest to see who wins. It is a shared pursuit of answers that can be reached by candid and knowledgeable use of intelligence. Deliberation is very different from the entertaining but usually unproductive telling of "war stories." If a class falls into mere exchanges of tales from the streets, practice at reasoning is forgotten.

The Fabric of a Life

Reasonable people deliberate about problematic cases because they understand that what they do matters. Some people who behave badly fail to grasp this. They seem to believe that a human life is made up of isolated actions that affect nothing else. Accordingly, an officer may believe that napping on duty, or "cooping," is all right because it affects nothing else; intemperance is all right because it affects nothing else; being needlessly confrontational is all right; and so on.

This kind of mistake has been made throughout history. It is the mistake of Macbeth and Lady Macbeth who believe that, by committing murder, they will change only one isolated thing—who will become the next king and queen. They do not expect to be haunted by the blood they spill or to be changed in any way by their behavior. In the Bible, when King David sends Uriah the Hittite to certain death in battle, he believes that he will get Uriah's wife, Bathsheba, for himself and that everything else will remain the same. But as the Prophet Nathan shows David, everything changes when David makes himself into a ruler so unjust. People who make such mistakes are weakened, made worse, or destroyed because they fail to realize that our actions weave a tapestry of our life—beautiful or indifferent or ugly.

Officers who sleep in a free hotel room while on duty require other officers to work and cover for them. They invite the contempt of hotel employees toward police, they risk returning to duty only half alert, and they steal from the public who pay their salary. In all this, their action reveals serious flaws of character and judgment. Similarly, officers who drink to excess privately are likely to be hung over on duty and more prone to errors of judgment and concentration than they have any right to be. They give less than their best to their colleagues and the public.

Neither does an officer who is needlessly confrontational commit some isolated action. By such rashness, as Aristotle observed more than two thousand years ago:

> he gives the impression of overacting the part, and his courage is a little suspect. At all events, he would like people to believe that he is animated by the same feelings as the brave man when danger threatens. So he imitates him whenever he can. For this reason, most rash men are of the forcible feeble type. They swagger a good deal when things look bright, but make themselves scarce in the presence of actual danger. . . .
>
> We may add that the rash man is foolhardy, ready for anything before the danger arrives; but, when it does, shearing off. On the other hand, the brave man is gallant in action but undemonstrative beforehand.[23]

Police officers who unnecessarily make a situation confrontational do not fear the right things. They ought to fear needlessly endangering the public, their partners, and themselves, and they therefore ought to be firm but not swaggering. They ought to fear boastfulness that leaves others no room for flexibility and inspires feelings of hatred toward themselves and other police. They ought not to fear the use of force when nothing less will do, but they should fear hasty and precipitous force. They ought to fear in themselves weakness and lack of self-confidence that tempt them to confrontation for fear of losing their dignity. Fearing the right things and seeking to address them forthrightly is neither soft nor irresolute. What is at stake in a needless confrontation is not isolated but woven into the fabric of all of an officer's life.

When I asked a street cop how far officers go in interrogating suspects, she replied that they used phone books—that is, they hit suspects on the head with a telephone directory to intimidate them without leaving bruises. When I asked whether that was department policy, she asked how anyone could be interrogated without a phone book.

Qualified interrogators know more effective legal ways to elicit information from a suspect. This officer clearly took for granted, however, that brutalizing suspects is an isolated action that bears on nothing else. She did not understand that it necessarily involves officers in a conspiracy of silence, since it violates legal rights of citizens. It also violates "official" departmental policy, it requires the preparation of false reports, and it may involve perjury. Our actions have broad consequences, not least in the kinds of people they make of us.

What is taught by academies about ideals should be woven into the realities of the streets and the kinds of cases officers routinely encounter. Just as academy instructors need rich police experience, their instruction should be reinforced by field training officers, who show that it applies in practice. Ethics learned in an academy will be forgotten if field training officers tell new police officers that it is irrelevant to the streets and to real police work.

Police must learn in field training the truth of their academy lessons. Without coherence between academy preparation and field training, and cooperation between teachers and FTOs, even very good academy programs will soon be forgotten by officers in the field.

11
Tragedy and "Noble Cause" Corruption

Every rational being exists as an end in himself and not merely as a means to be arbitrarily used. . . . Act so that you treat humanity, whether in your own person or in that of another, always as an end and never as a means only.

IMMANUEL KANT[1]

Education directed to excellence of character and judgment is incomplete without some treatment of tragedy. The treatment is likely to be brief in criminal justice programs, since not all the features of general theory need be covered.

Tragedy may, but does not always, arise from a character flaw, as when blind ambition destroys a person of promise, or pride or hubris brings King Oedipus to grief in Sophocles' drama. Tragedy can also arise from the nature of the human condition itself.

Suppose a doctor has two patients before him, both dying, but has the time and resources to save only one. The issue is not how he is to decide, but that he is to decide. If he cannot possibly save both—no matter what he does—he must decide. His deciding is not a case of "playing God"; it is a case of fulfilling the duties of a doctor.

That one patient dies, say, for lack of available blood, is tragic, but not something the doctor could have prevented. By saving one—as many as he could—the doctor has done the right thing. In such circumstances, a doctor of fine character may feel regret bordering on remorse that he could not do more, even though he acted rightly in doing all he could. He faced the ordeal of judgment without shirking. Because he has behaved rightly, and because only wrongful acts can logically be forgiven, we cannot respond to his regret or remorse with forgiveness. Instead, his friends and colleagues should offer comfort to him—and the humane reminder that sometimes the human condition causes tragedy, no matter how hard we try to prevent it.

Tragedy can also arise from the conflict of one undeniable good with another undeniable good, when no amount of effort, intelligence, or good will can bring the two into harmony. Sometimes we cannot have things both ways. To make the public safe, we must arrest and confine the criminally dangerous, but to make the public safe we must also restrain government from presumption of guilt and disregard for due process. Law enforcement officers sometimes know that someone is guilty of a serious crime but either lack evidence or have tainted evidence. The individual remains free to commit crimes against new victims. We are obliged to do everything in our power to safeguard the public and to make government just, but our best efforts cannot always prevent failure.

Despite the heartache, those who have to make practical decisions must acquire the fortitude to go on. They are obliged to give their best despite the stress that will otherwise grind down their aspirations. This is an irreducible element of taking the human condition seriously.

For these reasons, the possession of authority, discretion, and power leads reflective people from morally important but unproblematic cases to questions about extreme cases where tragedy may lurk. Often such cases are hypothetical, sometimes unrealistic. They are invariably extraordinary and distinct from commonplace decency in daily life. The principal value of examining them is that careful analysis can advance subtlety, good reasoning, and a sense of the tragic.

Although law enforcement officials do not always agree which cases are difficult, examples usually resemble the "lifeboat" type of problem. One question goes something like this:

> If you have a perpetrator in custody, and he has information that could save the life of an innocent victim, is it right to use extreme methods to get the information?

Such occurrences are removed from the daily realities of law enforcement. When the question comes up for discussion, I ask for more detail. Even hypothetical cases must be specific. Here is one response.

> Suppose you have a perpetrator in custody who is known to have kidnapped a victim. The victim is known to be buried alive, and the perpetrator is known to have the information sufficient to rescue the victim.
>
> Time is short. The perpetrator will not divulge the information under ordinary legal interrogation, even though it is

191

conducted very shrewdly. Is it morally right to exceed your authority and use physical coercion to get the information? Is saving the life of the innocent victim a sufficient end to justify such illegality? Does this noble cause justify a means we would normally consider wrong and evil?

This type of question is usually accompanied by others: Do ends justify means? Is there ever a cause so important that it justifies everything? Do noble causes justify illegality and immorality?

Many command personnel deny that this case is problematic or difficult. Police are sworn to uphold the law, they point out, and they have no right to violate it, certainly not by inflicting pain on a prisoner. The situation poses no ordeal, they argue, because the rules on prisoners are clear and unmistakable.

A smaller number admit that the rules are clear but still see a problem: What about the rights of the victim? They feel torn between a clear duty to obey the law and respect the rights of the suspect-perpetrator on the one hand and a sense of duty to try to save the life of an innocent victim on the other.

Some philosophers would direct the inquiry to another question. They say that mistreatment of the prisoner is wrong, but in such an instance—not as a rule—is it an excusable wrong? Should this person, who commits this wrong, under these conditions, this time, for the sake of this victim, be forgiven?

The questions raised by police can illuminate ways of thinking through such conflicts. Although character education would be incomplete without such illumination, hard cases cannot be the initial focus, and should not be the central focus, of academy programs in ethics.

Ends and Means

The meaning of the question, Do ends justify means? is neither simple nor clear. It might mean any or all of the following: (1) Do good ends make actions right? Do they contribute in part to the rightness of actions? (2) Should we take ends and consequences into account in deciding what to do? (3) Are a person's ends relevant to the quality of the person's character and to the praise or blame the person deserves for specific actions?

Clearly, having a good end contributes to the rightness of an act, just as having an evil purpose counts against it. And we do have to take consequences into account. A person's ends are relevant to the esteem the person deserves: one whose purpose is to benefit others deserves greater admiration than one whose purpose is to cause harm or than one utterly indifferent to everyone else.

But these answers do not lead to the conclusion that having a good end is sufficient to make an action right, or that ends and consequences are all we should consider in deciding what to do, or that having good ends is all that matters in a person's character. Furthermore, even if having good ends were the sole determinant of right action, we might still encounter conflicts about what we should do. Good ends can conflict with each other. They can pull us in contrary directions, just as worthwhile principles do.

Accordingly, the answer to the question is, Ends do justify means up to a point, and in certain ways, depending on what you mean, but not simply or unqualifiedly. Human life is just not that simple.

This is the lesson that the French Algerian author Albert Camus tried, in July 1943, to teach to a former German friend who had become a Nazi. Camus wrote to him:

> You said to me: "The greatness of my country is beyond price. Anything is good that contributes to its greatness. And in a world where everything has lost its meaning, those who, like us young Germans, are lucky enough to find meaning in the destiny of our nation must sacrifice everything else."
> "No," I told you. "I cannot believe that everything must be subordinated to a single end. There are means that cannot be excused. And I should like to be able to love my country and still love justice."[2]

Camus' love of justice is akin to Kant's recognition that people deserve consideration, deserve not to be just used, simply because they are people. A person is a repository of worth, of significance, even if that person appears without merit. This is why we oppose inordinate coercion; once we descend from reasoned persuasion— and respect for each other's freedom—to force, we deny the right to self-determination. Justice constrains us from going any further in this direction than we believe necessary.

American traditions affirm this principle. The right of due process and the prohibition against cruel and unusual punishment in the Eighth Amendment are based on the principle that human beings deserve to be treated as ends and never as mere means, never as objects, no matter how heinous their crimes. This moral tradition of America and other civilized nations contrasts with the gulags of the Soviet Union, where guilt is presumed, trials are a mockery, and cruel punishment routine. Where moral traditions are absent, the consequences are predictable.

Even in war, where enemy troops are often treated as mere obstacles to a nation's will, the Geneva Convention reflects the idea that nations still have an obligation to treat prisoners as human beings. These standards prohibit torture because it is inexcusable brutality against a defenseless person. They should apply even to prisoners who refuse to divulge highly valuable information, but they are often violated. The North Vietnamese, for example, tortured American POWs to make them assist in their propaganda efforts. The Americans were routinely treated as mere means to their purposes.

American traditions stand squarely opposed to use of the third degree in interrogating suspects. Such methods violate at least the Fifth and Eighth amendments, as well as Miranda and other judicial interpretations of those guarantees. These amendments are not pieces of advice to law enforcement—they are fundamental law, the foundation of our way of life.

Yet in law enforcement as well as other national affairs, we are driven to the question whether illegal actions that violate the rights of citizens are ever morally right or excusable. I call this the question of "noble cause" corruption. Are police ever justified, or do they ever deserve to be excused, in breaking fundamental laws, not for personal gain, but for a purpose that appeals to our basic moral sensibilities? This is a question about extraordinary situations, when we cannot stand for all the goods we judge to be of the highest order, fulfill our highest principles, and respond to our most strongly felt duties, in the treatment of all persons involved. The conflict between the rights of the innocent victim and the rights of the suspect-perpetrator is such a case.

Our response to this difficult question has crucial consequences. Since the literature about it leaves much to be desired, I have discussed it with philosophers and other scholars, lawyers, public officials, police chiefs, military officers, religious leaders, and corporate executives, whose counsel is paraphrased or quoted below. Sensible persons faced with hard problems should turn to the wisest people they know—the wisest friends, the best authors, and the historic figures and contemporaries they most admire. Their example is as precious as any moral precept and their judgment a powerful supplement to our own.

Three points are basic. First, since ends do not necessarily justify means, a good end cannot justify a means in a context that makes it wrong and evil. In a primitive setting where the law is nonexistent or ineffectual, and where conditions of due process are not yet established, we might argue that physical coercion of a prisoner is at times justifiable. A lone champion of justice who behaves with regard for morality could be the only criminal justice system in existence. Or if a public official has thoroughly corrupted the system and become impervious to its sanctions, our main question might be one about what justice requires, not one about ends and means. But where civilizing law does have a hold, as in America, violations of fundamental civil liberties and laws, violations of oaths of office, abuses of authority and power—all betrayals of the public trust—are wrong and cannot be justified by any end.

Knowing this, however, does not help much in deciding what to do or tell us whether as decent people we should ever use evil means. It leaves open the question whether we should ever excuse the use of evil means because the end is undeniably good, lesser means are ineffective, and the motives of the agent are unquestionably noble.

Second, revising regulations and rules cannot eliminate tragedy and conflicts of ideals. Although revisions can alter the mechanics of accountability, they cannot change elements of the human condition. After the United States restricted the use of weapons by its ships defending tankers from attack by Iran, thirty-seven Americans died in an attack on the U.S.S. *Stark*. After the restrictions were relaxed, the U.S.S. *Vincennes* mistakenly shot down an Iranian civilian airliner, killing all aboard. Both events were tragic, despite efforts to establish the best policies.

Third, inflicting pain sadistically, with pleasure and without regret, can never be excused. Even in a conflict in which allegiances have been staked out and the pursuit of information has become brutal, thrilling to the torture of others, viewing them at most as containers of information, is wrong. It is depraved and inexcusable—even if the victim is loathsome.

Interrogators may pretend to be sadistic, however, and use fear rather than pain as their instrument. In Bertolt Brecht's play, the pope—who wants Galileo to recant his scientific discoveries—addresses the cardinal inquisitor:

> POPE (exhausted): It is clearly understood: he is not to be tortured. (Pauses.) At the very most, he may be shown the instruments.

INQUISITOR: That will be adequate, Your Holiness. Mr. Galilei understands machinery.[3]

Who Is to Say (What to Do)?

To begin reflecting about a hard case, we should ask who should actually have to suffer the ordeal of making the decision. Asking whom we should trust differs from asking, What is the answer? Because hard cases must be approached with a knowledge both of particulars and of general principles, we must determine who in a police department should be faced with a moral issue so hard and of such profound consequence.

Most adults should reflect on and talk about painfully hard problems, which can contribute to the moral and intellectual maturation of younger people as well. Certainly, many police of all ranks can meet the challenge of demanding thought, but the issue here is, Who should actually have to make such a decision, not in thought, but in practice?

Not every moral question should require a decision by every officer, for some are beginners who are not qualified to decide problems of great magnitude. Beginners should not be asked to risk a career—for that may be at stake—in making decisions that go beyond their experience.

While citizens generally should try to develop informed opinions on public issues of all kinds, we would neither entrust policy making to amateurs nor ask them to live with the trials of setting policy. As Walter Lippmann said, such decisions call for "a kind of knowledge—not to speak of an experience and a seasoned judgment—which cannot be had by glancing at newspapers, listening to snatches of radio comment, watching politicians perform on television, hearing occasional lectures, and reading a few books. It would not be enough to make a man competent to decide whether to amputate a leg, and it is not enough to qualify him to choose war or peace, to arm or not to arm, to intervene or to withdraw, to fight or to negotiate."[4] Although we may disagree with them, we want officials with "experience and a seasoned judgment" to have the authority to make such decisions.

As history teaches, the ordeal of judgment may be dreadful. When France fell to Germany in World War II, for example, the French government advocated alliance with Germany, not merely submission, so the French Navy seemed likely to become part of Germany's arsenal. Winston Churchill, as Britain's prime minister, had to decide whether to attack those ships, manned by former allies, in order to deny them to the enemy. He did so, thereby preventing German naval dominance. Although the decision was not compounded by any question of illegality, he described it as the most painful one of his life. Such hard decisions are part of the ordeal of command, not of lesser rank.

Police are the constituted authority for the use of force within society. They are uniformed as a mark of their authority and competence. Police departments have a structure of command just so that problems beyond the scope of junior personnel will not fall to them. Only in this way can the police live up to the public trust and safeguard against erosion of morale, which results when daily responsibilities simply cannot be met.

In many departments, policies on weaponry, ammunition, and the use of weapons other than sidearms are made by command rather than patrol personnel. In well-run departments, supportive and trustworthy authority flows from the top. The hardest issues should therefore be faced by officers with the most seniority and highest rank. Officers who have risen to command rank are probably better qualified than anyone else inside or outside law enforcement to identify the hardest moral questions. They know from experience the temptation to twist the law or manipulate the facts in routine matters in the streets. They know the common view that some excesses in the use of authority are necessary. They should therefore consider where such views lead when the stakes are life, death, and fundamental law, and they may then help the next generation of police grapple with such issues.

Every person I have consulted on this issue insists that only mature adults with considerable experience should ever contemplate actually practicing extreme and illegal conduct. The moral burden is simply too heavy for personnel inexperienced in policing, who are not competent or prepared to make such decisions. They lack experience and information, they are less able to identify and apply legal means, and they have not had the opportunity to reflect on hard cases. These police would more likely guess than think their way to a decision.

My colleagues do not mean to suggest that patrol and mid-rank personnel are without deep moral insight and great personal maturity. The moral character of police forces often rests as much on the influence and training provided by sergeants as on higher officers, they say, and seasoned officers of all ranks can arrive at compelling conclusions about such issues. Considerations both of authority and of fairness, however, imply that the highest ranking personnel ought to make such decisions and live with the consequences.

The consequences of extreme illegality within law enforcement are so grave that only those in a position to appreciate their gravity should be involved. Police officers who step so far beyond their authority as to physically coerce a prisoner have ceased to function as legitimate enforcers of the laws under the Constitution. They must be prepared to lose their job, to see the courts dismiss all charges against the suspect, or to deny the admissibility of evidence, and to stand trial themselves for assault and battery or more severe charges.

If the suspect-perpetrator goes free because the evidence becomes inadmissible, the police official who violated the rights of the prisoner in custody will have turned loose on society a murderous kidnapper, who can again prey on the innocent. If the victim dies despite the efforts of police, the crime for which the perpetrator can no longer be prosecuted is first-degree murder. Furthermore, no matter how brutal the official becomes, the prisoner may still lie. In that case, the police official has forsaken duty and all else for nothing.

No less important, command personnel are obliged never to permit officers under their command to employ third-degree interrogations. Even if they are willing to act *in extremis* as individuals and accept the consequences, they cannot as officers tolerate such conduct in the ranks. And they cannot lead their subordinates effectively, or deserve their confidence, if they are hypocrites.

If senior personnel have a right to consider such action, how can they avoid hypocrisy and remain faithful to the central duties of command? Since any attempt to justify illegal behavior after the fact would come too late, the question is, How should they stand on the record in advance?

With respect to policy making, command personnel should keep in mind that most of us tend to go a bit beyond the set limits. If the speed limit is fifty-five miles per hour, for example, ordinary traffic will go sixty or more. Since minor illegal infractions are likely to be commonplace, setting the limits a bit tighter than we intend to hold is prudent, so long as they do not make policing impossible or render the limits ridiculous or yield an appearance of indifference to infractions. Departmental limits should therefore be set slightly tighter than the legal treatment of suspects allows. Then minor and predictable infractions will not violate the law.

If command personnel take a realistic view toward slight overstepping, they can specify some limits as absolute. They can make clear, for example, that prohibition of third-degree methods is absolute and that they delegate no authority whatsoever in this matter. They can say candidly that, should any discretion ever be exercised on this issue, it will be reserved to the highest authority only—with no exceptions. To follow this path, the command officers must be forthright and not hide from the decisions of high office. Although they would avoid hypocrisy, they would still have to answer why rank carries a right to consider lawbreaking.

The answer is that the hardest moral questions cannot be reduced to questions of legality. Reserving the right of decision to the highest authority exhibits respect for the law, and it discloses that no principle—including the law—is utterly inviolable by absolutely everyone under all possible circumstances.

Article I, section 9, of the Constitution says, "The Privilege of the Writ of Habeas Corpus shall not be suspended, unless when in Cases of Rebellion or Invasion the public Safety may require it." Yet, when Abraham Lincoln became president and feared that the Maryland legislature would vote to secede, he arrested many of its members and suspended habeas corpus. By this means, he pre-empted Maryland's possible secession and fulfilled his duty to preserve the union. A state of rebellion may not yet have existed, however, and the danger to the public safety may not have "required" the action. And, certainly, there was no "invasion."

In practice, our moral sensibilities sometimes seem to call for things to be done, even though they are illegal. To make them legal would require too many specific details; otherwise, the law would be systematically abused. When we consider the morality of some illegal acts that we do not believe should be made legal, therefore, we recognize that no principle can be inviolable. Churchill and Lincoln perceived that inviolable principles can kill people. A refusal to fire on innocent French sailors in World War II might have enabled Germany to kill greater numbers with the French fleet and perhaps win the war.

This ground is so slippery, especially in a nation that treats certain rights as inalienable, that only command personnel of the highest rank should ever step onto it. The complexity of human life seems to me to warrant their stepping onto it, to face the ordeal of judgment with all its consequences, rather than never to consider extreme measures. Not only does such a position foreclose future decisions; it also threatens command personnel in some future case with hypocrisy.

I understand why some in law enforcement say that no one ever has a right to consider illegal measures. They insist that command personnel should be told *never* and should be made to comply. They know the danger of a command officer's going beyond the law, and so do I. But I also believe that the human condition compels us to see that an unconditional position here is too strong.

Trying to Have It Both Ways

Since no one who can avoid it should ever step onto such dangerous ground, command personnel and departmental legal counsel must know the laws that may provide relief from a conflict between undeniable goods. The Crimes Code of Pennsylvania, for example, like many others, contains a section called General Principles of Justification:

> In any prosecution based on conduct which is justifiable under this chapter, justification is a defense. . . .
> (a) General rule. Conduct which the actor believes to be necessary to avoid a harm or evil to himself or to another is justifiable if
> (1) the harm or evil sought to be avoided by such conduct is greater than that sought to be prevented by the law defining the offense charged.[5]

Such provisions may apply to command decisions in hard cases. Because such provisions may be overridden by other laws and by the Constitution, however, command personnel must use their intelligence, imagination, and experience to reduce the area of conflict.

A specific hypothetical case about physical coercion for information may help us test our suppositions, to be sure they do not draw us too hastily onto dangerous ground. In this case, the police know that the person in custody is the perpetrator, and not just a suspect. They know the victim is buried, and alive, and they know that the perpetrator knows where. They know the perpetrator will not divulge the information under legal interrogation.

Are the police likely to *know* this much in the situations they face? Colleagues in domestic law enforcement and in military intelligence and interrogation say no. They stress the difficulty of knowing how much information a suspect has. Inexperienced officers often treat detainees disgracefully—and even commit atrocities—because they overestimate a prisoner's knowledge. Experienced officers would urge that the hypothetical situation be made more realistic by supposing that the suspect may have information on which a victim's life may depend. The victim may be alive, and whatever information is drawn from the prisoner by any means may be true, and therefore may be useful in the preservation of life.

These useful points show how the case becomes harder under plausible assumptions that call for intellectual humility. In these circumstances, a police command officer who is unsure of the facts contemplates the additional moral burden of wrongdoing, even while uncertain that the desired end can be achieved by any means. By contrast, he can be sure that a no-holds-barred interrogation is wrong.

This uncertainty of facts is quite different from the legal presumption of innocence. Police officers frequently know who committed a crime—they may even have apprehended someone in the act. Legally, however, the person remains a suspect entitled to due process of law and therefore to the presumption of innocence. Factual guilt and legal innocence are entirely compatible; if they were not, we could not bring evidence to a trial that proved beyond a reasonable doubt a suspect's legal guilt.

In the hypothetical case, my colleagues are not suggesting that the perpetrator be treated merely as a suspect. They are not saying that the conditions for admissible evidence at a trial must be satisfied here, although they want to preserve these conditions if possible. Rather, they are pointing to an uncertainty about what the perpetrator knows. Accomplices, for example, may have decided where to bury the victim. The officers are also uncertain whether the perpetrator under duress would be telling the truth, and whether any information could save the life of the victim.

Several of these colleagues point to extreme measures within the law that can be tried to obtain the information the perpetrator has. And some observe that a perpetrator may lie, even in pain or under threat of death, especially one who would bury a victim alive. One writes:

> A number of reasons might account for not telling the truth: buying time for an accomplice, placing blame on another person, and—the most difficult to deal with—complete lack of conscience with regard to the crime. If he lacks a conscience and the attendant guilt, the perpetrator has no interest in saving the endangered life as an act of personal redemption. To that type of individual, whom we can refer to as sociopathic, outwitting the police officer is a far more appealing goal than a cleansing confession. This would be the type of personality that would thrive on burying a child alive in the first place.

Sociopaths may understand that what they have done is perceived as wrong by society, but they have absolutely no sense that their behavior is wrong, and, as a result, they have no remorse. Misleading a bothersome police officer would be predictable behavior from a sociopath, and provoking the officer to act outside the law in order to extract information would give the sociopath the last laugh that he seeks. Fooling the stupid officer and being very likely beyond prosecution *and* committing the original crime makes for the perfect sociopathic success.

The expertness of interrogators in such a case becomes a central issue. As one colleague notes, police must be "well enough trained in interrogation that they are not likely to rush into extreme measures." A poorly trained interrogator is more likely to panic under the pressure of trying to save a victim's life and ignore rules and policies. "The more urgent the need, the less rational a person is likely to be," one of my colleagues writes. Although this may make us more tolerant of police behavior under pressure, it does not help the victim or achieve purposes within the law. Legal measures might have succeeded; at least they had as much potential as illegal ones.

Legal methods of interrogation may be distasteful, but they are preferable to illegal ones. If male perpetrators have kidnapped female victims, the interrogation may be more effectively conducted by women, so a department should have expert male and female interrogators.

As one colleague writes:

> Scrupulous attention to detail, intelligent and practiced interrogation techniques based on an understanding of human psychology, and decisiveness . . . stand at least as good a chance of yielding the desired result [as physical coercion]. [T]hey do so without the risk of losing the admissibility of evidence. There are ways to flatter a suspect, gain his trust, convince him of his "rightness," enlist his assistance or enrage him, that yield information that can be acted upon. The lay person might very well be shocked by some of these techniques, and many police officers are uncomfortable using them because it requires their serious and convincing acting of roles which they find personally repugnant (such as telling a child molester that you understand perfectly how those little girls lead men on, and how they truly want to be screwed, and that you wish you had been screwed by someone strong and good-looking like the suspect when you were six years old), but they are not illegal, and they are remarkably effective. The U.S. Supreme Court

has consistently affirmed the legality of the police use of these techniques.

And another concludes:

The word "necessary" is slippery. It is often used merely for what appears efficient or expedient. "We had no choice" can be a lame and dishonest substitute for "It was the quickest way." There are many techniques for interrogation that are not violent.

In any deliberation about interrogation of great urgency, command personnel should be in close consultation with their legal personnel. A police department does not have to act alone in such a matter. A colleague writes:

Historically, our courts have sought to resolve and adjust the conflict of legitimate rights and interests in our society. Were I representing law enforcement authorities in the case you pose, I would naturally consider an emergency application to a court of competent jurisdiction. A compelling factual presentation would have to be made as to the life-threatening consequences of a suspect's refusal to provide information. I would ask the court to consider ordering the supervised administration of sodium pentathol or the employment of some alternative practice which has gained a degree of acceptance in the medical community. For purposes of analogy, I would cite those instances where courts have ordered emergency medical intervention for minor children, despite the constitutionally protected religious scruples of their parents.

We should conclude that command officers who fail to exercise all the legal means at their disposal have failed in their duty. Those who proceed into flagrant illegality without doing so are neither justified nor excusable, and they thrust their departments into hazards of civil and criminal liability that might have been avoided.

Obviously, some illegal actions are more serious than others. Several of my colleagues point out that if they were questioning a suspect in a case of this sort in his home, they would listen illegally to a phone call from an accomplice if they could. Such a judgment would have to be made by an officer at the scene, without benefit of consultation or supervision. In my judgment, this action, though illegal, would be morally appropriate; it is not a flagrant violation of the suspect's rights, and it seems less than extreme given the peril to a life. Releasing a suspect to gain information by surveillance might be plausible in some cases, and it would be legal. An officer would be remiss, however, to spurn opportunities to secure information by intrusive but nonviolent means.

Thinking It Through

Given all these considerations, what should a conscientious high-ranking police official do in the extreme situation? Suppose he is certain neither that the victim is alive nor that the suspect-perpetrator can be made to divulge what he does know. Suppose the legal methods of interrogation have been tried, expertly (albeit quickly), and failed. The life of the victim may depend on information the suspect-perpetrator may have that physical coercion may yield.

Most thoughtful people will come down on one side of the issue with some feeling of respect and sympathy for those on the other. Even mature and experienced adults who agree with everything that has been said to this point will be divided on this issue.

Certainly, my colleagues are. Some envision circumstances that would excuse the use of third-degree methods or drugs, but others do not. One writes:

> If any end can justify all means, it would be the protection of innocent life. I would use all the instruments at my disposal to get information from someone who *clearly* possessed it to secure the safety of the blameless. And do so with the intention of taking the responsibility personally for such action. I would not consider putting such policy in writing; neither would I consider denying my actions afterward.

Another writes:

> I think that, for roughly utilitarian reasons, getting information from a suspect by hurting him could be justified . . . but I think that saying or writing to policemen that it could be justified is probably not itself justified. This is because policemen, being human, may fall short of their convictions about hurting suspects and hurt them more and more often than they really think they should.

Still another observes:

> I think it unwise to offer a solution to this problem based on general principles. The problem for a real policeman is not so much what principles to apply but how to apply them. Much depends on the policeman's estimate of the suspect's knowledge, the urgency of the case, and the failure of suc-

cessful interrogation by means less than physical coercion. . . . But I would want to make it clear that, when it is urgent to save human life, *any* rule is breakable.

Some who oppose these positions, including police, share the views of one colleague:

> I see the violation of rights as an easy way out. . . . I want to be able to look at myself in the mirror every day and believe that I have done the best I could have under the circumstances. To do so, I proceed under the belief that there is no situation that I can predict in which I will meet the circumstances with a studied and purposeful decision to violate a suspect's constitutional rights as the best—or only—solution.

Another colleague is even more direct:

> The rule of law requires all of us to submit to it. A cop who breaks the law, in order to enforce it more effectively, is a criminal. No one is above the law. If you can't live with it, quit. Anything else is a slope toward totalitarianism, and it is naive to have faith that command personnel or anyone else can avoid sliding downward once they break the law, and it *is* hypocrisy to say that anyone in law enforcement has the right to do so. It is wrong to agree to the slightest compromise in these matters.

Another concludes with a reflection on the human condition itself:

> My position is a *simple and plain* acknowledgment of a conflict between official duty and an obligation of a person to do all he can to save the life of another. We must refuse to blur the distinctions between our official positions and our individual felt obligations. Thus, we should acknowledge on the one hand that using extreme measures to gain information from a "suspect" is never justified. On the other hand, *as individuals* we should be willing to consider acting *in extremis* and accepting the consequences of our actions. . . . In a sense my view is that this is one of the conflicts in the human condition (it is *not* a dilemma) for which there is no solution, even though individual human beings must, finally, decide. It is because the human condition can call for so much from the best of us that we should feel compassion for those who must face such conflicts.

When reasonable people of good will disagree about how to handle a complex problem, we can only hope that those who actually decide will do so with profound regard both for the status

of the human beings involved as ends and for their own professional duties, including their duty not to bring the department
into bad repute. They must not choose their methods in anger and
passion, or in a vengeful or self-righteous spirit in the name of a
supposedly all-justifying principle. They should recognize the
moral peril of excess and take every measure to avoid it. Then, if
they do choose to break the law and commit a wrongful act, they
will at least not do so routinely or feel justified in cloaking their
behavior in secrecy or perjury.

Terrorists and other extremists—in the name of justice—consider their murderous actions entirely justified. They are devoid of
the humility that makes people trustworthy to bear authority or
exercise power. Because they believe they are entirely devoted to
justice, they always believe themselves innocent as well. Human
life is neither so easy, however, nor so simple.

The same tendency can be seen in law enforcement. In 1986,
officers of the 106th Precinct in Queens, New York City, were
convicted of assault in the second degree and coercion in the first
degree for using stun guns to get confessions from misdemeanor
suspects in custody. Also in 1986, in San Antonio, Patrolman
Stephen Smith was shot to death by another officer, his closest
friend, who believed Smith was about to kill him. Smith was at the
time suspected of a plot to assassinate city officials and of involvement in six vigilante murders. In an investigation by a local newspaper of what happens in a police department "when it has
dangerous officers but cannot fire them because of union protection," City Manager Lou Fox had earlier declared, "I've got a killer
cop I can't get rid of. . . . To know that there are renegade cops,
dangerous people, on your force and to be unable for so long to do
anything about it, that can scare hell out of you." Ballistics tests
revealed that "bullets used in two unsolved murders matched
slugs fired from one of Smith's AR15 rifles."[6]

This mentality of self-righteousness, which is absolutely incompatible with the public trust, was also exhibited by a Miami
police officer on trial in 1988 for the murder of nine alleged drug
dealers. According to the local press, his only regret was that he
had not killed ninety-nine dealers before being caught. "I enjoyed
what I was doing," he said, denying he was a murderer because
his victims were "not human beings." He acknowledged that he
worshiped Hitler and said, "This is called absolute justice. . . . I
took nine people with me. . . . They'll never sell drugs to your
children." Prosecutors contend, however, that not all of his victims
were involved with drugs.[7] The columnist William Safire put such

behavior in perspective: "Toleration of the cop who deliberately kills a suspect threatens our way of life."[8]

A further problem, even for well-intentioned and normally restrained public officials, is the corrosive effect of extreme, illegal measures on restraint in future instances. Those who employ extreme measures may find it easier to do so the next time a hard case arises, and perhaps easier in a case not quite so hard after that. Extreme measures can then become routine merely because they are convenient.

A point made in *A Man for All Seasons* applies here, because we are creatures of habit. After bribing someone to betray a trust, an official says, "There, that wasn't too painful, was it? . . . That's all there is. And you'll find it easier next time."[9] Once we go beyond the law for a noble purpose rather than a selfish one, we may feel we have committed ourselves to illegal means, as further extremes become natural. As one of my colleagues observed, "When we violate a suspect's Constitutional rights, we deviate from fundamental principles. That can be the beginning of a substantial erosion. There's a fine line in these things, but once you step over it, you tend to justify subsequent acts by the former one." An intellectual and moral humility and an appreciation of the gravity of what we have done are the only bulwarks I know against such deterioration of character.

Dirty Harry

In a well-known article, Carl B. Klockars, professor of criminal justice at the University of Delaware, writes, "The Dirty Harry problem asks when and to what extent the morally good end warrants or justifies an ethically, politically, or legally dangerous means to its achievement."[10] In the film *Dirty Harry*, a psychopathic killer, Scorpio, kidnaps a fourteen-year-old girl, buries her alive, demands a ransom, and reneges on the promise to provide information when the ransom is delivered. The main character, Inspector Harry Callahan, illegally searches the suspect's room, confirms that he is Scorpio, tracks him down, shoots him in the leg, and then "stands on Scorpio's bullet-mangled leg to torture the information out of him." Scorpio divulges the location of the girl, who is, as Callahan suspected, already dead. Since the physical evidence and the confession are inadmissible in court, Scorpio walks away a free man.

Klockars denies that the most difficult problem is what Dirty Harry ought to do:

On the contrary, I suspect that most people would want Harry to do something dirty in the situation. I know I would want him to do what he did, and what is more, I would want anyone who policed for me to be prepared to do so. I want to have men and women of moral courage and sensitivity as police officers.

All of us want morally courageous and sensitive police officers, and many audiences seemed thoroughly satisfied with Callahan's behavior. In fact, many would no doubt approve of inflicting pain as punishment on Scorpio even if Harry knew the victim was dead.

Yet, we must not allow moral outrage to blind us to facts. The inspector's behavior is justified, Klockars says, by the goodness of the purpose, by his knowledge that Scorpio has the information, and by the "small possibility" that the victim is still alive. "There appears to be no reason for Scorpio to confess to the girl's location without being coerced to do so," he adds. Although Scorpio would not divulge the information from any goodness in his heart, a shrewd interrogator might enrage or trick him or use deceptively sympathetic tactics to draw out the information. Harry Callahan does not try any such means, nor does he try to comfort Scorpio as a way of gaining his confidence, however offensive such false compassion might feel. Neither does he seek assistance from a court of competent jurisdiction. He goes from asking a direct question at gunpoint to torture.

Callahan's excesses are no more a mark of courage or sensitivity than calling on interrogation experts and deferring to higher authority are marks of cowardice or insensitivity. Trying to fulfill the purposes of law enforcement within the limits of the law takes as much courage as any other course. Command personnel can help by being forthright and resolute about departmental policy in training. Klockars acknowledges that "the department that trains its personnel well and supplies them with the resources—knowledge and material—to do their work will find that its policemen will not resort to dirty means unnecessarily." He should add that a multitude of inexcusable moral wrongs has sought, and found, refuge under the slippery argument that it was "necessary." As Shakespeare wrote, necessity is the plea of tyrants. "The troublesome issue in the Dirty Harry problem," Klockars writes, "is not whether a right choice can be made, but that the choice must always be between two wrongs. And in choosing to do either wrong, the police officer inevitably taints or tarnishes himself."

In conversation with me, Professor Klockars has explained his position: the fundamental tenets of one moral theory may be irreducibly at odds with those of another moral theory; since an individual cannot satisfy both, he is bound to be tainted by one or the other. Thus, if one moral theory holds that you must always try to achieve the best immediate consequences (such as saving the life of the victim) and another holds that you must honor fully the status of a person as an end and not as a means to some goal (such as torturing a suspect for information), then an insoluble dilemma results.

The conclusion does not follow, however, because a person who subscribes only to one theory or the other has no moral problem at all, let alone a dilemma. The person simply acts in accordance with the theory. The real conflict arises for a person who sees a measure of rightness in each tenet, when circumstances force a decision between them. The incompatibility of some moral theories with others, by itself, taints no one. If it did, a vicious moral theory holding that might makes right or that white males are superior to everyone else and have a right to all positions of power and authority would taint everyone who rejected it. Theories have no such power, because they are sometimes wrong, simplistic, or overstated, and sometimes foolishly applied.

Furthermore, when we use coercion to prevent a person from self-determination, we do so either with or without restraint. The two differ profoundly.

Still, is it in some sense inevitable that police will be tainted by tensions between the limits of the law and moral constraint on the one hand and noble purposes on the other? Is this what we expect courageous and sensitive police to accept as their fate? Shall we tell students at police academies that they must "inevitably" become "dirty"?

The answer is no. Although the world has in it the makings of tragedy, not everyone who faces its most grueling demands need become dirty. Is it not still true, however, as suggested by the Klockars argument, that police officers who fail to use every means to achieve a high purpose are morally tainted? And are not officers who fail to abide by the law legally tainted or morally tainted by infidelity to their oath of office, to the Constitution, and to the public? I do not see why command officials would be morally tainted if they used all legal means at their disposal but declined to use illegal means that might be viewed by patrol personnel as a license for excess.

A more powerful consideration is that the suspect-perpetrator may go free if his rights are violated. The command officer may know that the prisoner is not suspected of other crimes that might lead to another arrest, that police surveillance of him will be prevented by charges of harassment, that no officers are available for surveillance, and that civic-minded private wealth cannot be enlisted to hire private surveillance. Moreover, the liberty of the suspect-perpetrator may be a murderous threat to other possible victims. The officer may imagine the eyes of the family of the next victim and hear their question, How could you have allowed the killer to walk away from his last murder?

That is, the command officer may see that using every conceivable means to save today's victim risks creating new victims tomorrow. What, then, is to be done? The slippery slope of physical coercion leads to the question whether false reports should be prepared to keep the perpetrator in custody and perjury should be committed to get a conviction. If the officer will do anything to save the victim and keep the suspect-perpetrator off the street, but he will not lie or commit perjury, then he cannot avoid the question of whether he should murder the suspect-perpetrator.

I do not see how a person can be tainted by refusing to step onto this slope, toward which we are dragged by extreme illegal measures in law enforcement. Ignoring the slope, Klockars argues that the story of Dirty Harry is art, in the sense that at "all meaningful levels" it is "true." He means that the Dirty Harry problem demands attention and analysis, not that all the particulars of the story are realistic.

After Scorpio goes free, Harry uses off-duty time to watch him until he is charged with harassment and ordered to stop. Scorpio then takes a bus full of elementary school children hostage. After Harry manages to force him away from the bus and they engage in a running gun fight, Scorpio takes yet another child hostage before Harry wounds him. When the child flees, the two at last confront each other. Now in a position to arrest Scorpio, Harry instead taunts him and dares him to try for the gun he has dropped. When Scorpio rises to the bait, Harry Callahan kills him. The shooting is calculated murder.

I do not know any police who would describe this denouement as realistic or "true" at "all meaningful levels," or describe Harry as a police officer of "courage and sensitivity." Klockars and others say that Harry Callahan should be fired. After all, if arrested in these circumstances, Scorpio would almost certainly be prosecuted and convicted. For purposes of law enforcement or the safety of the public, murdering Scorpio is pointless. The murder does offer delicious gratification to the appetite for revenge, and it satisfies moral outrage and hatred of the perpetrator. Such gratification has no place, however, in real law enforcement. It is not extreme action for the sake of high purpose, but raw self-indulgence.

If police officials are not tainted by refusing to step onto the slope of illegal action, neither are officials of demonstrated probity necessarily tainted by a last-ditch illegal step. Such an act may be unjustifiable by any unconditional principle, but it also may be excusable. Even if committed without regard to self-interest and at great personal sacrifice, inflicting pain is an undeniably evil act when committed by one who has no right to punish. Although it would constitute a betrayal of the duties of office, it would not necessarily be condemned in any subsequent legal proceeding. An enlightened governor could justifiably pardon the act. Still less does it follow that those who commit such acts are bad, that their character is besmirched, or that their honor is tainted.

I doubt that we would describe officials who act either way as "dirty." Some would say they should have done more, and some less. We may condemn their judgment, but we would not therefore think them worthy of disrespect. Our respect for proven decency in service to the public is deeper, and more subtle, than this.

Persons cannot be held morally responsible because the human condition has cast them into situations where highly desirable ends are at least temporarily at odds with each other. Neither can they be held blameworthy when they have undeniably done their best. We can scarcely say that those who have done their best are tainted for failing to do better. To say otherwise is to be fundamentally wrong about the nature of moral life.

"Noble Cause" Corruption

What does taint us as moral agents is an arrogant appraisal of ourselves that concludes, "I am entirely justified in my means because my end was noble," or a cowardly response to demands, such as, "I'm damned if I do and damned if I don't, so it makes no difference." Giving everything we have when the issue is hardest does not taint us, but giving less suggests avoidable ignorance, weakness, or incompetence.

Such flattering self-appraisals and failures of nerve are the two forms of noble cause corruption. Arrogance and cowardice imperil the ideals of a constitutional republic, because they are marks of individuals who despair of rising to the ordeal of command. In my experience, the republic has little to fear from officials who face up to ordeals and do not try to get off the hook by complacently justifying themselves or by whining that "the world isn't fair." What is fearful are the officials who believe that their ends always justify or excuse their means or who give up in despair but remain in office nonetheless. The greater the responsibilities and authority of these officials, the less the country can afford such flight from tension and conflict. They are the marks of a human spirit that has admitted defeat. In practice, they undermine the judgment required to bear the public trust faithfully. Arrogance corrupts by obscuring the need for thought, and cowardice corrupts by denying the point of thought, thus forsaking judgment to the whims of impulse.

Excusable Wrongdoing

At this point, we may wonder whether we should consider well-intentioned and remorseful wrongdoing in terribly hard cases to be excusable. This is a tempting way to handle the problem of tragedy because it invites us to make a rule for excusing (or not excusing) high-minded wrongdoing. Then, when faced with a tragically difficult case, we can appeal to the rule and spare ourselves the ordeal of judgment.

This way of proceeding is dangerous. If certain considerations excuse illegal conduct in one case, they do so in sufficiently similar cases too, but each case must be treated in all of its particularity. The specifics force us to be morally humble and intellectually thorough. We sacrifice doing our best if we lapse into the self-assurance that what we are about to do is wrong, but we deserve to be excused. This form of complacency can be as remorseless as any other.

Temptations of this kind are another reason to avoid making beginners in ethics courses focus on hard cases, which are not the mainstream of moral life. Beginners are likely to look for simple rules when they are taught, to paraphrase Edmund Burke, "to make the extreme medicine of human life its daily bread." When this happens, Burke observes, people tend to become weak, because they develop the bad habit of speaking and thinking lightly about profoundly demanding matters, both before and after the fact.[11] This is as true in law enforcement as elsewhere.

The conclusion to be drawn is that illegal conduct in a specific case may or may not be excusable—and I believe that it could be—

depending on the particulars, and even the minute details, of the case.

Deciding

On more than one occasion, I have been asked whether I—as a command officer who believed that all legal means had been exhausted and that physical coercion was the only means of saving an innocent victim—would consider using the third degree.

My response is yes, in that I would not absolutely foreclose consideration. I would consider it in light of all the relevant facts available at the time: the condition and reputation of my department; the levels of respect for law among my subordinates and peers; recent episodes of brutality and corruption for profit within; the prospect of loss of departmental autonomy in any resultant political firestorm; the legal means available for subsequently keeping the suspect-perpetrator off the streets; and other matters considered relevant by any competent command officer.

Would I actually use the third degree? I would be unlikely to, but I might. I would certainly seek the advice of counsel about the outer limits of the permissible throughout the ordeal. I would use every form of psychological pressure on the suspect, while making sure he would have a difficult burden of proof if he sought to suppress evidence on grounds that his rights had been violated.

If I actually crossed the line to physical coercion, I would then request or commence a departmental inquiry, along the lines recommended by counsel, to minimize the hazards to the department and to try to keep the suspect in custody. I would not participate in a cover-up because such conduct betrays the law itself, inspires conspiracies against the rule of law, and undermines by deceit the public trust. But I would avail myself of all my rights under the Constitution, on the grounds that I had never casually or routinely disregarded anyone else's rights. At the same time, I would resign from my position—not necessarily from the department—to make clear that no one who has violated the standards of a position of authority should continue in it.

I hope that I would be decisive but aware of the shiver that ought to be felt by anyone facing the moral demands of the grimmest realities. I would have at hand words of the theologian Reinhold Niebuhr:

> The tragic element in a human situation is constituted of conscious choices of evil for the sake of good. . . . Tragedy elicits admiration as well as pity because it combines nobility

with guilt. . . . Our idealists are divided between those who would renounce the responsibilities of power for the sake of preserving the purity of our soul and those who are ready to cover every ambiguity of good and evil in our actions by the frantic insistence that any measure taken in a good cause must be unequivocally virtuous. We take, and must continue to take, morally hazardous actions to preserve our civilization.[12]

I hope I would remember that some actions are not just morally hazardous, but morally suicidal. And I would have in mind the deepest reservation: that some of those I respect most in the world have said to me that they could never physically abuse any person in custody.

12
Death and Bereavement, Deadly Force and Guilt

It is hard to have patience with people who say, "There is no death," or "Death doesn't matter." There is death. And whatever is matters. And whatever happens has consequences, and it and they are irrevocable and irreversible. You might as well say that birth doesn't matter. I look up at the night sky. Is anything more certain than that in all those vast times and spaces, if I were allowed to search them, I would nowhere find her face, her voice, her touch? She died. She is dead. Is the word so difficult to learn?

C. S. LEWIS[1]

The life of a police officer is more uncertain than most lives, frequently involving situations of danger and death. Violence, whether sudden and unexpected or anticipated and countered, is not part of the job for every sworn officer, but the potential for it is real. Many police officers lose colleagues, and even more are touched whenever a person in law enforcement dies in the line of duty.

Three ethical concerns are occasioned by these conditions and events that arise from them. All have to do with the role of character and wisdom in adversity. First, is their place in facing the death of a beloved friend; second, in responding to the bereavement of others; third, in facing the future after using deadly force by which another person is killed. The third area embraces the worst case of all—where an officer has accidentally or mistakenly killed another officer or some other innocent person.

The Death of a Friend, Partner, or Loved One

When a beloved friend or partner dies in the line of duty, he or she is usually in the prime of life. This makes the death especially hard to bear, rather like the death of any young person with much life yet to be lived.

The agony that follows arises in part from love and affection and in part from the fact that we are creatures of habit. When a loved one with whom we share much dies—whether the death is sudden or expected—many of our deepest and dearest habits are shattered.

We are irrevocably deprived of the activities that have become habitual in daily life with that person. No more can that face and its many expressions be with us in person, no more the conversations, the daily excursions, the shared enjoyments and sufferings, the mutual trust, the feelings of contentment when that person was happy. The commonplace connections of heart and mind that made up perhaps substantial portions of each day are severed. The shock is so powerful that a person feels it physically. Heartache hurts all over.

Living up to the Facts

Each individual death is a fact. We grieve because we know it is a fact—hard, cold, and permanent. There are two ways to treat facts: a person can live up to them or seek ways to evade them.

Living up to the fact of a death—say, of a partner—begins with learning that when death takes someone you love there is nothing to do but grieve with all your heart. However much anger, bitterness, guilt, or denial are involved, living up to the fact means learning to bear it, suffering what must be suffered, learning to live in a world that is less because a specific person is forever gone from it.

Evasion of the fact of death takes many forms: numbing oneself with alcohol or drugs; giving way to flights of impulsive self-indulgence, to self-pity, or to the self-aggrandizing conviction that *this* love was so special that no one else ever suffered such sorrow, so great a loss; and failing to meet one's normal obligations to others, while expecting everyone else to show extraordinary consideration and generosity in *this* case.

The most fundamental evasion, of which many others may be only symptoms, is preoccupation with one's own grief. When the response to the fact of death is trying to "cope with grief," the object of focus becomes a psychological reaction to the fact, not the fact itself. This evasion is unrealistic; it is a failure to give reality its due. The real issue is what one should do about the fact, not how one copes with grief. A powerful response lies in the nature of good character and its relation to love and dignity.

Love

The poet William Butler Yeats observed that human beings are creatures who love what vanishes. We choose other people to love, in greater or lesser awareness that in time they and we will vanish into death. Many people deny this fact even to themselves, but the wisest among us do not.

When we take seriously that all of us are mortal, we may love not less but more, with greater rather than smaller consideration and attentiveness. We try to put the very best of ourselves into the lives of those we love. This is one of the spurs of morality: knowing that death will one day part us all provides a powerful motive to treat each other's interests, concerns, well-being, and happiness with devotion.

Such devotion does not reflect a morbid preoccupation with death, but the courage to love with depth of heart in spite of death's heartbreak. Those who cannot or do not love fully and well may seem to risk less to death, but in fact lose more. For their days are emptier, and they are left in the end unable to say, "I tried to give the best of myself to you."

In this respect, habits of good character are habits of love; they make us most worthy and able to love others and to be loved. They give credibility to the words of love and friendship because our actions really do speak louder than words.

None of us ever becomes a perfect friend, any more than anyone achieves perfect character. Therefore, when death takes a dear friend, we are likely to feel guilt and remorse, as well as grief, over some of our past actions and words. But these will be less grinding if we have genuinely tried to be worthy friends.

Dignity

As we have seen earlier in the words of Frederick Douglass and others, our dignity does not turn on what others do to us, but on what we do ourselves. Neither does it turn on the circumstances of good fortune or adversity. Dignity rises or falls in our response to what befalls us.

Most of us think that our dignity is threatened by things we cannot control. When illness makes us dependent on others, helpless, perhaps forced to use a bedpan or rely on others to feed us, we are embarrassed, and our feelings of modesty and independence are offended. But dignity is much more at stake in matters we can control, particularly in the habits of feeling and acting we establish as aspects of our character.

When we have forged the habit of giving the best of ourselves to the people closest to us, the habit does not disappear when our hearts are breaking. Our dignity is never greater than when we can reach into ourselves, despite our own anguish, and find what it takes to comfort another. Such character emerges from firmly established habits of temperance, unselfishness, compassion, and courage.

Sometimes in face of the death of a person very dear to us, we seek consolation in the promise that "time heals all things—this, too, shall pass." Yet when John and Abigail Adams lost their daughter, they heard from Thomas Jefferson, who had lost five children and his wife, that the only ultimate relief from such losses is in one's own grave.

The power of time to heal us lies largely in our own power to control our lives by sustaining our best habits. We can direct ourselves to other friends and family with the constancy of character we brought to the friend who is gone. We do not need to form new habits of character, but rather to apply them faithfully to others.

The memories of the one who is dead never entirely fade away. Although our longing diminishes over time, we have not thereby forsaken the one who is gone, any more than the fading of that person's face in our mind means that we are forgetting.

We have seen that a person does not become happy by trying to be happy or have fun by trying to have fun. Neither does a person learn to live with the fact of death by trying to overcome or cope with grief, as so many current theorists assert. Just as happiness depends largely on doing and giving our best, we live best with loss when we bring our best habits of feeling and acting into our daily lives with others.

Sometimes the pain makes this very difficult, and the anguish may be made worse by feelings of lassitude, lethargy, and lack of will power. If, in the past, we have practiced accomplishing difficult and disagreeable things by diligent application of our will, we will be able to call up will power when we need it most, and when others need it from us. Thus do habits of good character sustain us—and our family and friends.

The Bereavement of Others

When others lose someone they love, we may think we can do little. We may avoid those who are suffering, confidently assuring ourselves that they would rather be alone when, in fact, it is we who do not want to face death. Certainly, we should be respectful of the wishes of friends who truly do want to be alone in their heartache, but we should not generalize that everyone feels that way.

We say too easily that words cannot help. This is sometimes a way of sparing ourselves the effort of finding words that will help. Words make a difference, the right ones said in the right way. Words can become right by the manner of their delivery. Sometimes words comfort by their tenderness; they may evoke bittersweet memory; or they may simply express sympathy. Sometimes the right words recall something funny and cause laughter. The appropriate words and manner can be known only by careful, thoughtful, wise appraisal of the people and the circumstances. Sometimes silence is called for, but not because words do not make a difference.

Grieving people may believe they will never smile again. They may even believe they are somehow doing wrong if they smile. Friends who recall them to occasions for smiling can slowly erase such misunderstandings. Even the silent nearness of a friend serves to remind a bereaved person that not all love and caring are gone, not all intimacy and kinship are lost.

Responding to the needs of our friends in such circumstances is demanding. But if we are friends, we want most of all to respond when their needs are greatest. Practice at rising to those needs in ordinary circumstances gives us greater power to sense their feelings and to see things as they do. We learn not only to comfort but also to encourage them when they are suffering most deeply.

Deadly Force

A law enforcement colleague tells of an undercover episode in which he believed that his cover had been blown. Two things occupied his mind: how to get out without killing anyone, and how to avoid being killed. No one of good character takes either question lightly.

In Phoenix an FBI agent on a fugitive arrest team is accidentally shot to death by other agents. In Dallas, two elderly people call for police assistance and, in the ensuing confusion, both are mistakenly shot by police and die. In Montgomery County, Maryland, when a specially trained squad begins to break into an apartment suspected of containing weapons and drugs, the leader of the team is killed by police gunfire after a noise inside is mistaken for a shot. No weapons are found with the suspects.

Deadly force is deadly—and sometimes in the least intended ways. Because law enforcement can become chaotic and life-threatening and require immediate action, preparedness is fundamental.

Most people do not know exactly how they will behave in sudden danger, and most who take an innocent life—even when they acted with good judgment of what seemed necessary—are devastated by it. The guilt may be ineradicable.

The ability to perform must therefore be kept sharp. Weariness and stress take enough of a toll without the added burden of drugs, excessive alcohol, indolence, and the like. The most professional exercise of skill and judgment requires alertness. Not having been at one's best adds immeasurably to the anguish of taking a life.

Wisdom also cautions against unnecessary distractions, such as leaving home on a quarrelsome note, falling into excessive debt, complicating one's life with messy entanglements, living a lie of one form or another, or entering a fray after having had harsh words with a partner. They all distract and hamper alertness. After using deadly force, we would not want to face the ugly truth that our mind was elsewhere.

Guilt

Although a person who feels ashamed of avoidable errors is far better than one who does not, guilt can be corrosive. It may turn our minds so intensely to the past that we become indifferent to the present and the future. It can lead us to despair.

Thus, while a certain measure of character is required to feel guilt, greater character is required to avert its most pernicious effects. The first problem is the person who feels more guilt than is deserved. The second is the person who is to blame for a deadly error, and suffers dreadful feelings of guilt and shame, but must somehow turn to the future.

An officer may accept too much blame for the death of an innocent person or a fellow officer. Some deaths, especially in high-speed pursuits and in shootings occur because departmental training standards are not good enough. If officers are not well-taught how to work together in dangerous raids, levels of competence and expectation vary. A sudden and unpredictable movement by a suspect, bystander, or officer can cost a life. A department may find such factors hard, perhaps impossible, to admit, and so may a victim's family.

An officer whose action directly caused the death may believe that considering such facts is only a cowardly search for excuses. Those who feel guilty may be unable to give themselves the benefit of an honest appraisal of the facts. Their friends and colleagues may have to press such an appraisal upon them. For inordinate guilt, the antidote is truth.

In the worst cases of all, persons who really are to blame can lose their capacity to go on, because of guilt. For those whose religious faith embraces the forgiveness of sins, repentance and confession may lift the burden of guilt. For others, various kinds of counseling and professional guidance may be helpful. In any case, humility is essential, and strength of character is irreplaceable— the strength to look in a mirror, acknowledge blame, bear guilt— perhaps always—and resolve not only to endure but to aspire. No evasions, no rationalizations, no attempt to escape the facts. This takes the honesty to face what one has done and the courage to recognize that it cannot be undone. It also takes the fortitude to exert effort despite suffering; it depends on habits—formed or yet to be formed—of applying oneself when doing so is most disagreeable.

Rising above the destructive effects of guilt—as opposed to rationalizing guilt away—is also a matter of wisdom. It consists in seeing that if we ever had reasons to aspire to do our best, we always have reasons for such aspiration. No failure, however massive, changes this.

We would be foolish to discount our past by celebrating today as the first day of the rest of our lives. Today has a past, which cannot be erased, because habits are not formed overnight. Today and tomorrow matter because we still have lives to live, however grievous our mistakes of yesterday may have been. Failure to grasp that is tantamount to self-annihilation; if it does not result in literal suicide, it may still destroy all purpose in life. And one mistake may thus become the basis for a host of further errors. We can at least begin to redeem ourselves by avoiding that.

13
Taking Our Lives Seriously

Moral performance begins in individual self-discipline on the part of officials, involving all that is meant by the word "character." But this is not enough. . . . The official individually and organizationally must be concerned to go beyond simple honesty to a devoted guardianship of the continuing reality of democracy.

PAUL APPLEBY[1]

As we have seen throughout this book, living up to the highest ideals of policing calls for character and wisdom. Genuine professionalism always does. Technology may change, specific problems may become more or less severe, but this fact of life remains the same.

The Extra Mile

Police can live up to these ideals in a number of ways: by trying to inspire and deserve public confidence even when public expectations are inordinate; by exercising proper discretion on and off the job; by living up to higher standards of conduct than the general public; by acting with largeness of spirit in response to unfair personnel policies and laws; by behaving honorably undercover; by remaining compassionate and just despite exposure to human weakness and depravity; by bearing the ordeal of making judgments in complex circumstances; by sustaining one's best self despite disappointment and grief. To sum up, the police officer must often "go the extra mile."

Many police I know realize this and do not lament it. They understand that the rule of law is intended to promote the public good and that it cannot do so unless the guardians of that rule are devoted to it, willing to sacrifice for it. They share the realistic expectations expressed by the columnist Walter Lippmann in 1930:

> The American ideal of government as a public trust to be carried on by disinterested men represents not the actuality

but a long step ahead in the evolution of man. . . . It is a very difficult ideal to attain, and I know of no man in America even in our time who has felt able to be completely loyal to it. . . . The campaign . . . on behalf of the idea of trust is no mere repairing of something perfect that has broken down, but the implanting of a new habit of acting in the ancient consciousness of man.[2]

The best law enforcement personnel aspire to acquire that habit of acting—the habit of going the extra mile.

The Morality of Aspiration

The legal scholar Lon Fuller writes that the morality of aspiration consists in the will and resolve to become and behave as "a human being functioning at his best."[3] Fuller contrasts this high ground of morality with the lower ground of law and duty couched in terms of prohibitions of the form "Thou shalt not." Good law enforcement agencies reflect this distinction by stressing what police can do, not merely what they are not permitted to do. On the lower ground a person may respect the letter and limits of the law, while taking advantage of omissions and loopholes. That would require no aspiration to fulfill the spirit of the law or the purposes of law in a free country, and no sense of what behavior is worthy of oneself.

A person who respects the prohibitions of law would not use illegal drugs but might indulge himself with them where they are legal. Such a person would refrain from gambling where it is prohibited but might gamble for high stakes where it is allowed. But a person who aspires to excellent character would not debilitate himself with drugs anywhere. Neither would he waste time on "deep play," as high stakes gambling is sometimes called. He would consider the action not as illegal but as beneath him. As Fuller explains:

> We are concerned not so much with the specific harms that may flow from gambling, but with the question whether it is an activity worthy of man's capacities. We would recognize that in human affairs risk attends all creative effort and that it is right and good that a man engaged in creative acts should not only accept the risks of his role, but rejoice in them. The gambler, on the other hand, cultivates risk for its own sake. Unable to face the broader responsibilities of the human role, he discovers a way of enjoying one of its satisfactions without accepting the burdens that usually accompany it. Gambling for high stakes becomes, in effect, a kind of fetishism. . . .

223

The final judgment that the morality of aspiration might thus pass on gambling would not be an accusation, but an expression of disdain. For such a morality, gambling would not be the violation of a duty, but a form of conduct unbefitting a being with human capacities.[4]

A police officer must meet much more real risks and challenges: a command officer must decide whether to authorize subordinates to try to shoot a hostage-taker or try to save both the hostage and the perpetrator; a police officer must enter a dark hallway to answer the cries of a victim inside; an officer must resist the sapping of his alertness by boredom during a stakeout; an officer must remain cool in the midst of abusive citizens. These are risks and challenges of reality, not fabricated, seldom enjoyable, and yet genuinely worth our best capacities.

Recognizing what is worth our best capacities—and devoting our lives to such activities—builds self-respect. Aspiring to make ourselves worthy of demanding responsibilities invests our lives with purpose and meaning. The ultimate power of moral aspiration is that it reduces the likelihood of using the failures or faults of others as an excuse for one's own. Genuine aspiration in a person tends to inspire sadness, pity, or disdain for the self-indulgence and corruption of others. Those who aspire to become the best they can be recognize that they are far from perfect. Their aspiration prevents them from becoming self-righteous, holier-than-thou, or permissive toward their own failings just because "others do it." Our most secure bulwark against moral weakness and wrongdoing is always the conviction that it is beneath us. It is inestimably more durable and reliable than the fear of being caught at wrongdoing, and it is therefore a guarantee of trustworthiness that no prohibition can ever provide.

Those who aspire to strength of character hold themselves answerable for their faults. Though accountable to others, perhaps in a chain of command, they become worthy of trust by being genuinely accountable to themselves. Surely the answer to the ancient question of Juvenal—Who guards the guardians?—lies partly in procedures for supervision and accountability; but it also lies partly within the levels of aspiration in each individual who is entrusted with authority. For finally, the "unsleeping sentinels who guard the outposts of society," in Chesterton's words, must draw a fair portion of their vigilance and honorability from within.

In this crucial way, good character—and the moral aspiration to become better—is "the bottom line." Few people go the extra mile out of fear. They go because of devotion and self-respect, and because it is second nature to them.

Taking Our Lives Seriously

In our actions and aspirations, we discover how seriously we take our lives. The idea of good character can be summed up in taking our lives seriously—not humorlessly, but seriously—in good fortune and in adversity. Each of us has a life to live. Although it will come to an end, it will remain always and indelibly *that* life that was lived.

That we cannot entirely accomplish our purposes—that the mission of the police cannot be fully realized—is no reason for despair or cynicism. That we fall short of our best expectations of ourselves is no reason to settle for less. That we and our loved ones are mortal is no reason for indifference or for preoccupation with short-term gratification.

Instead, all these facts of the human condition are reasons to do the best we can with what we have for as long as we have it. Doing so, becoming wise and forging habits of fine character, *is* success in the conduct of a life.

Morality, to paraphrase a philosopher of long ago, is the proper calling of human beings. It is not only the measure of whether we have any right to consider ourselves members of a profession dedicated to the service of others. It is also the measure, finally, of how we have sought to live.

14
Fatalism, Microcosms, and Therapeutic Reductions

Humility, on the one hand, and true, noble pride on the other, are elements of proper self-respect; shamelessness is its opposite. . . . A low opinion of oneself in relation to others is no humility; it is a sign of a little spirit and of a servile character.

IMMANUEL KANT[1]

Throughout *Character and Cops*, I have argued for the tradition that public servants are obliged to live up to higher ethical and intellectual standards than those expected of the general public. Obviously, the public cannot be morally bankrupt and still expect to draw individuals of high quality into public service; no one will make sacrifices for a public that is unworthy of personal sacrifice.

Though the United States, like the other nations of the world, leaves much to be desired in public dedication to justice, the people are not morally bankrupt. Huge numbers of people are law-abiding, make commitments to ideals that transcend their own private desires, and invest their best efforts in their private and work lives. In more than twenty years of work on the streets with police, I have never seen a neighborhood, even where homicide and drug-trafficking are at their worst, that did not include substantial numbers of decent people. They may be frightened of their environment, suspicious of police, or reluctant to get involved, but they are not unworthy of fine public servants.

Since 1989, however, and especially since the widely publicized videotaped beating of Rodney King in 1991 by Los Angeles police officers, three developments have increased the difficulty of maintaining higher standards for public servants.

The first is a certain fatalism about institutions and individuals charged to bear the public trust. I call this fatalism the microcosm argument. The second is a progressive obliteration by political leaders of the distinction between higher standards for public servants and double standards within government itself (a problem discussed earlier, in chapter 5). The trend away from higher standards transcends all party politics and threatens excellence in public service to the core.

The third adverse development is the uncritical acceptance of a therapeutic vision of human beings, which sees human beings merely as victims of a host of diseases that require treatment and compassion. The therapeutic account of human nature dims the vision of human beings as agents largely responsible for their own fate. The notion that human beings are primarily objects of therapy underlies features of the Americans with Disabilities Act (ADA) that threaten to impair policing. It is also implicit in unreliable forms of sensitivity training for police.

Fatalism and the Microcosm Argument

Responses to the police assault on Rodney King have varied among the police, the public, and academic circles. The most dangerous responses have been the most fatalistic; if widely accepted, they will tend to drive policing back to the situation described in chapter 5, in the statement made by August Vollmer in 1931: "Law enforcement agencies are usually held in contempt and law enforcement is [taken as] one of our national jokes."

Fatalism insists that police departments are no more than microcosms of society itself. Since the general public includes a great range of excellence, mediocrity, and depravity, every police department must be expected to include the same characteristics. In the broad society are to be found brutality, incompetence, excessive consumption of alcohol and drugs, financial corruption and other forms of lawbreaking, and racism, sexism, and other forms of bigotry. Therefore, the argument runs, a roughly proportionate incidence of such attitudes, ineptitude, and misconduct will inevitably find its way into police departments. The brutal beating of King simply reflects this "fact."

The obvious flaws in the microcosm argument do not prevent it from being viewed favorably by some police, academics, citizens, and media figures. Fatalism always enjoys some popularity, because it puts the solution to problems beyond our reach and thereby spares us responsibility for them.

The most obvious flaw in the microcosm argument is that most people become members of society, citizens or subjects, simply by being born. They do not select their society, and their society does not select them. Since 1957, it has been illegal in the United States to deprive a person of citizenship as punishment for a crime. In *Trop v. Dulles*, the Supreme Court ruled that deprivation of citizenship as punishment for a crime constituted cruel and unusual punishment and therefore violated the Eighth Amendment.[2] In a police department, however, no one has a right to membership by virtue of birth, and no one has a right to remain a police officer irrespective of criminal misconduct.

A police department *is* selective—the more selective, the better. People born into a society do not have to meet eligibility requirements and standards, submit to background investigations, complete instructional programs, undertake probationary terms and field training, learn and perform in accordance with departmental policies, cooperate with internal investigations, or, ultimately, retire from service. Police do. In every good department, such features elevate the department and its sworn and civilian personnel beyond the norms for society as a whole.

No selective institution can be a mere microcosm of any larger nonselective society. No flaw in a selective institution, therefore, can be excused on the grounds that it is a microcosm. Indeed, we establish principles for service in a selective institution, dedicated to the public trust, precisely because we know that mere membership in society is insufficient as a mark of fitness to serve the public. Selective institutions are designed so that they will *not* be microcosms.

Still, a police department cannot be impervious to the society around it. It cannot reasonably be expected to screen out all unfit candidates or to prevent all wrongdoing. The realistic goal is to minimize the adverse social influences through selective recruiting, rigorous training, able supervision, deft leadership, and so on. A police leader must make clear that the department is not intended to be a microcosm of society. The bigotry, brutality, corruption, and incompetence in the society at large are among the very facts that compel the department to live up to higher standards.

Every serious account of standards of ethical policing illuminates this point. In *Power and Restraint: The Moral Dimension of Police Work*, for example, Howard S. Cohen and Michael Feldberg argue for "five ethical standards against which police work can be judged":

> Standard I: *Fair Access.* As a social resource, police must provide fair access to their services.
> Standard II: *Public Trust.* Citizens, having limited their right to enforce their own rights, have made police work a public trust.
> Standard III: *Safety and Security.* Police must undertake

law enforcement within the framework of maintaining safety and security.

Standard IV: *Teamwork*. Police are part of a system that includes legislators, other law enforcers, prosecutors and judges, so their behavior must meet the tests of teamwork: coordination, communciation and cooperation.

Standard V: *Objectivity*. Police work is a social role that often requires the officer to set personality and feelings aside, and demonstrate objectivity.[3]

These standards are drawn from ideals of justice expressed in the Constitution, such as impartiality of judgment and regard for domestic tranquillity. They cannot be met except by fidelity to the public trust and an understanding of the place of policing in the governmental framework designed to advance the public interest. Like other summaries of ethics in policing, this account shows that a department capable of responsible policing cannot be conceived as a mere microcosm of the general society.

The public has a right to expect police departments to try to live up to such ideals, despite the flaws in the general population. Neither police nor the public can afford to be fatalistic in matters of such consequence. Police who have a proper self-respect, which embraces humility toward the magnitude of their duties, will not consider themselves mere microcosms of society-at-large. By contrast, a complacent self-esteem—feeling good about oneself while thinking of the department as no more than a microcosm of society—is self-deception.

Rising above Microcosm

In "Police Integrity and Public Expectations," my colleague, Scott R. Stripling, and I wrote:

> The public has a right to expect that police recruits will be chosen on the basis of moral, intellectual, psychological, and physical fitness to bear the public trust as established by thorough background investigations, rigorous testing, and professionally conducted personal interviews. Procedures for identifying suitable recruits should focus on the candidates' behavioral history—with emphasis on the question of whether they have displayed a settled disposition to act reasonably and with regard for others rather than impulsively and selfishly. That is, the criteria for fitness to serve should include the achievement of personal integrity, including established habits of justice, self-control, and trustworthiness.
>
> The public has a right to expect that police departments

will provide excellent academy and field training for their recruits and ongoing inservice education and training for experienced personnel. Every aspect of policing deserves attention—not only peacekeeping, crime prevention and law enforcement, but also the delivery of social services, and the cooperative support of families and the business, civic, religious, educational, and medical institutions whose successful work is indispensable to neighborhood self-protection and the reduction of criminal predation.

Police should be expected to achieve high levels of competence through training in communication and verbal skills, physical fitness, weapons, law, departmental procedures and policies, management of informants, conduct of interrogations, paramedical services, suicide prevention, domestic violence control, crowd and riot control, traffic enforcement, and preparation of reports. They should also be well-instructed about the nature of the communities they are to serve and about the public- and private-sector service agencies with which they must work to advance public safety and the overall public good. And because the fulfillment of the mission of policing necessarily involves the exercise of discretion by police of all ranks, the public has a right to expect that police will be trained not only in the limits to their discretion, but also in the exercise of good judgment within those limits.

The public has a right to expect that the supervision and accountability of police will be rigorous and thorough, based on the same high standards and unequivocal policies that inform reliable training. By these dimensions of recruitment, training, and supervision, police departments have the best chance of providing wise and virtuous service of the sort Madison had in mind, and of safeguarding the public against betrayals of their trust.

Measures for fulfilling the public's rightful expectations continue to advance. Many police departments use psychological testing to screen candidates, and some are required to do so by state law. Drug testing and polygraph examinations have become part of the screening process in some agencies. Many states have instituted standards that require completion of some course work in postsecondary or higher education for police certification. Educational opportunities of the highest quality are offered for state and local police by the federal government through the programs of the FBI Academy and at the state level by a number of state police academies.

Some individual departments have established career development programs that link supervisory promotion to accomplishment in higher education. Because the number of open supervisory positions is always limited, and because many good officers do not want to be supervisors, some departments are also offering increased compensation and nonsupervisory promotion as incentives to pursue higher education. In these departments, police officers who do not desire the supervisory responsibilities of a sergeant are encouraged to continue their special training and education in order to be named, and receive the higher compensation of, a master police officer.

Few police leaders are so naive as to suppose that higher education provides a guarantee of character excellence or professional performance. But they know that much of policing consists of talking with people—asking the right questions, listening diligently, giving people room to tell their stories—and keeping accurate records of the interviews. In the interest of professionalism most police leaders, therefore, take very seriously the habits of successful communication and systematic learning by study that higher education helps to inculcate.[4]

Various commission studies of police departments conducted in recent years have also stressed means by which the expectations of the public can be met. None of these studies seems to me to be very sophisticated—even about such straightforward matters as community policing, problem-solving policing, and their relation to other police practices in crime prevention and law enforcement—but some do contain instructive passages.

The Mollen Commission, a mayoral panel established to report on conditions in the New York City Police Department, issued an interim report at the end of 1993. Under the chairmanship of Milton Mollen, the commission asserted that the "police culture" of the NYPD tolerates corruption, brutality, and other forms of misconduct. The report alleged that the behavior of the Buddy Boys—robbing and brutalizing drug dealers—is copied by other groups of officers. The panel also claimed that command officers sustain a "code of silence" to protect their own careers from discovery of corruption in their units, and that "a deep-rooted reluctance to uncover corruption" is to be found in all ranks.[5] Whether or not all these charges are confirmed, any pockets of officers in the department who behave as the commission claims draw it downward toward the mere microcosm—or worse.

Political and police corruption in any prominent city sets a bad example for the rest of the nation. For more than two hundred years, wise leaders in the United States have understood urban corruption as a threat to the vision, and therefore the quality, of public service everywhere. Endemic urban corruption lends persuasiveness to—and obscures the flaws in—the microcosm argument. As the philosopher Francis E. Rourke explained in 1964, for over a century reformers have held

> a deep conviction that the corruption of urban politics reflected a very fundamental malaise in American life, the growth of a commercial spirit and a weakening in the moral fiber of the population that was endemic in society and the economy as well as government. "The boss is not a political, he is an American institution," wrote Lincoln Steffens, and this point of view was widely shared. What was needed from the reformer's perspective was a moral regeneration of American life—a "great awakening" which would cleanse and purify not only local but national politics as well, since the movement for urban reform was only part of a much larger reform effort directed at uplifting the tone of public life in every sector of the nation's business, including the practices of private institutions where they impinged on the public interest.[6]

In 1898, Josiah Strong, author of *The Twentieth Century City*, cautioned that "unless the reform of urban politics is successful, the boss will certainly rule the city when the city rules the nation." Strong reported that abolitionist and reformer Wendell Phillips, who died fourteen years earlier, had prophesied, "The time will come when our cities will strain our institutions as slavery never did."[7] Our contemporary urban crises may yet prove him right.

The magnitude of that strain may be even more evident in Los Angeles than in New York. Perhaps the most prominent of recent police department studies is the *Report of the Independent Commission on the Los Angeles Police Department*, published in August 1991. Warren Christopher, who later became secretary of state, was chairman of the commission. I have been told by public servants I trust thoroughly that the commission or members of its staff did not keep promises of confidentiality made during the preparation of the *Report*. Furthermore, although Los Angeles Mayor Tom Bradley's published charge to the commission promised the involvement of a distinguished scholar as a senior adviser to the commission, the scholar never served as an adviser. Because of these and other flaws in the *Report*, I do not assent to all the commission's practices, affirm all its findings, advocate all its recommendations, or encourage its use in academy training and criminal justice education. Nonetheless, the *Report* does stress important features of policy for background investigations, academy standards, field training, and supervisory accountability, which merit the attention of police and their leaders.

While acknowledging that the Los Angeles Police Department has been admired for its professionalism in some dimensions of law enforcement and for its support of background investigations and field training, the commission reported:

> [T]he background investigation offers the best hope of screening out violence-prone applicants. Unfortunately, the background investigators are overworked and inadequately trained. . . . The training problem is magnified because a number of investigators have been selected with only patrol experience, despite the apparent policy of the Unit to select officers with significant investigative experience. . . . In a number of files, drug use and sexual background were marked for attention, but a candidate's discussion regarding losing his or her temper or engaging in fights was not.

To this potential source of departmental problems in policing generally, the commission added its concerns about reduced academy standards. For Los Angeles, the commission lamented the low numbers of "minority officers in management positions," but observed that "the LAPD has made substantial progress in hiring minorities and women since entry of the Blake Consent Decree in 1981." The commission insisted that neither the achievement of diversity in personnel composition nor any other consideration should be permitted to reduce academy standards:

> At present approximately 90–95% of each entering Academy class graduates. Less than ten years ago that rate was closer to 60%. Some of this difference undoubtedly is due to changes in teaching practices, the availability of remediation programs, improvement in prehiring screening efforts, and reduction in physical training requirements. A portion of this change, however, seems attributable to an unwillingness to terminate poorly performing recruits, especially those protected by the consent decree or other similar mandate, for fear of civil liability or legal challenge or simply not meeting Departmental guidelines. The Commission urges that unqualified recruits not be retained for any reason. To do so only threatens the well-being of the public and the police force.

Background investigations and academy standards are as important today as they have ever been in policing. A few departments show signs of repeating the mistakes made by the Miami Police Department in the instance of the River Cops in 1980 (described in chapter 1), an entirely avoidable debacle that should never be allowed to happen again.

The LAPD, according to the commission, also failed to select and train field training officers in accordance with reasonable standards:

> At present there are no formal eligibility or disqualification criteria for the FTO position based on an applicant's disciplinary records. Fourteen of the FTOs in the four divisions the Commission studied had been promoted to FTO despite having been disciplined for use of excessive force or use of improper tactics. There also appears to be little emphasis on selecting FTOs who have an interest in training junior officers, and an FTO's training ability is given little weight in his or her evaluation. . . .
>
> Twelve of the FTOs in the four divisions studied had been disciplined for dishonesty. For example, the officers had failed to report misconduct they witnessed, lied about their own involvement in an incident, or agreed to lie about other officers' involvement in an incident.

Similar problems were identified in supervision and discipline in direct testimony by one high-ranking LAPD official:

> In my judgment, we do a very poor job of management and supervisory accountability. . . . [H]igher command officers when learning of [incidents of excessive force] having occurred took no action or very indecisive action, very weak and slow approach to doing something. Let me tell you that none of those people [the higher command officers], with rare exceptions, have been disciplined. And, in fact, I'm not even sure they've been counseled in many of these incidents. . . . And so, that's an area that I believe we have failed miserably in, is holding people accountable for the actions of their people.

The commission stressed few new problems in policing. But the importance of sound background investigations, high academy standards, good field training, and accountability at all ranks cannot be prudently neglected anywhere. All are fundamental to the integrity of a department and its personnel, and indispensable to any effort to rise above the microcosm.

More on Higher Standards and Double Standards

Nothing stands more in the way of rising above the microcosm than the collapse of higher standards into double standards. Double standards generate not aspiration to excellence in public service but rather cynicism among public servants and within the public.

Such problems persist in government at all levels. The nomination of Zoe Baird as attorney general of the United States showed how government leaders have either forgotten or never understood the differences between a higher standard and a double standard. After her nomination in 1992, Baird admitted that she and her husband had hired two illegal aliens from Peru to serve as their chauffeur and nanny. Baird, a corporate lawyer, and her husband, a Yale Law School professor, had paid no Social Security taxes for these employees. Even though Baird paid $12,000 in back taxes and a $2,900 fine after her nomination, opposition to her confirmation led her to request, on January 22, 1993, that the president withdraw her nomination. The president agreed to Baird's request and, on the same day, wrote the following letter to her:

Dear Zoe:

I have received your letter asking that I withdraw your nomination as Attorney General of the United States from further consideration by the Senate. With sadness, I accept your request that the nomination be withdrawn.

You are an exceptionally gifted attorney and a person of great decency and integrity. You have responded to the call of public service with energy and a firm dedication to the mission of the Justice Department. *I realize that it was your candid disclosure of the child care matter that led to the circumstances we face today. I believe that the concerns raised about your child care situation were unique to the position of Attorney General.* [Emphasis added.]

You are highly qualified to be Attorney General. Your stated goals for a non-partisan, independent and strongly managed Department of Justice were fully in accord with my own. I believe you would have been a fine Attorney General.

Hillary and I value your and Paul's friendship. We look forward to seeing you often. I hope that you will be available for other assignments for your country in my administration.

Sincerely,
Bill Clinton[8]

Significantly, the president said that Baird's confirmation problems came from her "candid disclosure" of her lawbreaking, rather than from her lawbreaking itself and her indifference to law. Then he asserted that such lawbreaking was relevant only to "the position of Attorney General"—a declaration of a double standard as pronounced as those that had been made about the position of secretary of defense during the confirmation hearings for John Tower.

In reaction to the withdrawal of Baird's nomination, some academics and government officials insisted that opposition to her was really a sign of a higher standard for women than for men nominated for high office. The president fueled this view and the concerns about justice that it raised by his later nomination of Bobby Ray Inman as secretary of defense. Like Baird, Inman failed to pay the required taxes for employees in his household but was nominated all the same. Had he not withdrawn, his confirmation would have shown either that there is a lower standard for men than for women, that there is a lower standard for one cabinet position than for another, or that in the aftermath of the Baird controversy the president, Congress, and the media lowered their standards for everyone.

All these alternatives threaten further erosion of the tradition of higher standards for public servants than for the general public. Justice Leah Sears-Collins, of the Georgia Supreme Court, said, "If [Baird] had been up for environmental secretary, this probably would not have been as big an issue and would not have axed her appointment. But above all, an attorney general needs to have absolute integrity and be very tough."[9] If this view dominates thinking about public service in American life, no public servants except law enforcement personnel will be expected to have integrity. That is an ominous prospect for all of our institutions, for the status of obligations to the public trust, and for the way police view public service.

The Therapeutic Vision of Human Beings

Double standards and their erosion of higher standards take on staggering proportions with the rising popularity of a therapeutic vision of human beings, which views human beings not as Homo sapiens (man the thinker) but as Homo victus (man the victim). A credulous public seems to be accepting the social science ideology that human beings are neither free nor responsible for their actions. Instead, an article of faith in many academic circles holds that adults and children are merely victims of genetic or environmental circumstances beyond their control.

When people misbehave, according to this ideology, they do so because they are ill, or because of needs for which they are not responsible, or because of suffering that could have been counseled away, or because of externally inflicted damage to their psychological health—their self-esteem. Those who criticize "life-styles" different from their own merely disclose their own illness, their own phobias.

This therapeutic reduction of all human misconduct to illness differs dramatically from the obvious truth that some wrongful human actions do spring from afflictions. Some people, after all, are sick. The therapeutic reduction, however, denies that persons are ever moral agents, responsible for their actions, and implies instead that they can never be understood and reasoned with as autonomous equals. People are only patients under therapy in an endless state of either recovering from their afflictions or suffering relapses.

No one familiar with the quasi-metaphysical pronouncements of social science for the past several decades will find such unsupported claims for determinism unusual. For years, one school of thought on policing has contended that people thrust into corrupt institutions have no choice but to become corrupt. The many police in corrupt environments who remain entirely honorable and morally upright do not shake proponents of this dogma.

The therapeutic vision is equally indifferent to evidence from other walks of life. In our lifetime, we have witnessed unprecedented progress in medical research, medical treatment, medical technology, and health care. Advocates of therapy want to treat everything in human life as a medical issue, as if we are beset by daunting new diseases unknown in former times. This range of putative diseases continues to expand, in ways that border on the ridiculous, but are, in practice, very dangerous. The Health and Environment Department of New Mexico released a report, *Let Peace Begin with Us: The Problem of Violence in New Mexico* (1990), by Dr. Victor LaCerva, who said, "[T]he most important aspect of the report is to realize that violent behavior is a disease."[10]

Attempts to classify dispositions to violence as a disease disclose an ignorance of the many forms of violence and dispositions to it. Dante, in the *Inferno*, and his translator Dorothy Sayers were right that "wrath, lust, and the will to dominate" are fundamental causes of violence. All of them are integral features of human nature at some times, but not always, and none is a disease. The therapeutic vision also ignores the times and circumstances in which violence, unlike disease, is justifiable and even obligatory.

The therapeutic vision threatens both liberty and justice because it lends itself to the tyrannical subjection of individuals to "treatment" in disregard of due process, of individual responsibilities, and of individual rights. Such diminution of human beings offers only the illusion of mercy, at the expense of respect for achievement and contempt for depravity.

The therapeutic vision is, however, gaining momentum worldwide. When South Africa's anti-apartheid religious leader Allan Boesak resigned his ministry amid charges of adultery, his wife told the media, "I think it is just a sickness among men over 40."[11] Stephanie Jefferis, serving as student coordinator in Pennsylvania State University's peer sensitivity and diversity training program, routinely tells students: "I consider myself a recovering racist, sexist, and homophobic. It's ridiculous for anyone to say they're not."[12] Mary Abowd, a senior at Notre Dame, explained at a "conference on women's ordination" that "a lot of feminists, former Catholic feminists, call themselves 'recovering Catholics,' like it's an ailment that they're getting over."[13]

Frank Riessman, codirector of the National Self-Help Clearinghouse, says addiction "is becoming a major problem—not just alcohol and drug addiction, but gambling, overeating, sex certainly, money," and adds, "I would be hard pressed to find anyone I know who doesn't have one kind of addiction or another."[14] Describing herself as a "recovering psychotherapist," Anne Wilson Schaef says she has "never met anyone who only has one addiction." When she told "a national conference of female Lutheran ministers in Los Angeles" that "they are all addicts of . . . some kind," the ministers gave "her a standing ovation."[15]

Responding to charges of ethical misconduct, Senator Dave Durenberger described his immersion in work after the death of his wife as his "grief counseling" and lamented the difficulty of his life at that time, when "ethics, like beauty, is in the eye of the beholder."[16] He spoke in the words of health professionals, funeral directors, and other counselors, who view grief as an illness and offer therapy for it. In the same way, dependency on drugs, narcotics, or alcohol is considered a disease. "Drug addiction isn't an issue of morality," says one such professional. "It isn't an issue of willpower—it's a disease."[17] Not to be outdone, sex therapists write of promiscuity as an illness called sexual addiction. Sexaholics Anonymous, with 20,000 members in America, joins the growing list of "Anons" for putative victims of their own genetic make-up.[18]

A popular rock 'n' roll song blares, "Might as well face it, you're addicted to love." *Newsweek* defines rape as men's "preempting of another person's body for the gratification of their own *needs*."[19] [Emphasis added.] A talk show host trumpets the question, "Are you a hostage of your own emotions?"

New Age retreats and spas offer treatment to "de-stress" customers they call guests, and provide therapy to promote "mind-fitness."[20] A Beverly Hills "psychiatric script consultant" for television dramas and situation comedies announces that "a psychological consultant should be part of the crew for each show." The *New York Times*, oblivious to distinctions between the subject matter of psychiatry and psychology and that of ethics, mistakenly identifies this consultant as a "connoisseur of character."[21]

A movie idol refers to videotaping his own sex acts with teenage females not as something he did, but as something that "happened" to him and his career. Similarly, the convict who masterminded the primary cocaine-trafficking organization in Washington, D.C., says, "I'm a good guy, and just something bad happened to me."[22]

New heights in the popularity of the ideology of illness may have been reached by the aggrandizement of celebrity addicts. Glorification of celebrities who tell all as if doing so were heroic, courageous, honest, and inspirational tells more about America's love affair with addiction than about anything else, including the nature of good character. We should, after all, scarcely want to identify the limit of human aspiration as recovering one day at a time. Neither should lust for the limelight rank high among credentials for admiration and self-respect.

In keeping with the therapeutic vision, a California Task Force on education advocates "*healthy* self-esteem" as a "*social vaccine*" to inoculate us "against the lures of crime and violence, alcohol and drug abuse, premature pregnancy, child abuse, chronic dependence on welfare, and educational failure." It recommends that "training in [promoting self-esteem] be a part of the teacher credentialing process and a part of all in-service training."[23] It also urges that courses in raising children with self-esteem be given in all schools, which should appreciate the "uniqueness . . . and address the special needs . . . of each child," by "serving to liberate rather than domesticate" all children, and to prepare every student "to become fully competent in . . . Relationships"—one of the six R's.[24]

As teachers are taught not to be critical of their students' performance for fear of impairing their self-esteem, students learn to feel good about themselves no matter how shabby their work or disgraceful their behavior. The report tells us, "Ultimately, we also need to learn to accept and treasure ourselves. . . . The point is not to become acceptable or worthy but to acknowledge the worthiness that already exists . . . [to] accept, appreciate, and celebrate ourselves as we are . . . unique."[25] Furthermore, the task force insists, "as a result of cultural conditioning . . . most of us feel some shame when we honestly express our innermost feelings," and so we must always create an environment for healthy self-esteem, "an atmosphere in which honest expressions are in fact encouraged, accepted and affirmed."[26] Presumably, this includes affirmation of even the most depraved forms of self-indulgence.

At no other time in history has self-esteem been vaunted as *the* social vaccine against grave problems at the very time it was practiced so self-indulgently by so many people. Of America's high school seniors in 1988, only 5 percent could read well enough to do college-level work. Seventy-four percent could not write "an adequate persuasive letter, and a third did not know that the Mississippi River flows into the Gulf of Mexico."[27] Yet, of these same students, "eighty percent 'take a positive attitude' toward themselves, eighty-three percent judge themselves to be 'person(s) of worth,' seventy-nine percent claim to be generally satisfied with themselves, and . . . only fifteen percent agree with the statement 'I feel I do not have much to be proud of.' "[28]

Rather than self-esteem, in the sense of feeling good about themselves no matter what, people, including children, need to acquire a proper self-respect, a respect for *selves* that involves taking others seriously by considering the effects our actions will have on them. We also need to learn that we deserve our own esteem and the esteem of others because of our achievements. Self-confidence should be acquired from activity that brings intellectual and moral powers to life, as in good schoolwork and acceptance of daily responsibility at home and with friends. To lead responsible lives, all of us must learn to discipline our emotions, including our feelings of self-love and pride.

Some advocates of the therapeutic vision even go beyond the effort to promote self-esteem and inordinate self-love. They claim that particular groups of people are exempt from the fallibilities and weaknesses of others because they were *born* exempt. Academics and political figures define some human failings as a disease and then insist that only certain groups of people can catch it. In an article in the influential *Phi Delta Kappan*, two professors of education declare, "Racism is a mental illness." It "may be thought of as a sick belief system," a "stubborn disease

. . . characterized by perceptual distortion, a denial of reality, delusions of grandeur (belief in white supremacism), the projection of blame (on the victim), and phobic reactions to differences."[29]

Since only white supremacism counts as a delusion of grandeur, only some groups identifiable by race can be afflicted with the illness. "A colonizer may be a racist, but a victim cannot be so,"[30] announce the professors.

Their message echoes Illinois Congressman Gus Savage's declaration, "Racism is white. There is no black racism."[31] And despite the obvious capacity of some members of every racial, ethnic, gender, and economic group to discriminate against others, these educationists subscribe implicitly to the dogmatism of Detroit's former mayor Coleman Young: "I think racism is a system of oppression. I don't think black folks are oppressive to anybody, so I don't consider that blacks are capable of racism."[32] Perhaps Mayor Young never noted the sexist bigotry of the black activist Stokely Carmichael, a member of the Student Nonviolent Coordinating Committee, who said, "The only position for women in SNCC is prone."[33] Similarly, the anti-Semitism of Louis Farrakhan and Khalid Abdul Muhammad, black leaders of the Nation of Islam, and the murder of a black civil rights leader by the white racist Byron de la Beckwith prove that a person's color tells nothing about his character.

Such alleged exemptions by birth of groups of people from specific forms of human fallibility demean them. All of us are fallible and flawed because we are human. To exempt any group is to claim that they are more than human or less than human—a grotesque falsehood.

Similar difficulties emerge in discussions of homosexuality. Some religious fundamentalists call homosexuality an addiction, sometimes "demonic oppression."[34] Gay rights activists classify all objections to homosexual conduct as "homophobia," an irrational fear and hatred of homosexuality, which they call a "lifestyle." Neither homosexuality nor heterosexuality, however, is a lifestyle. The lives of homosexuals differ as much from one another in substance as do the lives of heterosexuals. Some of each group are honorable persons, some are not. Some are courageous, fair-minded, and trustworthy; others are not. Some are promiscuous; others are not. Some of each group indulge sexual tastes that involve predation on children and commit acts of domestic violence against their partners. Homosexuals no more think alike on every issue than heterosexuals do; and many homosexuals and heterosexuals agree on some issues. Opposition is widespread to the North American Man/Boy Love Association, an association of pedophiles that asserts their right to respect as a minority and the right of children to the alleged benefits of sexual involvement with adults. In NAMBLA, we see how the popular doctrine that all "lifestyles" are morally equivalent ends in nihilism. Failure to take individuals into account is bigoted, no matter where it occurs: in exempting black people from racial prejudice, in indicting all religious people as prejudiced, or in claiming all homosexuals are bad or all homosexuals are good.

The therapeutic vision also implies an assault on the traditional family. Self-help guru John Bradshaw, the author of *Healing the Shame That Binds You*, estimates that "there are 131 million addicts in the U.S. of various stripes." Almost all of them, he says, can blame their illness on what he describes as the fundamental premise of his work: "All families are dysfunctional . . . distorted by the addictions and compulsions of one or more members, usually to the detriment of each individual."[35]

The movement against the family, for the therapeutic agenda, and against personal responsibility depends on what Charles Krauthammer calls "defining deviancy up." This means, for example, generating or inventing data to show that the traditional family is so riddled with child abuse that the "middle class lifestyle" is deviant. Then illegitimacy can be viewed as perfectly normal, even though it results in unwed teenagers bearing children who will be destroyed by neglect, abandonment, and exploitation in the streets.[36]

The description of all families as dysfunctional, together with the insistence of the "self-esteem" movement that we must "liberate rather than domesticate" children, recalls earlier ideological claims that the family is an instrument of repressive power, "the factory of reactionary ideology and structure," as the Freudian Marxist Wilhelm Reich called it.[37] Some educational traditions have treated society, culture, and the institutions of both as affronts to freedom and self-fulfillment, which fraudulently sustain themselves by pretending to advance the formation of character in the young and to safeguard morality. Today, the bitter fruit of such indefensible practices is the decline of schooling and the family—with 1.2 million children born annually in the United States out of wedlock and frequently abandoned to their own devices.

At the same time, the movement for moral equivalence depends on what Daniel Patrick Moynihan calls "defining deviancy down."[38] One example is the view of staggering levels of homicide as normal rather than as deviant; another is the assertion of R. D. Laing and Thomas Szasz that mental illness is a myth and a coercive instrument of political and social control. Since the late 1960s this view has contributed to the dramatic increase of homeless people in the United States and to criminal predation within the homeless population. In this and other respects, the therapeutic agenda has become highly politicized.

Still another instance of the therapeutic vision is graphically identified by Krauthammer:

> Consider this advice from one of the more popular self-help books on sex abuse, *Courage to Heal:* "If you are unable to remember any specific instances [of childhood sex abuse] . . . but still have a feeling that something abusive happened to you, it probably did." And "if you think you were abused and your life shows the symptoms, then you were". . . . Whenever a patient complains of depression, low self-esteem, or any of the common ailments of modern life, the search begins for the underlying childhood sexual abuse. As the book says, if your life shows the symptoms, then you were abused. This new psychology is rooted in and reinforces current notions about the pathology of ordinary family life. . . . So much for the family.[39]

Police will recognize the illogic of these claims in *Courage to Heal* and the spectacular contempt for evidence and due process they convey.

Police and law enforcement leaders should recognize the threat to their standards in the therapeutic agenda, which holds that human beings are bundles of addictions who cannot be genuinely responsible for their actions. All of us are victims except those born into groups of victimizers, who are identifiable by color or sex. These tenets influence social and criminal justice policy at the federal, state, and local levels. A surgeon general, urban mayors, and other public servants have suggested that crime and violence should be viewed as *health* issues; that their "root causes" are illnesses bred in perpetrators by their victimization at the hands of a perverse society; that law enforcement is not central to policy on drug trafficking and consumption; that minimum sentences for drug and firearm violations should be eliminated; and that public policy in these areas should focus on the expansion of health and social services.

Many of these positions reveal a startling incoherence. On December 7, 1993, for example, Joycelyn Elders, the surgeon general of the United States, recommended that the government consider studying the legalization of drugs as a means of reducing violent crime. Given the popularity of the therapeutic agenda, this recommendation is surprising not in itself but only in conjunction with a pronouncement of the surgeon general a week earlier, when she was asked whether it was immoral for people to have children out of wedlock. She replied, "No. Everyone has different moral standards. You can't impose your standards on someone else."

Why, then, should the surgeon general be concerned about violence? If you can't impose your standards about anything, all moral standards fall. By denying moral standards that transcend the individual, Joycelyn Elders denies that violence against the innocent is wrong. Neither are drug consumption, murder, abandonment and neglect and abuse of children, sexual harassment, rape, discrimination, injustice.

In one broad sweep, the surgeon general rejects both morality and law—the two principal instruments of civilized life—as means of safeguarding the public. In rejecting moral standards, she denies that individuals are responsible for their behavior: we must not "impose" standards of responsibility on anyone, even in their treatment of helpless children.

Is drug legalization worthy of consideration? Would it reduce violent crime and illegal drug trafficking? No. Drug users would still commit crimes of violence for money to buy other things—food, clothes, liquor, entertainment, and the like. And they would commit violent acts because they would be on mind-altering drugs. Drug traffickers would market drugs to children who could not buy them legally and would wage war over market share. They would introduce new free-based drugs that have not been legalized. They would sell the drugs in any quantity to anyone who wished to buy. And they would use murder, hijacking, extortion, and bribery to secure shipments of legal drugs to sell cheaply—just as they now operate a multibillion dollar industry in the criminal diversion of legal prescription drugs. Can drug legalization reduce the consumption of harmful drugs? It is not likely.

At present, as Dr. Herbert Kleicker of Columbia University's Center on Addiction and Substance Abuse explains, "There are 50 million nicotine addicts, 18 million alcoholics or problem drinkers, and fewer than 2 million cocaine addicts in the United States. Cocaine is a much more addictive drug than alcohol. If cocaine were legally available, as alcohol and nicotine are now, the number of cocaine addicts would probably rise to . . . perhaps 20 to 25 million."[40]

Even if all these arguments were invalid, drug legalization could succeed only if education, peer pressure, family influence, and drug treatment were geared to dissuade people against using harmful drugs. Since the surgeon general has said that we should never "impose" our standards on anyone else, however, teachers, peers, parents, and health care providers should not be allowed to say that use of harmful drugs is *wrong*.

Anyone who wonders about the logical consequences of the therapeutic vision of humanity for our institutions need only ask, What would be the consequences for the Americans with Disabilities Act if every human failing were treated as a disability and thus outlawed as a reason for denying employment—just as the law now prohibits institutions from treating a history of illegal drug consumption as a reason for denying employment? One therapeutically inclined federal official recently said to me, "Within ten years, we will have everything classified as a disease, and then we can hope for justice and the end of discrimination in this country." Insofar as his goal has already been achieved, the idea that we are normally responsible for our lives is dimmed. There can be no greater threat to the dignity of human beings or to the ideals of constitutional government than this slippery slope.

The Americans with Disabilities Act

Although the therapeutic vision threatens integrity in all human institutions, its most immediate adverse consequences for policing may lie in features of the Americans with Disabilities Act and of multicultural sensitivity training for police. The Americans with Disabilities Act, signed into law in July 1990, became effective in July 1992 for all institutions with twenty-five or more members and in July 1994 for smaller institutions. In many respects, the law is wise and should be welcome; it prohibits employment discrimination for a variety of disabilities that should never have led to disadvantage for the people who suffer them.

But according to the Bureau of National Affairs, the act provides that "individuals who have successfully completed a supervised drug rehabilitation program and who are no longer engaging in the illegal use of drugs, or who have otherwise been successfully rehabilitated, or who are participating in supervised programs and are not using, or who are erroneously regarded as engaging in such use, are protected by the statute."[41] Police department policies that disqualify candidates because of a history of illegal drug consumption are threatened by this feature of the act. Although federal officials say that this is not the intention of the law, few laws are applied and enforced over time only in accordance with their original intent. The act not only ignores the limits to our knowledge of how to treat drug habituation but also neglects the failures of personal responsibility, the weaknesses of character, the disregard for other people, and the contempt for the law that often accompany such habituation.

Some police departments will find deficiencies of character related to illegal drug consumption compelling reasons for dis-qualification and will do their best to maintain standards without violating the law. Others will be intimidated by the possibility of lawsuits, just as they feel constrained by possible lawsuits from establishing policies of zero tolerance for lying in internal investi-gations. If these departments discard standards related to prior drug consumption, they are likely to deteriorate.

My experience confirms that some police departments are already lowering standards to avoid difficulties with the Ameri-cans with Disabilities Act. In some large urban departments, physical standards—strength, endurance, stamina, agility, fit-ness, weight in relation to height—are being entirely set aside, and background investigations either are not being conducted at all or are being ignored for fear of diminishing applicant pools. The result is not only that drug users are becoming police, but also that drug traffickers are entering police departments. A crisis of corruption, brutality, and incompetence looms in these departments. Drastic problems are appearing, as officers steal weapons held in evidence, traffic in illegal substances, threaten the lives of other police, commit acts of grievous incompetence, and commit rape, murder, and kidnapping. This crisis deepens where departments disregard records of serious juvenile crimes, as some departments now do.

Many police leaders are utterly opposed to suspension of high standards and high expectations, but there are exceptions. A few police executives have told me that they consider the use of juvenile records and background investigations an instrument of racist efforts to minimize the diversity of departments. One prominent police executive has told me—in the presence of other command officers—that the idea of "competence" is purely sub-jective, that there actually is no such thing as competence in policing or any other walk of life. Police training for the sake of competence, he said, only establishes racially biased ideas of how to do a job.

Academy and field training can surely fuel racial, gender, and other biases and do other harm. But assertions that literacy is irrelevant, that deftness of communication is unnecessary, that the powers of observation police sometimes call street eyes make no difference, that acting in accordance with the law and with departmental policy is unnecessary, and that knowledge of the languages, customs, and habits of the public to be served can be neglected with impunity are as dangerous. Police leaders who spurn rigorous standards of candidate fitness and training because some are ill-conceived bring ruin to their own departments and heartache to the public.

Therapy and Multicultural Sensitivity Training

While many police departments understand themselves to serve a diverse population in terms of color, gender, ethnicity, cultural heritage, religion, and economic condition, the more crucial fact is that all police departments serve a diverse population. All police departments serve the individuals who make up the public, and no two individuals are alike in every respect. This fact must be heeded if police are to avoid thinking of people merely as members of one group or another. Real sensitivity to human beings consists of taking them seriously as individuals.

When police departments help their officers become competent in the native languages of residents or to understand their customs and traditions, they take a step toward excellent police service. If they treat their officers as students who need such training in order to do their jobs ably, they advance their departmental missions.

But the therapeutic vision leads to multicultural sensitivity training that treats police as if they were patients rather than students—patients who have an affliction that calls for treatment. This view of police is demeaning, it ignores aspirations to excellence, and it tends to be discriminatory. The author Ralph Ellison was right to insist that "our task is that of making ourselves individuals. The conscience of a race is the gift of its individuals."[42]

Some programs of multicultural sensitivity training arbitrarily treat police officers as if they were disposed toward racism, sexism, xenophobia, homophobia, and the like. The claim that all white people are racists and that only white people are racists is

247

no less malign than any other form of racism. Yet textbooks used for sensitivity training often make this claim. In *Counseling the Culturally Different*, Derald Wing Sue and David Sue assert:

> First, racism is a basic and integral part of U.S. life and permeates all aspects of our culture and institutions. Second, Whites are socialized into U.S. society and, therefore, inherit the biases, stereotypes, and racist attitudes, beliefs, and behaviors of the society. In other words, all Whites are racist whether knowingly or unknowingly.[43]

The same textbook charges that America is utterly intolerant of diversity:

> Many of the Asian immigrants to the United States tend to hold very positive and favorable views of their own culture. What happens when they encounter a society that views cultural differences as being deviant?[44]

The proposition that all and only white people are racists refutes itself, since it is itself racist, and not everyone who asserts it is white.

Any intelligent police officer, regardless of background, will recognize the perniciousness of such assertions and will resent them. Educational programs designed on this model impair the mission of the department. Nothing is more certain to undermine real integrity in a department than the attempt to make officers feel guilty for harboring prejudices that they do not actually harbor.

Such sensitivity training is designed, not to increase knowledge or competence, but to spread the view that all lifestyles must be accepted as morally equivalent. Such programs celebrate differences as if every difference were good, and they sentimentalize other cultures as if all were models of justice and respect for human dignity. Celebration of all differences denies that even the worst forms of human depravity are wrong. Serial killers, after all, are different. Sentimentalization of all cultures amounts to falsification, since no culture can be wise and just in every respect. Today various regions of the world are plagued by problems of corruption, discrimination, bigotry, sweat shops, de facto slavery, genital mutilation of girls and women, ethnic cleansing, and genocide. No population in history has been exempt from flaws or fallibility, but programs of sensitivity training often lie about that.

Education about cultures and cultural differences should be educational, not therapeutic. It should be reliable, rather than sentimental, and should never uncritically celebrate differences.

Training should advance competence rather than instill guilt or treat putative afflictions. It should teach that cultural differences provide no warrant for indifference to basic decency and lawfulness.

Police executives must show more wisdom and circumspection than federal lawmakers did when they adopted a "Congressional Declaration of Purpose" for the National Endowment for the Humanities and the National Endowment for the Arts:

> The arts and the humanities reflect the high place accorded
> by the American people to the nation's rich cultural heritage
> and to the fostering of mutual respect for the diverse beliefs
> and values of all persons and groups.[45]

The United States and other nations have police departments precisely because the diverse "beliefs and values of all persons and groups" do *not* merit respect. Predatory gangs and their members, for instance, believe that they have a perfect right to behave violently and ruthlessly in pursuit of their own pleasure or profit.

Finally, educational programs should not be perceived as reactions to misconduct by individual officers. Police resent it as much as anyone else when they are presumed to be insensitive or bigoted because someone else happens to be. Judiciousness and freedom from prejudice are as essential to educational programs as to other matters of policy.

If educational programs about cultures and differences are conducted without attributing character flaws to the members of the department—if police are treated as students—such programs can be assets in a department's efforts to rise above the microcosm. If they presume that police should be treated as patients, they will drive wedges within the department and solidify us-against-them attitudes toward the public.

15

Ethical Ideals, Youth Violence, and Gang Enforcement

If we heedlessly trash the minds, indeed the very souls, of our children; if through reiterated models of violence and the false promise of endless instant gratification we produce generations incapable of self-discipline and restraint; if we encourage the development of insatiable men and women who put the pursuit of pleasure before the pursuit of happiness; if by shortening the attention span we create persons incapable of complex analysis and responsible judgment; if we distort events of the day, garble the words of our leaders, simplify the character of nations, positing a false equivalence between democratic and totalitarian governments—there can be only one result. A dictatorship may survive by virtue of the strength of one man and an army that stands behind him, but the survival of democracy depends upon the moral virtue and reasoning power of all its people and on their participation in government as responsible, understanding citizens.

JOHN SILBER[1]

When state and local police executives, sheriffs, and other leaders of federal law enforcement agencies ask me for a thumbnail sketch of an ethically ideal law enforcement agency, I offer one with the strong caveat that such an institution is impossible to forge. Moreover, unrealistic expectations breed cynicism, and ignoring human limitations invites tyranny. Unrealistic expectations lead to the idea that a powerful government—fascist, socialist, or communist—could make life perfect. Tyrannies always betray justice as their inevitable failures become more desperate. Any sketch of an ideal department is at best a rough template of what to strive for in policing and law enforcement.

Conversations about the difficulties of approximating the template sometimes focus on gangs, juvenile career criminals, and youth violence. Ruthless and violent antisocial behavior by girls and boys and youths who grow up without adult supervision have reached intolerable levels. Juvenile justice systems are inadequate because they were never designed for such staggering levels of depravity in the young.

Violence is on the rise even in the elementary, middle, and junior high school grades. In New York City, 900 elementary and junior high school students were suspended for carrying illegal weapons in school in 1992 alone.[2] Many states show dramatic increases in juvenile crime over the past decade. In 1992, in Florida, which suffers the highest crime and violent crime rates in the country, "149 juveniles were charged with murder or manslaughter . . . compared with 69 a decade earlier. During the same period, attempted murder cases involving juveniles rose to 249 from 13, armed robbery cases to 1,972 from 645, and aggravated assault and battery cases to 7,083 from 2,688."[3]

William J. Bennett, the former U.S. secretary of education, points out in his *Index of Leading Cultural Indicators* that in the past thirty-three years

> there has been a 560 percent increase in violent crime; more than a 400 percent increase in illegitimate births; a quadrupling in divorces; a tripling of the percentage of children living in single-parent homes; more than a 200 percent increase in the teenage suicide rate; and a drop of 75 points in the average S.A.T. scores of high-school students. . . . Today 30 percent of all births and 68 percent of black births are illegitimate. By the end of the decade, according to the most reliable projections, *40 percent* of all American births and *80 percent* of minority births will occur out of wedlock. . . . And then there are the results of an ongoing teacher survey. Over the years teachers have been asked to identify the top problems in America's schools. In 1940 teachers identified them as talking out of turn; chewing gum; making noise; running in the hall; cutting in line; dress code infractions; and littering. When asked the same question in 1990, teachers identified drug use; alcohol abuse; pregnancy; suicide; rape; robbery; and assault.[4]

Surely, no greater crisis faces us than the spawning of generations of young bereft of regard for civility, restraint, and law. And because large segments of the public are inclined to think of this as a crisis only for police, no social phenomenon is likely to cause deeper or more persistent ethical problems in policing. How, then, should ethical ideals be brought to life in relation to youth violence and gang enforcement?

A Sketch of the Ethically Ideal Institution

Foremost, an ethically ideal organization would be one with integrity, in which policies and practices were forged for moral reasons—such as the dignity of human beings—rather than from impulse, whim, desire for personal gratification, and the like. There would be no us-against-them attitudes against the public and no disrespect for the limits of the law. Everything done in private would be done exactly as if the public were watching.

Conduct would be informed by considerations of justice, not only in dealing with the public but also in all reward and accountability structures. Merit would be recognized, and mistakes made in good faith would be treated as opportunities for instruction rather than punishment. By definition, there would be no bad-faith errors or misconduct, but everyone would be fully aware that bad-faith errors should be punished and treated differently from good-faith mistakes. There would be no bigotry of any kind.

Members of the organization would draw upon deep reservoirs of temperance and courage; no one would sacrifice duty to personal desire and gratification or show cowardice, or rashness. Accordingly, they would show probity rather than financial corruption, restraint in use of force rather than brutality, and healthful personal habits, without problems of drug consumption or excesses with alcohol.

Since integrity embraces honesty, the leaders would be faithful to sworn and civilian personnel by giving them clear policies and acting in accord with stated policies. There would be no falsified reports, no perjury, no covert uses of the badge for private gain of any kind, and no acceptance of gratuities. In such an organization, there would be no peer pressure against the faithful fulfillment of the police mission, so no one would be unsuited to be police. Recruitment programs would have to be flawless.

Because in ethics we recognize that people have a duty to be competent at their work, in an ideally ethical institution there would be no crucial weaknesses in academy or in-service training, no acceptance of personnel who were unable or unwilling to perform well and honorably. And the institution would give its personnel whatever resources they need to perform the work required by their mission.

Finally, inexperienced personnel would not be left to their own devices without guidance in the field, and no one would be deprived of ample supervision. Because the leaders would recognize the pressing need to know what their personnel must contend with, open lines of communication would be routinely used throughout the ranks, upward, downward, and laterally. This same level of communication would be maintained with the public and the media: police policies and actions would generate few surprises.

This is, roughly, what an ethically ideal organization would be like. Obviously, no human being or group of human beings, no matter how ethical or wise, could create or maintain such an institution. It would have to be exempt from all the contingencies of the world in which we live and be made up of angels, not human beings. So it is, when we describe the ideal. Nothing real is ever utterly ideal; the challenge is to make intelligent use of the ideal as a standard of judgment.

Youth Violence and Gang Enforcement

How, exactly, are these ethical ideals to be realized in contending with youth violence and gangs? The answer begins with courage—the courage to tell unpleasant truths.

School officials sometimes manipulate data to show student performance as better than it really is (for example, by excluding various groups of students from the data samples) or to show that everyone in school is learning well (by making tests so trivial as to be meaningless or by graduating students on the basis of accumulated credits rather than on scholastic performance). School officials also downplay violence and pressure school police to deny the existence of gangs. Political leaders also may minimize reports of violent crime and gang predation to mollify prospective tourists and local residents. Broad segments of the public commonly regard crime as someone else's problem—a problem only for those whose neighborhoods are hardest hit or whose children are imperiled.

Since such matters become politically volatile, police candor on youth violence and gang activity may be unwelcome. Many political leaders even call gang enforcement units by some euphemism to obscure gang problems. Nonetheless, it seems to me obligatory for police leaders to be forthright in alerting the mayors, city managers, governors, or others to whom they are accountable. They should also issue warnings about gang activity likely to have impact on youth organizations, drug treatment centers, and hospitals, as well as on the streets and in schools. Disputes about whether a pack of youths who cruise in search of racial confrontations is properly called a gang should not delay or prevent proactive steps by police.

If youth violence and gang activity are ignored or denied, gangs acquire a head start in recruitment and criminality that is difficult to overcome. A city that believes it has no problems will not mount unified opposition to gang incursion and recruitment by schools, youth organizations, civic groups, corporations, the media, police, prison and probation officials, prosecutors, judges, private foundations, and health and other social service agencies. Without such a unified front, the odds against reversing gang activity can become overwhelming.

Enlisting the help of the media may be difficult but must be attempted. Publishers and editors must learn that gang activity resembles guerrilla theater in that gangs use publicity to aggrandize themselves and to promote recruitment. Public visibility, like conviction for violent crimes, is a mark of success and honor.

I have seen local police plead with television reporters not to interview a gang member because they knew he would declare war on rivals and, once publicly committed, could not back down. Yet, the television reporters interviewed the gang member on camera and precipitated the violence.

Some reporters who write feature stories are susceptible to manipulation by gangs that present a false picture of themselves as civic-minded youth organizations. Such well-organized criminal conspiracies as the Latin Kings, also known as the Almighty Latin King Nation or the Almighty Latin Charter Nation, and the Latin Queens have become skilled at manipulating community leaders, youths, and the media. Concealing their ruthlessness and violence, they seek 100,000 members by the year 2000 to control large markets in drugs and weapons smuggling, while professing to be dedicated to education, good citizenship, ethnic pride, and the self-esteem of the young. Not even the most convincing evidence the police can provide persuades reporters to acknowledge the facts. Reporters who get a voyeuristic thrill from being around violent criminals may slant their stories to extend their access to a gang.

Despite such difficulties, police have to try to work with the media for the sake of the public interest, without pandering to their every desire. Police leaders must have their own agenda for media interviewers. They should think of themselves as teachers of the public whenever they speak for the record, rather than as objects of media interviews. No matter what questions are asked, police spokesmen and women should say the things the public most deserves to know and not be diverted by the reporter. Police departments should videotape extended interviews in full so that they can respond if sound-bite editing misrepresents the department or jeopardizes the public.

At the same time, police should resist the temptation to inform the media of search and arrest warrants to be served and the like. Some departments yield to that temptation in the hope of currying media favor and showing the public that police are effective. When camera crews arrive, however, crowds—including many police and police command officers—follow them, and confusion reigns. I have seen episodes where warrants served on the wrong address or the wrong person made the police a laughingstock on the next day's news. The work of policing is hard enough without courting such unnecessary impairments.

To the courage of telling unpleasant truths and the wisdom of trying to work with the media in the public interest should be added the virtues of wise planning and preparedness. In gang enforcement and the prevention of youth violence, the most essential of all resources is the capacity to gather intelligence and to use it effectively. Departments should also make a commitment to the education of nonpolice organizations in their own areas and of neighboring police departments. If local police alone know what needs to be anticipated and opposed, their efforts will be isolated and less than effective. Officers who learn to read gang graffiti can teach others that graffiti are not harmless art work or trifling vandalism.

Gang graffiti are declarations of terror that mean, "If you can see this, you are under our dominion. Here you have no rights, no public space. This space belongs to us, and you live only at our sufferance and with our permission." Police teach school officials and city officials that to lose the graffiti wars is to lose immeasurable ground, so they stress graffiti eradication every day, before school starts. Although we spend several billion dollars on graffiti eradication annually in the United States, and succeed only about 20 percent of the time, this form of opposition to gang power remains imperative. The basic principle is James Q. Wilson and George Kelling's "broken window" principle: leave a broken window unrepaired, and other forms of neighborhood decline will follow. So, too, with graffiti.

Gathering gang intelligence and keeping it current are always crucial. This includes information about recruitment, weaponry, agendas, graffiti, tattoos, codes, signs, mobility, affiliations and

enmities, prison associations, wealth, vehicles, patterns of criminality, and gang colors, dress, jewelry, and paraphernalia. Some
departments assign pregnant officers and officers who are temporarily disabled for patrol duty to update computer records daily.
Informing patrol personnel, detectives, gang enforcement units,
and other personnel of the most current information is essential
to proactive enforcement.

Some gangs use computers in gathering intelligence on police. I have seen raids of gang houses, some of them fortified,
where police discovered computer records of police assignments,
patterns of patrol for marked and unmarked vehicles, movements
of the spouses and children of police officers, and the activities of
rival gangs. Police departments have been forced to relocate
spouses and children under names that conceal their ties with
gang intelligence or enforcement officers. Departments must
know what the gangs know and are capable of discovering to
protect their own people.

It has never been unusual for prostitutes and other lawbreakers to keep careful track of police. As one Chicago officer put it:

> Streetwalkers organize their lives around cops' schedules.
> They keep close watch on the vice cops and the district tac
> teams. They know the guys they can outrun and outfox.
> They know when we're out there and when the watch
> changes. Their peak times are shift changes. They can do a
> lotta, lotta stuff in half an hour. Sometimes we switch
> shift times to confuse them. They get real perturbed at
> us—"What you doing out here? You're not supposed to be
> here *now*. You're not playing by the rules."[5]

But the stakes are dramatically higher now, and underestimating
them can be deadly.

Unfortunately, some departments are inept at gathering and
using gang intelligence, and some create gang enforcement units
in name only—as a sop to the community or the media. I have
worked with departments that assigned officers to gang enforcement who had no training in managing informants or in gang
activities. Where gangs are involved in drug trafficking—and, of
course, not all of them are—I have seen narcotics and gang
enforcement officers who had no real knowledge of drugs or
narcotics and who would not have recognized them had they
encountered them. I have also seen weak officers assigned to drug
and gang education programs in schools and youth organizations,
officers who were not very good on the streets and were even
worse in classrooms. Such imprudent steps by police thwart their

own investment in gang and drug enforcement and undermine their credibility, especially with the young.

Departments that deal well with youth violence and gangs assign to these units very good people who teach leaders in civic, educational, foundation, and corporate affairs what they need to know, and they formulate plans for coordinated activities. If officials want to rely on youth curfews and related measures, the police are straightforward about the resources and personnel needed to make them useful. Police leaders stress the risks of enacting policies and laws that cannot or will not be enforced and that parents will not support, especially if they have given up hope of controlling their children. They explain that isolated measures without a comprehensive plan accomplish little.

Abilene, Texas, has a well-conceived and coordinated plan, which reduced known gang members from 650 to 75 from 1988 to 1993. Boys and girls club gymnasiums and youth centers, built adjacent to lower-level schools in high-crime areas, led in each area to at least a 46 percent reduction in reported crimes. They serve as gyms for schools during the day and as facilities for youth recreation and entertainment at night. A local foundation bought a motel, restored it, and currently underwrites its operations to prevent the erosion of a neighborhood; other business leaders, encouraged by this anchor, succeeded in reversing the decline of the area. Schools have fought graffiti daily. Police have focused on prevention of prostitution, in cooperation with health officials, to avert a rise in addiction and the market for crack that prostitution brings. The city has eliminated buildings that provided haven for drug trafficking and other gang activities, and the police have concentrated patrols in areas beset by drive-by shootings. They have made drug-criminal business sufficiently difficult that gangs have looked for more promising markets elsewhere.

Nothing of this magnitude can be accomplished in a city that views youth violence and gang predation as police problems or problems of a specific area or group of residents. In my experience, it is unusual for anyone except police to provide the initial leadership in educating the community and advising investments of money and time. Excellent personnel must therefore be assigned to these tasks. Their work may not appear as exciting as kicking down doors, but it reduces the dangers to the community, including the officers who have to kick down doors.

Gathering intelligence can be especially difficult where language barriers interfere, as with some Jamaican posses and Asian gangs. Immigrants frequently come to the United States from parts of the world where governmental corruption is the norm and police are only another gang to be feared. Securing the trust of these newcomers is time consuming and may yield only modest success. Large, diverse populations of immigrants who speak little or no English may resist all police efforts to be of service, particularly if they fear prompt and fatal gang reprisals. I know of no remedies except persistence, making and keeping promises faithfully, recruiting officers whose backgrounds give them access to the public, maintaining high visibility, and working with prosecutors to ensure mutually supportive agendas. Even these efforts may take years to produce results, and the results may be disheartening.

Wise police and sheriffs' departments establish close ties with state and federal agencies. They look for opportunities to have violators prosecuted under the statutes with the stiffest penalties, thereby dissuading outside gangs from incursion. Although joint law enforcement task forces can be effective, their operations call for care. When agencies with different standards work together, the lower standards may dominate the task force, and impair the better departments. When officers supervise personnel from other agencies, they do not always take accountability seriously. Officers may be faced with temptations without benefit of supervision or clear policy.

A chief or sheriff or agency head cannot afford to assign personnel to a task force and expect it to run smoothly by itself. Vigilant maintenance of institutional standards is as crucial here as in undercover work within the department.

Noble cause temptations can be as dangerous as temptations for private gain, especially if asset forfeiture is involved. When departments imprudently suggest that they seek to acquire assets, perhaps to sustain a portion of the operating budget, officers may be tempted to skim. Some of the worst corruption cases involve skimming to "cut out the middle man" in asset forfeiture and to buy equipment for the department or the task force with the stolen money. Inevitably, it seems, the noble cause theft becomes plain theft by the members of the unit as they begin taking money for themselves.

Falsification of reports, planting of evidence, and perjury can also become tempting, especially in departments or task forces that reward outcomes too heavily and conscientious performance too weakly. Supervisors too much concerned with outcomes may turn the other way when officers cut corners in violation of policy or law, thus undermining their ability to enforce any other policy and to stand for integrity in any respect. Poorly trained officers may also be tempted to gratify the wishes of area residents who ask them to beat up gang members and drive them out of the neighborhood. Officers who yield to this temptation may not learn until too late that the person they assaulted is someone's son, nephew, cousin, or lover. Friends and relatives of gang members will file complaints, and the public will turn on brutal police. A disregard for policy and law by officers turns into a source of tension between police and the public and makes their cooperation virtually impossible.

As gangs turn from territorial organizations concerned principally with turf and reputation into criminal conspiracies for profit resembling organized crime, they learn the advantages of bribery and the value of "friends in high places." When a willingness to take violent reprisal against adversaries and competitors is joined with a sophistication in co-opting public servants, the result is an institution capable of profoundly undercutting the public interest.

Some gangs, rich enough to hire prestigious lawyers and shrewd enough to enlist the sympathy of civil rights groups, persuade the media or the public that police investigations and arrests are motivated by racism. Mere denials by police count little. Here, only a deserved reputation for fairness can safeguard a department. Such a reputation can be secured only by the high quality of daily performance, by great care in classifying individuals as gang members, and by due restraint in the use of force.

Perhaps prompted by suspicion of racism among police, several mayors proposed that all police data and crime statistics should be color blind, though they are unlikely to opt for color blindness in matters such as personnel recruitment, employment opportunities, departmental composition, and the proportion of complaints filed against police departments by members of minority groups.[6] The mayors may argue that crime statistics that are not color blind fuel racial bigotry and prejudicial stereotyping. Color blindness of crime data seems unlikely to advance the safety of the public, however, including the minorities that are disproportionately the victims of violent crimes, nor will color blindness in data reporting prevent the perpetuation of racism. Instead, the proposal will be seen as special pleading, an effort to cover up facts about crime. The proposal risks solidifying racism among those who are tempted to believe the vicious falsehood that a person's color indicates character or criminality.

Some youth violence and gang activity *are* racist. Wilding

packs of youths of one color do look for individuals of another color to assault or kill. The disgusting history of racist violence shows that no one is exempt from racist feelings by virtue of color or other accident of birth, and we must be willing to acknowledge the facts of history to improve the future. Disputes about presentation of statistics will not advance education against prejudice, encourage contempt for racism and other forms of bigotry, or further the prosecution of racially motivated crimes of violence.

The very real challenges of safeguarding the public become more grim when juries decide that individuals have less responsibility for their own violent acts if they are part of a mob. This proposition demeans us, because it implicitly denies that we are free and therefore accountable. Denial of personal responsibility threatens to dim public perceptions of the savagery of wilding crimes and gang-inspired riots. This makes prevention of youth violence and gang predation more difficult for police, schools, and other institutions of civility and civilization. Toleration of excuses for violence add to the already powerful influences that corrupt the young.[7]

Gangs, Education, and the Heroism of Cowards

Although police have no hope of combating these corrupting influences without the help of schools, parents, and other public- and private-sector institutions, police know more about gangs and the threat they pose than anyone else does. Their educational programs—about the malevolence of criminal conspiracies, about the signs of gang membership, and about constraints against gang involvement—can be central to crime prevention and gang enforcement.

Police must therefore know thoroughly the criminal conspiracies their communities face. They must be prepared to make concrete proposals for community and parental action. The basic points to follow would be the same whether a city suffers an incursion by a white supremacist motorcycle gang trafficking in amphetamines or some other type of criminal conspiracy, but Jamaican posses are so spectacularly dangerous that they provide a good illustration. Originally formed as strong-arm political street gangs in Kingston, Jamaica, they took their name from the cowboy posses in western movies.

Federal agencies estimate that at least forty posses, with between 10,000 and 20,000 members, now operate in Jamaica, Great Britain, and the United States. The most infamous are the

Jungle, Spangler, and Shower Posses, based in, but not restricted to, America's eastern seaboard. Most members are black Jamaicans, but Chinese, white, and Indian Jamaicans are also members. The human capacity for evil has no racial boundaries.

These posses are beneficiaries of the demand for crack in the United States. Incredibly brutal (some of their members were trained by Cuban guerrilla warfare specialists), the posses have been implicated in more than 2,000 drug-related murders since 1985. The posses are so powerful in the United States that they buy and fortify crack houses for retail distribution of drugs and other houses for wholesale distribution to their retail outlets, with local juveniles running the supplies. Sometimes they buy whole sections of neighborhoods to shelter their facilities. They control almost half the crack marketed in America.

Confidential law enforcement documents confirm that the posses launder drug money through the purchase of record stores, supermarkets, and car dealerships. For a steady supply of vehicles altered to conceal narcotics, they purchase and operate automobile repair shops. To divert law enforcement agencies, they use women as assassins. They can also be extremely effective in recruiting and exploiting girls and boys. They are utterly indifferent to the fate of those they recruit.

Late one night in a chilling fog outside the main entrance to a tenement, I stood with several uniformed and plainclothes police as they prepared to execute a warrant to search an apartment, believing it was a stopover place for a leading Jamaican posse.

Police went up the stairs quickly, and pounded on the apartment door, which was quickly opened. A fast search of the three rooms revealed only two women, however, both high on crack. The high did not last through fifteen minutes of questioning, which revealed that the apartment had been used by Jamaican gang members transporting drugs.

Although crumbling plaster, garbage, urine, and vomit were pervasive throughout this tenement, a staggering odor of filth and decay rose and assaulted our senses when we entered this apartment. The bathroom had not worked for many days; the sink, the toilet, the floor, and the bathtub were covered with excrement and befouled paper towels. The floor was a soggy swamp of waste that no one was willing to search by hand. The living room, littered with drug paraphernalia and broken-down furniture, was dimly lit by two bare light bulbs. Oilcloth covered a window, and rotting food, fist-size piles of roach droppings, and crusted stains of semen covered the bed and the sofa. The kitchen sink and counter were piled with dirty dishes wedged all the way up to the cupboards overhead and might have tumbled down at a touch. The freezer, running constantly with a door that would not close, was filled with one huge block of ice dripping blackened icicles. Everywhere—on table and counters, refrigerator and floor—roaches fed on garbage, cast-off chunks of fast food. There were ratholes in the walls, and the noises of rats close-by.

One of the women sat crying; the other flopped, limp, against the wall. Still young girls, they were prostitutes whose lives revolved around drugs. Although they were paid to let posse members stay in their apartment, the police would not arrest them. The one being questioned could not conceal that she was calculating how much she must say to satisfy the police without risking gang reprisal against herself. After she struck a deal for information with an officer, and a threat and a promise were exchanged, we left. A tenement hallway never smelled so clean.

These girls resembled many used by Jamaican posses. Their business is the betrayal of our children. Despite their contempt for the lives they manipulate, criminals such as posse members often achieve hero status in the eyes of inner-city youths. By acquiring wealth and power through ruthlessness, these criminals seem to possess a shortcut to fame, fortune, and pleasure. The shortcut, the quick fix, has enormous appeal for youths who have failed in school and are bereft of decent adult companionship. Like adults, youths who want shortcuts often band together to commit wrongs in greater security and safety. Not surprisingly, the levels of behavior of urban gangs seldom rise above the depravity of their meanest members. "Mobocracy," writes columnist Sidney J. Harris, "is the heroism of cowards."[8] This point should be emphasized in educational programs on gangs, at the same time that the record of the specific gang is made clear.

According to long-time gang enforcement officers Robert Jackson and Wesley McBride, the tendency toward remorseless wrongdoing rises in part from the belief that the youths are themselves victims of an evil society. When mothers of delinquents meet law enforcement authorities, they often make excuses for the children in "the form of accusations against society in general. Thus, children are taught early that they are not responsible for their actions. . . . By the time the youngsters reach their mid-teens . . . they truly believe that they are victims and that they have the absolute right, if not the duty, to do whatever they want, whenever they want."[9]

Nothing worse in the way of education can befall girls and boys than to be taught that they are mere victims of society. Such teaching, however well-intentioned or grounded in desperation it may be, diminishes children in their own eyes to such a degree that a hopeful sense of their own real possibilities for achievement, decency, and happiness may be forever obscured to them. The consequences of thwarting youthful aspiration in this way threaten always to be dreadful; as C. S. Lewis said, "Famished nature will be avenged."[10] Police and schoolteachers should emphasize these points, too, with parents.

Like police departments, school districts around the country lack lines of systematic communication with one another, so they learn little from the experience of others. Addressing problems alone is staggeringly inefficient and slow. Much of the readily available literature about gangs lacks analytical power and offers recommendations that are banal, unrealistic, or utopian.

Many writers on gangs simply follow the media, which in turn chase ambulances in accordance with the maxim of many local television stations, "If it bleeds, it leads" (the news broadcast of the day). Because these writers ignore the emergence of gangs in suburbs and rural areas, they identify the "root causes" of gangs with inner-city social conditions. They overlook human nature, the fact that all of us are creatures of habit and imitation, and cannot say how to try to bring out the best in the young. Police and school teachers and administrators need to know how to do so.

The most experienced police I have worked with offer advice along these lines:

> What my work with gangs and schools has taught me is that school officials must control the walls; they must paint out all graffiti every morning, preferably before the students arrive. The worst possible mistake is to legitimize the gangs by setting special walls aside for graffiti.
>
> There has to be a strict dress code: no gangbanger or wannabe clothes allowed, no colors, no caps. Administrators must not kow-tow to kids. When a kid does something wrong, *do* something; get the parents involved. If they won't get involved, discipline the kid yourself. And the kid who won't stop must be put out of school.
>
> You cannot be heavy handed, and you must not destroy face, or try to make object lessons of gang members. You must treat them like men, since that is what they insist they are. If you humiliate them, they will commit not only vandalism, but arson and murder. Every gang member is a

potential death wish, an absolute advocate of "vengeance is mine."

Give your attention to the good kids. And, believe me, there are a lot of gang kids you cannot reach or rescue. Give them a steady diet of the cops.

Instructive, generous, and patient school officials and teachers echo those views; here is a distillation of the counsel I have gathered from the most experienced of them:

Much of the time, parents, teachers, and administrators don't understand about gangs. They don't even know the meaning of colors. Parents will deny gang, alcohol, and drug problems and insist, "Not my kid!" You have to bring in experts to talk with teachers, parents, and student assistants about what to look for. Everybody has to learn that education is impossible unless there is peace and order everywhere on school property and in the streets adjacent to campus.

In some schools, we brought in Hispanic police officers, who had been raised in the neighborhood and could communicate, and introduced them to everybody, including gang members, as our "Homeboys." And we quietly brought parents in so they could see the gang members their kids were actually hanging around with.

The police who work in and with your schools have to be in agreement with your administrative philosophy. Once they're working in the schools, they're more than cops, they're really school administrators, too.

Once kids are in the gangs, there's not much you can do for them. We told them, "You follow *your* rules out there on the streets. You follow *our* rules in here." Some of us had school police bring each gang leader into the boiler room to meet privately with the principal to establish the schools as neutral ground: "No gang wars on campus, no hanging around after school." After a while, the gangbangers saw the advantage to schools as "islands of safety" just as we did.

We faced graffiti everywhere, and we learned to read it on the kids' notebooks, on the underside of their baseball-cap visors, on the soles of their tennis and basketball shoes. Parents, grandparents, and cops helped us paint over graffiti on the walls every morning. It took us six months to win, but eventually we had clean doors, tables, elevators, water coolers, everything. We proved that the schools were our turf, and the more determined we were, the more the decent kids rallied to the cause.

Top administrators went door to door, to everyone who lived near the schools, and personally gave them telephone numbers to call anonymously if they saw anything bad happening. Principals rode perimeter blocks to get kids to school on time, and police moved loiterers out of the area after the morning bells had rung. We locked the gates and the doors all day, and we covered the tops of our exterior fences with printer's ink, so that anyone who climbed over and managed to get in would be easily identifiable.

We made police welcome on our campuses all the time. They had to be there often—not just to arrest people, but to make communication easy and natural. We trusted each other. If something went down over a weekend between the gangs, the police told us before school started on Monday who to keep an eye on and what to look out for.

The police constructed two curriculum units on gangs for us as part of their DARE (Drug Abuse Resistance Education) program. We had many kids who couldn't read or write, and they would make all kinds of trouble in class to hide their illiteracy. We had to keep them out of the gangs while we taught them to read.

We supervised our hallways closely. There were always adults available and visible everywhere. Principals visited every classroom at least once a week, and many classrooms once a day. Every non-classroom staff member had to supervise activities before, during, and after school.

We couldn't have made it without gaining the support of the parents. We told them the truth: "Move away. Your son's going to be killed if he stays here. If you stay, fight him now, or bury him soon."

With the support of parents and community advisory councils we were able to enforce a dress code. No colors. No gang jewelry or paraphernalia. No caps indoors, including the baseball caps and watch caps the gangbangers fancied. No suspenders left hanging down in back. No canes. No bandannas, no shoelaces in gang colors. And no blasters. The only things you bring to school are books, pencils, and tablets. Many kids changed clothes when they got to school and again when they left. We let them keep straight clothes in their lockers overnight and gang clothes during the day.

We also got a lot of mileage from "opportunity rooms," where we sent trouble-makers. They had to stay in the rooms, closely supervised, do all their assignments, eat all their meals, with all their privileges suspended. Sometimes this worked better than sending them home or throwing them out. If they straightened out, they got the same chances for extracurricular activities as everybody else. We tried to treat everybody as an individual, and we required all school activities and school organizations to be integrated—cheerleaders, teams, student councils. At dances, nobody's favorite music got all the play.

We became friends with parents and colleagues, police and community leaders, alumni. We looked out for each other and for our students.

In some of our schools, levels of achievement and pride are now so high that enrollments have risen dramatically, drop-out rates have declined, and faculty and staff retention and continuity exceed 90 percent over periods of several years. It was hard and exhausting, but we stuck to it. And, in the end, it became fun.

Police departments may also benefit from instructional programs on gangs such as the Gang Resistance Education and Training (GREAT) program of the Bureau of Alcohol, Tobacco, and Firearms. First mounted in 1991 in cooperation with the Phoenix Police Department, GREAT is designed to teach "middle school children to set goals for themselves, resist pressures, and resolve conflicts without violence. GREAT provides at-risk teenagers with the necessary skills and information to say no to gangs. In 1992, the Federal Law Enforcement Training Center joined the partnership to assist with the national expansion of the program." The program rightly focuses on educating "teachers, parents, and the community about pre-crisis indicators showing that gang involvement or activity is in their geographical area." More than four hundred police from thirty-six states have been trained in GREAT. Eligibility for participation requires a formal agreement of mutual cooperation between local police and schools and on the local selection of highly able officers.[11]

The GREAT program is well-designed in many respects. But in the program's emphases on cultural sensitivity and self-esteem, trainers and trainees will need to be alert to the problems described in chapter 14. Similarly, GREAT instructors charged to prepare officers to teach the young skills of conflict resolution will need to avoid conceptual errors rife in such programs in higher education. Many of these programs teach that the way to resolve conflict is to "acknowledge [the] other person's position as legitimate."[12] Clearly, not all positions are legitimate, and students should not be taught that they are—or that all beliefs and actions are tolerable or excusable. Learning resistance to gangs necessarily includes learning that much of what they do is grievously *wrong*. Making this clear becomes imperative where gangs hold sway. As Evan Simpson observed in his writings on violence, "In a hostile environment one may become inured to almost anything, including injury, and it is to be expected that what from a more favored standpoint is violent may fail to be so regarded by one raised in the midst of turbulence or social decay."[13]

Neither the police departments nor the ATF can advance the interests of children and youths on the ideological premises accepted by many conflict resolution specialists. The National Institute for Dispute Resolution in Washington, D.C., for example, provides instruction about "Alternative Dispute Resolution" in *Peaceful Persuasion: A Guide to Creating Mediation Resolution Programs on College Campuses.*

> Mediation requires acceptance of certain assumptions about human nature and human beings: that there is a genuine desire to cooperate; that disputants know best how to resolve their own disputes; and that people can be trusted to negotiate in good faith. In educational settings, the goals and language speaking to trust, cooperation, learning, and growth as applied to students are often at variance with individual and institutional ways of actually dealing with students. A dispute resolution process that assumes a high level of trust in students may be consonant with rhetoric, but not with actual assumptions and institutional practice. When the institutional norm is to prescribe for students, to intervene, direct, solve, and discipline—mediation requires a major reorientation.
>
> It is important to realize that mediation is not a total substitute for conventional conflict resolution mechanisms. It is not appropriate for all conflicts. Some disputes need to be dealt with publicly in order to develop or reinforce community standards on issues or behavior patterns. Others, by their nature, require a response that will deter others from similar action. However, mediation is useful when there is a need for a conflict resolution approach that may be less intimidating than the Dean of Students Office, when greater sensitivity to disputants' concerns than that afforded by evidentiary proceedings is sought, when one seeks to produce the feeling that grievances are actually heard, or when one wishes to empower disputants by enabling them to retain more control over the resolution of problems.

Mediation programs could be dramatically improved if they were designed to produce not merely "the feeling that grievances are actually heard," but the fact that they are actually heard. Programs would be strengthened if they showed disputants that respect for evidence and for truthfulness is irreplaceable in genuine sensitivity to the concerns of our fellows. We need not be misologists to care about each other—and we cannot care about each other responsibly if we disregard the real effects of our intentions and actions.

The *Guide* continues:

> Mediation can be used in a variety of ways to handle a wide range of individual and social problems and needs as is illustrated in the case studies found in this manual. It can be incorporated into disciplinary codes as an option for handling specified code violations or it can be structured to handle student conflicts in which no code violations are involved. It's a useful intervention tool for short-term crises that over the long-term may require therapy. Or conversely, in a violent dispute, arrest may be used to control the immediate situation while mediation might be part of the longer range solution. *In a broad context, mediation provides a forum for resolving any conflict involving personal, institutional, or policy difference.*[14] [Emphasis added.]

In the event that the reader does not find this account persuasive, the authors offer an ad hominem argument, disguised as benevolent therapy, and attack the background of the reader. Instead of offering reasons for accepting what they say, they disparage individual judgment of evidence in pursuit of the truth. All forms of inquiry intended to discover the truth and enable responsible evaluation are illogically equated with the imposition of punishment.

> It is difficult to overestimate the importance of acquiring a full and deep understanding of mediation whether one is preparing to become a mediator or preparing to initiate a program. It is not easy to readjust one's inner assumptions about how a dispute should be settled. Growing up with the idea that breaking the rules results in punishment, makes it very difficult to accept the notion that rule breaking can be resolved without punishment. If punishment for misdeeds is fair, then how can it be fair for there to be no punishment? *If one is socialized to believe that disputes are settled by obtaining evidence that points to the truth of a situation, it is very difficult to accept fully a process in which evidence and objective truth are not the focus. In order to embrace mediation, one must give up judging. Giving up the notion of analyzing a dispute in terms of who is right and who is wrong is hard.*[15] [Emphasis added.]

No one should be taught "to give up judging." Resistance to gangs depends on judging. Neither should people be taught to spurn the relevance of right and wrong. Some conflict resolution programs, however, demand not only this but also that participants must surrender facts. In its Human Resources Leadership Strategies, the Program on Negotiation at Harvard Law School provides "stop-action video analysis [to] help you learn the six key lessons of successful fact-finding." The first is, "There is no such thing as a 'fact' . . . fact finding is really a process of documenting differing perceptions." In addition, "Each person presents information according to the outcome she/he desires." Therefore, the human resources leader must learn "how to separate 'facts' from reactions to facts—while being sure to validate the feelings of each person being interviewed." Not surprisingly, once the very idea of fact has been undercut, the reader is cautioned, "After fact finding, your recommendations will be subjective and value-laden."[16]

This skepticism about the capacity of human beings for intellectual honesty is self-refuting. In political theory, it is well to establish the safeguard that no person shall be a judge in his or her own cause. Indeed, this is one element in the genius of the United States as a constitutional republic. But political safeguards do not make epistemological theories, especially not when the advocates' description of conflict resolution implies that everything they say is only their own "presentation of information according to the outcome [they] desire." On this premise, no distinction can be drawn between truth and falsity within conflict resolution theory itself. Validation is reduced to making people feel good; it no longer has anything to do with being reasonable or thinking rationally. This marks the intellectual bankruptcy of the theory.

Children and youths deserve better than this. They need better instruction if they are to acquire the backbone necessary for real resistance to gangs and other corrupters of the young. Many conflict resolution programs misinform by downplaying resistance and giving the impression that the avoidance of conflict is easy.

I know of no place where efforts to combat youth violence and gang activity have gone easily. Most school and police policies generate disputes, and parents may be the last to cooperate. Accordingly, efforts to get the various institutions to work hand in hand call for great levels of fortitude. They usually draw encouragement from their cooperation and reciprocity. Otherwise, resistance to cynicism and despair would be much more difficult.

Unconditional Obligations

Even if legislators and others admit publicly the gravity of youth violence and gang activity, they may remain unwilling to combat them. When drug trafficking is disrupted by arrests and successful prosecution, the short-term homicide rate tends to rise in turf and market wars. Politicians who understand that reform of juvenile justice systems costs real money may be reluctant to propose anything requiring new taxes.

Politicians must expect to draw fire it they advocate the establishment of orphanages for dispossessed children, boot camps for juvenile criminals, prosecution of juveniles as adults, expulsion of convicted felons from schools, and prohibition of increased welfare payments to unwed mothers who have additional children. Only those who care more about the public interest than their own political survival or advancement will risk it. The great cultural historian Jacques Barzun is right to caution that "there are few statesmen or good politicians who can govern."[17] Accordingly, police are unwise to expect rationality and courage in legislation and public policy. They are obliged to do their best even when officials fail to take the most obvious steps.

A group of political leaders abroad who faced a massive scandal of noble cause police corruption proposed to announce that the public had a right to trustworthy police and that the police had a right to a trustworthy criminal justice system. Those leaders could not have been more wrong, or less informed about the obligations to the public trust, when they implied that police lawfulness and integrity depended on whether the criminal justice system convicted and punished every guilty suspect. Fortunately, with the benefit of outside consultation, those leaders ultimately took the correct position when they went public: police lawfulness and integrity are unconditional obligations. The force of the obligation does not depend on the effectiveness of anything else, including the criminal justice system as a whole. Many political leaders will, however, continue to bungle the most important issues involving gangs and juvenile crime.

This is a hard lesson; it can be difficult to teach police that their obligations remain unconditional despite it. But it lies at the heart of ethics in policing, as it does in every other walk of life that involves the public trust. In my experience, no area of police work makes the ideal of principled conduct harder to live up to than work on juvenile crime, gang activity, and drug trafficking, particularly when they involve murder. Pursuit of serial killers also dramatically tests the fortitude and mettle of police, but there the police have the citizens and political leaders on their side. They do not always have either the public or the politicians on their side on juvenile crime, youth violence, and gang predation—far from it.

Accordingly, my police and law enforcement colleagues seem to me to be exactly right to raise questions about how to live up to ethical ideals as they try to bring policing to bear on grim realities of contemporary life. Our future as a people rests in the balance.[18] When I am with police leaders, and our discussions of ethical ideals in policing draw toward a close, I remind them how very much will be asked of police in the years to come. The magnitude of public expectation should serve to remind all who bear the public trust, all police: *Nothing is incorruptible except personal character that will not be corrupted.*

A Guide to the Further Study of Ethics in Policing

Those who read *Character and Cops* will see that the opening paragraph of chapter 1 speaks of "being a good person and doing what is right." Ethics is the branch of philosophy that asks such questions as: What is a good person? What is good character? What makes actions right or wrong? What are the principles for deciding how individuals and human institutions should behave? How can we identify our obligations and our rights?

These questions are universal. They do not ask what a good person is according to one society or another, or how different individuals behave in fact. Rather, they seek answers that apply to all of us, because we are all human beings capable of rational thought, capable of giving and appreciating reasons for and against specific ways of behaving. Answers to such philosophical questions must also be universal. Ethical standards and principles cannot be one thing for public servants and another for business executives, one thing for farmers and another for coaches, one thing for parents and another for police. Any answer that is relevant to the questions must hold for all of us. This is why *Character and Cops* refers to ethics in policing and never to police ethics.

Still, fundamental ethical principles must be applied in specific circumstances. Accordingly, police instructors should know both the fundamentals of ethics and how to apply them in policing. They must know the departmental policies, the codes of ethics, and the laws that establish the context and boundaries for applying fundamental ethical principles in policing. Since the moral obligations of policing or any other profession depend on professional competence, officers with a strong record of professional achievement will gain the most from the study of ethics.

Instructors should have taken an ethics course at the college level. Most courses involve reading either classics and masterpieces in ethics, or an anthology or survey textbook, or both. The more that can be gained from philosophical sources, the better. Even studying a textbook for an introductory course is better than nothing.

Some ethics courses, however, focus only on real or imagined dilemmas and do not advance knowledge of ethics. Reading the sections on "Moral Problems," "Habits," and "Current Fashion in Ethics Education," in chapter 9 of *Character and Cops*, along with the introductory section of chapter 10, will safeguard against the conceptual weakness of such courses.

Whether through a formal course or through a program of reading on their own, officers will want to address questions about the nature of good character, the criteria for identifying right and wrong actions, and the principles for deciding what we should do. They should be familiar with portions of *Character and Cops* that deal with character, integrity, and the formation of dispositions and habits that make up our character for better or worse—especially chapters 1, 3, 9, 12, 13, and pages 99–103 of chapter 7. They should reflect on the nature of moral deliberation—thinking about fundamental principles and deciding what we should do—as presented in chapters 7, 8, 10, and 11. And they should concentrate on the context for policing provided by the law and by the Constitution as presented in chapters 2 and 4.

For further background, they will find Plato's *Apology* and *Crito* a valuable introduction to principled conduct and careful ethical reasoning as Socrates embodied them. Aristotle's *Nicomachean Ethics*, accompanied by J. O. Urmson's little book *Aristotle's Ethics*, captures much about character and decency. Nonphilosophers find a number of short essays by the American philosopher William James very readable. They include "Habit," especially the sections on the practical effects of habit and on the ethical and pedagogical importance of the principle of habit. "On a Certain Blindness in Human Beings" and "What Makes a Life Significant" are instructive about justice and compassion.

John Stuart Mill's *Utilitarianism* deliberates on the identification of right actions as those that produce the best results, by one standard or another of "best." Such ethical theories are called teleological—from the Greek words *telos* (end, goal, or desired result) and *logos* (account), in the sense of giving an account from the perspective of the goal or end result.

Immanuel Kant's *Foundations of the Metaphysics of Morals* is irreplaceable for grasping moral life as self-directed actions performed because of the justifiable belief that they are right or obligatory. To behave rightfully, we must "treat all persons as ends in themselves and never as means merely"; we must act on principles that rational beings can universalize and therefore respect, whether these principles are applied in the treatment of other persons or in their treatment of oneself. Such ethical theories, called deontological, hold that some ways of behaving are obligatory because they are required by fundamental principles of rationality and justice, and others are wrong because they violate such principles and not because of actual consequences. The term *deontological* comes from the Greek words *deon* (duty, that which is binding or right) and *logos* (account), in the sense of giving an account from the perspective of duty.

Kant's account of rightness denies that mere consideration of consequences is adequate to responsible moral deliberation. Martin Luther King, Jr.'s "Letter from the Birmingham City Jail" shows how respect for justice involves more than producing good consequences. *Ecclesiastes* 3:1–9 suggests the importance of learning how to decide when specific conduct is justified:

> For everything there is a season, and a time for every matter under heaven: a time to be born, and a time to die; . . . a time to kill, and a time to heal; . . . a time to love, and a time to hate; a time for war, and a time for peace.

Those who find this difficult to cover on their own may want to study some secondary sources. Introductory books on ethics that have served undergraduates for many years include William K. Frankena's *Ethics* and Richard B. Brandt's *Ethical Theory*. More recently such books as Edmund Pincoffs' *Quandaries and Virtues*, David Falk's *Ought, Reasons, and Morality*, Fred and Christina Sommers's *Vice and Virtue in Everyday Life*, James Rachels's *The Elements of Moral Philosophy*, Louis P. Pojman's *Ethics*, and John Silber's essays "The Ethics of the Sword" and "The Gods of the Copybook Headings" in *Straight Shooting* have served readers well.

Chapter 2 of *Character and Cops*, "The Mission of Police," should be read with direct attention to the constitutional and ethical heritage and traditions of America. Papers from *The Federalist* are especially useful, particularly those written by James Madison, including numbers 10, 51, 55, and 57, and number 1, 6, and

78 by Alexander Hamilton. Boston University's National Center for America's Founding Documents produces a fine *Manual for Teachers on The Declaration of Independence* and *The Annotated Federalist* for *Federalist Papers* Nos. 1, 10, 39, 47, 51, 78, and 84, both written by Steven S. Tigner. The Declaration of Independence is must reading:

> We hold these truths to be self-evident, that all men are created equal, that they are endowed by their creator with certain unalienable rights, that among these are life, liberty, and the pursuit of happiness—that to secure these rights, governments are instituted among men, deriving their just powers from the consent of the governed.

This is the philosophy of government declared in the founding of the United States to which every police officer should be committed. It is enriched by the statement of purposes of the preamble to the Constitution:

> We, the people of the United States, in order to form a more perfect Union, establish justice, insure domestic tranquility, provide for the common defense, promote the general welfare, and secure the blessings of liberty to ourselves and our posterity do ordain and establish this Constitution for the United States of America.

Police ought to learn from the outset that the Constitution is not advice but the fundamental law of the land. The existence and authority of police are justified by this philosophy and these purposes. Even though no country or institution ever fully achieves the highest purposes for which it is established, even though we fall short in our pursuit of justice and public safety, police never have any right to exceed the limits of the law to achieve their goals.

The philosophy of government declared here stresses the equality of human beings. In providing services to the public and enforcing the law, police should understand that all discrimination on grounds of race, sex, ethnic background, religious affiliation, or economic condition is wrong. The philosophy of government to which we as a nation are committed confirms that no form of prejudice or bigotry is tolerable within the work of police.

A Short Bibliography in Ethics

To supplement *Character and Cops: Ethics in Policing*, the following books are recommended.

Aristotle. *The Nicomachean Ethics.* Translated by David Ross, revised by J. L. Ackrill and J. O. Urmson. New York: Oxford University Press, 1988.

Baier, Kurt. *The Moral Point of View: A Rational Basis of Ethics.* New York: Random House, 1965.

Bennett, William J. *The Book of Virtues.* New York: Simon and Schuster, 1993.

Brandt, R. B. *Ethical Theory.* Englewood Cliffs, N.J.: Prentice-Hall, Inc., 1959.

Cohen, Howard S., and Michael Feldberg. *Power and Restraint: The Moral Dimension of Police Work.* New York: Praeger, 1991.

Delattre, Edwin J. *Against Brutality and Corruption: Integrity, Wisdom, and Professionalism.* Tallahassee, Fla.: Florida Criminal Justice Executive Institute, Florida Department of Law Enforcement, 1991. For information on cost and to order, contact Florida Criminal Justice Executive Institute, Florida Department of Law Enforcement, P.O. Box 1489, Tallahassee, FL 32302; tel. (904) 488-1340.

Falk, David. *Ought, Reasons and Morality.* Ithaca: Cornell University Press, 1986. See especially, "Morality, Self and Others."

The Federalist. Edited, with Introduction and Notes, by Jacob E. Cooke. Middletown, Conn.: Wesleyan University Press, 1961.

Frankena, William K. *Ethics.* 2d ed. Englewood Cliffs, N.J.: Prentice-Hall Inc., 1973.

Fuller, Lon L. *The Morality of Law.* Rev. ed. New Haven: Yale University Press, 1975.

James, William. *The Writings of William James: A Comprehensive Edition.* Edited and with an introduction by John J. McDermott. Chicago: University of Chicago Press, 1977.

Kant, Immanuel. *Foundations of the Metaphysics of Morals.* Translated by Lewis White Beck. 2d ed. New York: Macmillan, 1990.

———. *Lectures on Ethics.* Translated by Louis Infield. New York: Harper Torchbooks, 1963.

King, Martin Luther, Jr. *A Testament of Hope: The Essential Writings of Martin Luther King, Jr.* Edited by James Melvin Washington. San Francisco: Harper and Row, 1986. See especially, "Letter from the Birmingham City Jail."

Mill, John Stuart. *Utilitarianism.* Edited by Samuel Gorovitz. Indianapolis: Bobbs-Merrill, 1971.

Pincoffs, Edmund. *Quandaries and Virtues.* Lawrence, Kan.: University of Kansas Press, 1986.

Plato. *The Trial and Death of Socrates.* Translated by G. M. A. Grube. 2d ed. Indianapolis: Hackett Publishing Company, 1988.

Pojman, Louis P. *Ethics: Discovering Right and Wrong.* Belmont, Calif.: Wadsworth, 1990.

Rachels, James. *The Elements of Moral Philosophy.* New York: Random House, 1986.

Silber, John R. *Straight Shooting: What's Wrong with America and How to*

Fix It. New York: Harper and Row, 1989. See especially, "The Gods of the Copybook Headings" and "The Ethics of the Sword."

Sommers, Fred and Christina, eds. *Vice and Virtue in Everyday Life: Introductory Readings in Ethics.* 2d ed. New York: Harcourt Brace Jovanovitch, 1989.

Story, Joseph. *A Familiar Exposition of the Constitution of the United States.* Lake Bluff, Ill.: Regnery Gateway, 1986.

Tigner, Steven S. *The Declaration of Independence: A Manual for Teachers.* Boston: National Center for America's Founding Documents at Boston University, 1989. To order, contact the National Center for America's Founding Documents, Boston University School of Education, 605 Commonwealth Avenue, Boston, MA 02215; tel. (617) 353-6278. ($7.50, plus $2.00 shipping and handling.)

————. *The Annotated Federalist, Nos. 1, 10, 39, 47, 51, 78, & 84.* Boston: National Center for America's Founding Documents at Boston University, 1990. To order, see above.

Ulich, Robert, ed. *Three Thousand Years of Educational Wisdom.* 2d ed. Cambridge: Harvard University Press, 1954.

Urmson, J. O. *Aristotle's Ethics.* Oxford: Basil Blackwell, 1988.

The following periodicals are also useful:

Criminal Justice Ethics. Published semiannually by the Institute for Criminal Justice Ethics in association with the Department of Law, Police Science and Criminal Justice Administration, John Jay College of Criminal Justice/CUNY, New York.

FBI Law Enforcement Bulletin. Published monthly by the U.S. Department of Justice, Federal Bureau of Investigation, Washington, D.C.

Law Enforcement News. Published bimonthly by John Jay College of Criminal Justice/CUNY, New York.

Notes

CHAPTER 1: EXCELLENCE OF CHARACTER

1. *The Ethics of Aristotle: The Nicomachean Ethics Translated*, 2.1, trans. J. A. K. Thomson (Hammondsworth, Middlesex, Eng.: Penguin Books, Ltd., 1953, 1958), p. 56.

2. J. O. Urmson, *Aristotle's Ethics* (Oxford: Basil Blackwell, Ltd., 1988), p. 25.

3. M. F. Burnyeat, "Aristotle on Learning to Be Good," in *Essays on Aristotle's Ethics*, ed. Amélie Oksenberg Rorty (Berkeley and Los Angeles, Calif.: University of California Press, 1980), p. 86.

4. *The Ethics of Aristotle*, 3.5, p. 91.

5. Urmson, *Aristotle's Ethics*, p. 26.

6. Immanuel Kant, *Education*, 1.4, 1.5, trans. Annette Churton (Ann Arbor, Mich.: University of Michigan Press, 1960), pp. 3, 4.

7. John Stuart Mill, "Moral Influences in Early Youth," in *Autobiography* (Indianapolis, Ind.: Bobbs-Merrill, 1957), p. 35.

8. Alasdair MacIntyre, *After Virtue* (Notre Dame, Ind.: University of Notre Dame Press, 1984), 2d ed., pp. 3, 4.

9. Urmson, *Aristotle's Ethics*, p. 22.

10. William Ker Muir, Jr., *Police: Streetcorner Politicians* (Chicago: University of Chicago Press, 1977), pp. 3, 4.

11. I am grateful to personnel from the Miami Police Department and other law enforcement agencies in Florida who have shared their knowledge of the River Cops with me. See Morris S. Thompson, "Miami Vice: Police Trafficking in Drugs," *Washington Post*, February 7, 1988; and "Miami Jury Convicts Two in Drug Ripoffs," *Washington Post*, February 10, 1988.

12. I appreciate the assistance of personnel from the New York Police Department in my review of the Buddy Boys. See Mike McAlary, *The Buddy Boys: When Good Cops Turn Bad* (New York: G. P. Putnam's Sons, 1987); CBS News Transcript of "60 Minutes," February 14, 1988, vol. 20, no. 22.

13. This position can be drawn from experience and is articulated by Aristotle in the *Nicomachean Ethics*. It is described in detail by J. O. Urmson in "Aristotle's Doctrine of the Mean," in *Essays on Aristotle's Ethics*, ed. Amélie Oksenberg Rorty, pp. 157–64.

14. Muir, *Police: Streetcorner Politicians*, p. 4.

15. Don L. Kooken, *Ethics in Police Service* (Springfield, Ill.: Charles C. Thomas, 1957), pp. 21, 23.

CHAPTER 2: THE MISSION OF POLICE

1. Aleksandr Solzhenitsyn, *The Gulag Archipelago*, 2 vols., trans. Thomas B. Whitney (New York: Harper and Row, 1973), p. 163.

279

2. Alexander Hamilton, James Madison, and John Jay, *The Federalist Papers*, No. 47, Introduction by Clinton Rossiter (New York: Mentor Books, 1961), p. 301.

3. Ibid., No. 51, p. 322.

4. Ibid., p. 324.

5. "Continentalist No. 1," July 12, 1781, in *The Papers of Alexander Hamilton*, ed. Harold C. Syrett et al., 26 vols. (New York, 1961–1979), vol. 2, p. 651.

6. Benjamin Rush, "An Address," Philadelphia, 1787, in *Principles and Acts of the Revolution in America*, ed. Hezekiah Niles (New York, 1876), p. 234.

7. Robert Goldwin, "Of Men and Angels: A Search for Morality in the Constitution," in *The Moral Foundations of the American Republic*, ed. Robert H. Horwitz (Charlottesville, Va.: University Press of Virginia, 1979), p. 11.

8. Ibid., pp. 4, 5, 12.

9. Charles E. Silberman, *Criminal Violence, Criminal Justice* (New York: Random House, 1978), pp. 4, 5.

10. Adam Walinsky, "What It's Like to Be in Hell," *New York Times*, December 4, 1987.

11. "Frontier Justice," *Wall Street Journal*, June 16, 1988.

12. Julia Preston, "Letter from Nicaragua: Deterioration Is Now a Way of Life," *Washington Post*, December 16, 1988.

13. Ibid.

14. Jack Anderson and Dale Van Atta, "Fearful Khomeni Turns on Own," *Washington Post*, December 19, 1988.

15. Solzhenitsyn, *The Gulag Archipelago*, p. 173.

16. O. W. Wilson, ed., *Parker on Police* (Springfield, Ill.: Charles C. Thomas, 1957), p. 13. Psychologist Stanton E. Samenow writes in *Inside the Criminal Mind* (New York: Time Books, 1984), pp. 204–5: "The criminal has long stood apart from the community, contemptuous of people who lived responsibly. . . . It is not his self-esteem that needs building. . . . Rather, he thinks of himself as an exceptional person who is superior to others."

17. Solzhenitsyn, *The Gulag Archipelago*, p. 307.

18. Ibid., p. 309.

19. Leon Radzinowicz and Joan King, *The Growth of Crime* (New York: Basic Books, Inc., 1977), p. 3.

20. "A Look at Crime Statistics," *Soviet Life* 8 (383) (August 1988), pp. 24, 25.

21. *Experiments in Police Improvement: A Progress Report* (Washington, D.C.: The Police Foundation, 1972), p. 9.

22. David A. Hansen, *Police Ethics* (Springfield, Ill.: Charles C. Thomas, 1973), p. xiii.

23. Lee W. Potts, *Responsible Police Administration: Issues and Approaches* (Tuscaloosa, Ala.: The University of Alabama Press, 1983), p. 8.

24. Ibid., pp. 8, 9.

25. August Vollmer, *The Police and Modern Society* (Berkeley, Calif.: Bureau of Public Administration, The University of California, 1936; reprinted College Park, Md.: McGrath Publishing Company, 1969), pp. 1, 3.

26. Silberman, *Criminal Violence, Criminal Justice*, pp. 203, 204.

27. Egon Bittner, *The Functions of the Police in Modern Society* (Rockville, Md.: National Institute of Mental Health Center for Studies of Crime and Delinquency, 1970), p. 7. See also my essay, "The Police: From Slaying Dragons to

Rescuing Cats," *FBI Law Enforcement Bulletin* 50 (11) (November 1981), pp. 16–19.

28. See, for example, Lawrence W. Sherman and Richard A. Berk, "The Minneapolis Domestic Violence Experiment," *Police Foundation Reports* (April 1984), pp. 1–8.

29. The President's Commission on Law Enforcement and Administration of Justice, *Task Force Report: The Police* (Washington, D.C.: U.S. Government Printing Office, 1967), p. 120.

30. Elijah Adlow, *Policemen and People* (Boston, Mass.: William P. Rochfort, 1947), p. 13.

31. Vollmer, *The Police and Modern Society*, p. 237.

32. Ibid., p. 81.

33. Joseph Story, *A Familiar Exposition of the Constitution of the United States* (Lake Bluff, Ill.: Regnery Gateway, Inc., 1986), p. 326.

34. Silberman, *Criminal Violence, Criminal Justice*, pp. 46, 47.

35. United States National Commission on Law Observance and Enforcement, *Report on Police*, No. 14 (Washington, D.C.: U.S. Government Printing Office, 1931), p. 17. This study is also known as the Wickersham Report, after the Commission's chairman.

36. Leonard V. Harrison, *Police Administration in Boston* (Cambridge, Mass.: Harvard University Press, 1934), pp. 28, 29.

37. William J. Bopp, *"O. W.": O. W. Wilson and the Search for a Police Profession* (Port Washington, N.Y.: Kennikat Press, 1977), pp. 138, 139.

CHAPTER 3: PUBLIC TRUST AND PROBITY

1. George Washington, "Farewell Address," in *A Collection of Orations from Homer to McKinley*, 25 vols., ed. Mayo W. Hazeltine (New York: P. F. Collier and Sons, 1902), vol. 6, pp. 2511, 2513.

2. Quoted in Philip Greven, *The Protestant Temperament: Patterns of Child-rearing, Religious Experience, and the Self in Early America* (New York: Alfred A. Knopf, Inc., 1977), p. 346.

3. B. C. Brymer, *Abraham Lincoln in Peoria, Illinois* (Peoria, Ill.: Edward J. Jacob, Printer, 1926), p. 103.

4. *The Mind of the Founder: Sources of the Political Thought of James Madison*, rev. ed., ed. Marvin Meyers (Hanover, N.H.: The University Press of New England, 1981), p. 158.

5. Dan Meyers, "Roofers Jury Hears Parade of Officials Get Cash," *Philadelphia Inquirer*, October 27, 1987.

6. Lynne Duke, "Operation Clean Sweep Net Snares Atlanta DEA Agent," *Washington Post*, March 13, 1988.

7. Jeff Barker, "Sen. Specter Calls for Appointment of Judges," *Philadelphia Inquirer*, March 21, 1988.

8. Howard Kurtz, "28 New York City Restaurant Inspectors Accused of Extortion," *Washington Post*, March 25, 1988.

9. Philip Shenon, "Enemy Within: Drug Money Is Corrupting the Enforcers," *New York Times*, April 11, 1988.

10. Robert E. Shalhope, *John Taylor of Caroline: Pastoral Republican* (Columbia, S.C.: University of South Carolina Press, 1980), p. 160.

11. John Adams to Mercy Warren, January 8, 1776, in *Warren-Adams Letters, Being Chiefly a Correspondence among John Adams and James Warren, 1743–1814*, 2 vols. (Boston, Mass.: The Massachusetts Historical Society, 1917–1925), vol. 1, pp. 201, 202.

12. Francis Hutcheson, *A System of Moral Philosophy in Three Books* (Glasgow: R. and A. Foulis, Printers to the University of Glasgow, 1755; reprint, New York: August M. Kelley, 1968), p. 285.

13. Ibid.

14. Ibid., p. 335.

15. Joanne Giza, "A Policeman's Lot," *Newsweek*, November 24, 1980, p. 31.

16. Ibid.

17. Forrest McDonald, *Novus Ordo Seclorum: The Intellectual Origins of the Constitution* (Lawrence, Kans.: The University Press of Kansas, 1985), p. 93.

18. Marvin Meyers, ed., *The Mind of the Founder: Sources of the Political Thought of James Madison*, p. xxix.

19. Alexander Hamilton, James Madison, and John Jay, *The Federalist Papers*, No. 49, Introduction by Clinton Rossiter (New York: Mentor Books, 1961), p. 315.

20. Albert A. Seedman and Peter Hellman, *Chief!* (New York: Avon Books, 1974), pp. 43, 44.

21. Elijah Adlow, *Policemen and People* (Boston, Mass.: William P. Rochfort, 1947), p. 71.

22. Ralph Lee Smith, *The Tarnished Badge* (New York: Arno Press, 1974), p. 227.

23. Seedman and Hellman, *Chief!*, p. 44.

24. Patrick V. Murphy and Thomas Plate, *Commissioner: A View from the Top of American Law Enforcement* (New York: Simon and Schuster, 1977), p. 184.

25. Thomas Hardy, *The Return of the Native* (New York: Washington Square Books, Inc., 1959), p. 34.

26. Cicero, *On Duties*, II, 12, 42; in *Cicero: On the Good Life*, trans. Michael Grant (Baltimore, Md.: Penguin Books, 1971), p. 142.

27. Xenophon, *Memoirs of Socrates*, II, 6, 39, in *Xenophon: Memoirs of Socrates and the Symposium*, trans. Hugh Tredennick (Baltimore, Md.: Penguin Books, 1970), p. 104.

28. James Madison to Ambrose Madison, October 11, 1787, in *The Papers of James Madison*, vol. 10, ed. Robert A. Rutland et al. (Chicago: University of Chicago Press, 1977), p. 192.

CHAPTER 4: DISCRETION

1. T. H. White, *The Once and Future King* (New York: Berkeley Books, 1958), p. 247.

2. Herman Goldstein, *Policing a Free Society* (Cambridge, Mass.: Ballinger Publishing Company, 1977), p. 107.

3. *Standards for Law Enforcement Agencies: The Standards Manual of the Law Enforcement Agency Accreditation Program* (Fairfax, Va.: Commission on Accreditation of Law Enforcement Agencies, Inc., 1984), pp. 1–1, 1–2.

4. Goldstein, *Policing a Free Society*, pp. 106, 107.

5. Philadelphia Police Study Task Force, *Philadelphia and Its Police: Toward a New Partnership* (Published by the City of Philadelphia, 1987), pp. 130, 131.

6. Kenneth Culp Davis, *Police Discretion* (St. Paul, Minn.: West Publishing Co., 1975), p. 171.

7. Ibid., p. 93.

8. Ibid., p. 65.

9. "New York Racial Tensions Run High since Verdict in Howard Beach Case," *Washington Post*, January 18, 1988.

10. Dick Dahl, "Mean Streets," *Twin Cities* (November 1984), pp. 69, 70.

11. Ibid., p. 61.

12. Ibid., pp. 61, 62.

13. "Police Probers Say Two Officials Gave False Data," *Washington Post*, January 17, 1988.

14. "Strengthen Kidnap Laws," *News Tribune*, Woodbridge, N.J., January 15, 1988.

15. Patricia M. Wald, "The Unreasonableness Test for Fourth Amendment Searches," *Criminal Justice Ethics* (91) (Winter/Spring 1985), p. 2.

16. Ibid.

17. Ibid.

18. United States v. Place, 462 U.S. 696, 703 103 S.Ct. 2637, 2642 77 L.Ed.2d 110, 118.

19. Wald, "The Unreasonable Reasonableness Test for Fourth Amendment Searches," p. 90.

20. Howard Cohen, "Overstepping Police Authority," *Criminal Justice Ethics* 6(2) (Summer/Fall 1987), p. 52.

21. Ibid.

22. Ibid., pp. 52, 53; taken from George Kirkham, *Signal Zero*, pp. 95–97.

23. Ibid., p. 53.

24. Ibid., p. 54.

25. Ibid., p. 59.

26. Roger Wertheimer, "Regulating Police Use of Deadly Force," in *Ethics, Public Policy, and Criminal Justice*, ed. Frederick Elliston and Norman Bowie (Cambridge, Mass.: Oelgeschlager, Gunn, and Hain, Publishers, Inc., 1982), p. 97.

27. The National Commission on Law Observance and Enforcement, *Report on Lawlessness in Law Enforcement* (Washington, D.C.: U.S. Government Printing Office, 1931), p. 5.

28. Wertheimer, "Regulating Police Use of Deadly Force," p. 95.

29. Ibid., p. 98.

30. Ibid., p. 96.

31. Ibid., p. 99.

32. Ibid., p. 107.

33. Ibid.

34. *Standards for Law Enforcement Agencies: The Standards Manual of the Law Enforcement Agency Accreditation Program*, section 1.3.3, p. 1–2.

35. Wertheimer, "Regulating Police Use of Deadly Force," p. 109.

36. "NW Sex Assaults Raise Question: Should Police Warn Area Residents?" *Washington Post*, January 18, 1988.

37. Ibid.

38. Ibid.

CHAPTER 5: CORRUPTION FOR PROFIT

1. Robert Bolt, *A Man for All Seasons* (New York: Vintage Books, 1962), p. 4.

2. *The Ethics of Aristotle: The Nicomachean Ethics Translated*, 4.7, trans. J. A. K. Thomson (Hammondsworth, Middlesex, Eng.: Penguin Books, 1958), p. 132.

3. *Virtue's Friend: Essays on Subjects Connected with the Duty and Happiness of Mankind*, 3d. ed., vol. 1 (Ormskirk, Lancashire, Eng.: R. Cocker, 1816), p. 114.

4. *Moral Issues in Police Work*, ed. Frederick A. Elliston and Michael Feldberg (Totowa, N.J.: Rowman and Allenheld, 1985), p. 251.

5. Iris Murdoch, *The Sovereignty of Good* (New York: Schocken Books, 1971), p. 59.

6. CBS News, "60 Minutes," November 22, 1987, vol. 20, no. 10, p. 10.

7. CBS News, "60 Minutes," February 14, 1988, vol. 20, no. 22, pp. 3, 4, 5.

8. Ralph Lee Smith, *The Tarnished Badge* (New York: Arno Press, 1974), pp. 191, 192.

9. Ibid., pp. 193, 194.

10. Ibid., p. 194.

11. Ibid., p. 212.

12. Jerry Knight, "Give Us that Old-Fashioned 'Honest Graft,'" *Washington Post*, June 21, 1988.

13. Arthur Niederhoffer, *Behind the Shield: The Police in Urban Society* (Garden City, N.Y.: Doubleday Company, Inc., 1969), p. 70.

14. Ibid. (Quoting from Mort Stern, "What Makes a Policeman Go Wrong," in *Journal of Criminal Law, Criminology, and Police Science* 53 [March 1962], pp. 98–99.)

15. Ibid., p. 97. (Quoting from William A. Westley, "The Police: A Sociological Study of Law, Custom, and Morality," Dissertation, p. ii. Later published as *Violence and the Police: A Sociological Study of Law, Custom, and Morality* [Cambridge, Mass.: MIT Press, 1970].)

16. Ibid., pp. 98, 99.

17. Julian B. Roebuck and Thomas Barker, "A Typology of Police Corruption," in *Social Problems* 21 (1974), p. 425. See also Barker and Roebuck, *An Empirical Typology of Police Corruption: A Study of Organizational Deviance* (Springfield, Ill.: Charles C. Thomas, 1974).

18. Mark Pogrebin and Burton Atkins, "Probable Causes for Police Corruption: Some Theories," in *Police and Law Enforcement*, vol. 3, ed. Robert J. Homant and Daniel B. Kennedy (New York: AMS Press, Inc., 1985), p. 215.

Pogrebin and Atkins summarize the view of Wallace Sayre and Herbert Kaufman, in *Governing New York City: Politics in the Metropolis*, and the concern of the 1967 President's Commission on Law Enforcement and Administration of Justice.

19. Ibid.

20. Ibid., p. 212.

21. Ibid.

22. Morris S. Thompson, "Miami Vice: Police Trafficking in Drugs," *Washington Post*, February 7, 1988.

23. "Miami Jury Convicts Two in Drug Ripoffs," *Washington Post*, February 10, 1988.

24. Thompson, "Miami Vice."

25. *Virtue's Friend*, pp. 15, 17, 18.

26. Michael Feldberg, "Gratuities, Corruption, and the Democratic Ethos of Policing: The Case of the Free Cup of Coffee," in *Moral Issues in Police Work*, p. 267.

27. Patrick V. Murphy and Thomas Plate, *Commissioner: A View from the Top of American Law Enforcement* (New York: Simon and Schuster, 1977), p. 213.

28. Feldberg, "Gratuities, Corruption, and the Democratic Ethos of Policing," p. 276; referring to William K. Muir, Jr., *Police: Streetcorner Politicians*, chap. 3 (Chicago: University of Chicago Press, 1977).

29. Lawrence W. Sherman, "Becoming Bent," in *Moral Issues in Police Work*, pp. 259, 260; referring to Ellwyn R. Stoddard, " 'The Informal Code' of Police Deviancy: A Group Approach to 'Blue-Coat Crime,' " *Journal of Criminal Law, Criminology, and Police Science* 59(2) (1968).

30. New York City Commission to Investigate Allegations of Police Corruption and the City's Anti-Corruption Procedures, *The Knapp Commission Report on Police Corruption* (New York: George Braziller, 1972), p. 4.

31. Herman Goldstein, *Policing in a Free Society* (Cambridge, Mass.: Ballinger Publishing Company, 1977), pp. 193, 194; quoting the *Knapp Commission Report*, p. 65.

32. CBS News, "60 Minutes," February 14, 1988, pp. 4, 5.

33. Leonard Schecter with William Phillips, *On the Pad: The Underworld and Its Corrupt Police, Confessions of a Cop on the Take* (New York: G. P. Putnam's Sons, 1973), p. 278.

34. Albert A. Seedman and Peter Hellman, *Chief!* (New York: Avon Books, 1974), p. 175.

35. Patrick V. Murphy, "Spotlight," *National Centurion* 1 (1983), p. 57.

CHAPTER 6: AUTHORITY AND REFORM

1. *Selected Writings of Lord Acton*, in vol. 3: *Essays in Religion, Politics, and Morality*, ed. J. Rufus Fears (Indianapolis, Ind.: Liberty Classics, 1985), p. 570.

2. James F. Richardson, "Berlin Police in the Weimar Republic: A Comparison with Police Forces in the Cities of the United States," in *Police Forces in History*, ed. George L. Mosse (London: Sage Publications, 1975), p. 86.

3. *The Police Community*, ed. Jack Goldsmith and Sharon S. Goldsmith (Pacific Palisades, Calif.: Palisades Publishers, 1974), p. 7.

4. Richard H. Ward and Robert McCormack, *An Anti-Corruption Manual for Administrators in Law Enforcement* (New York: The John Jay Press, 1979), pp. 4, 5.

5. *The Autobiography of Lincoln Steffans* (San Diego, Calif.: Harcourt Brace Jovanovich, 1968), pp. 280, 281.

6. Ward and McCormack, *An Anti-Corruption Manual*, p. 5.

7. Ibid., pp. 79, 80.

8. Herman Goldstein, *Police Corruption: A Perspective on Its Nature and Control* (Washington, D.C.: The Police Foundation, 1975), p. i.

9. Ibid., p. 52.

10. "You Need to Know," *Baltimore Police Department Newsletter*, February 7, 1973.

11. Donald C. Pomerleau, "Whistle Blown on Police Payoffs," in *Baltimore Police Department Newsletter*, October 31, 1973; reprinted with permission of the *Baltimore Sun*.

12. Herman Goldstein, *Police Corruption*, p. 30.

13. Ward and McCormack, *An Anti-Corruption Manual*, p. 9.

14. Ibid., p. 51.

15. Ibid., p. 67.

16. William K. Stevens, "Gains by Philadelphia Police Are Seen," *New York Times*, January 2, 1988.

17. "Ex-Narcotics Unit Officers Indicted in Philadelphia," *Washington Post*, July 20, 1988.

18. Stevens, "Gains by Philadelphia Police Are Seen," p. 9.

19. Ibid.

20. Christopher Hepp, "Residents and Cops: Partners against Crime," *Philadelphia Inquirer*, February 3, 1988.

21. Ibid.

22. Stevens, "Gains by Philadelphia Police Are Seen," p. 9.

23. Robert C. Wadman and Robert K. Olson, *A Miscarriage of Justice: Police Theory in America*, chap. 1, p. 12.

24. Ibid., chap. 4, p. 6.

25. Ibid., chap. 8, pp. 13, 14.

CHAPTER 7: LEADERSHIP AND CHARACTER

1. Booker T. Washington, *Up from Slavery* (New York: Viking Penguin, Inc., 1986), pp. 99, 100.

2. Hillary Robinette, *Burnout in Blue: Managing the Police Marginal Performer* (New York: Praeger Publishers, 1987), p. 4. (Quoting Lance Morrow, "The Burnout of Almost Everyone," *Time*, September 21, 1981.)

3. Ibid., p. 5.

4. David Maraniss, "Death in the County Jail," *Washington Post*, January 10, 1988.

5. Tom L. Beauchamp, "The Justification of Reverse Discrimination," in *Moral Issues in Business*, 3d. ed., ed. Vincent Barry (Belmont, Calif.: Wadsworth Publishing Company, 1986), p. 391.

6. Ibid., p. 394.

7. Ibid., p. 391.

8. William T. Blackstone, "Reverse Discrimination and Compensatory Justice," in *Moral Issues in Business*, ed. Vincent Barry, p. 399.

9. Civil Rights Act, Title VII, Sec. 703, 42 U.S. Code 2000e–2(a).

10. American Enterprise Institute, "A Conversation with the Reverend Jesse Jackson: The Quest for Economic and Educational Parity," *AEI Studies* 209 (1978), p. 4.

11. Terry Eastland and William J. Bennett, *Counting by Race: Equality from the Founding Fathers to Bakke and Weber* (New York: Basic Books, Inc., 1979), p. 136.

12. Carl Cohen, "Why Racial Preference Is Illegal and Immoral," *Commentary* (June 1979), p. 42.

13. *Atlanta Journal and Constitution*, September 22, 1974.

14. See Thomas Nagel, "Equal Treatment and Compensatory Discrimination," *Philosophy and Public Affairs* 2 (Summer 1973), pp. 348–63.

15. 110 *Congressional Record*, p. 1518.

16. Ibid., p. 1540.

17. Ibid., p. 7213.

18. United Steelworkers v. Weber, 443 U.S. 193,208 99 S.Ct. 2721,2730 61 L.ed. 2d 480, 492.

19. Harvey C. Mansfield, Jr., "The Underhandedness of Affirmative Action," *National Review*, May 4, 1984, p. 28.

20. Ibid., p. 26.

21. Ibid., p. 30.

22. DeFunis v. Odegaard, 416 U.S. 312,334,336–337 94 S.Ct. 1704,1715 40 L.Ed. 2d 164,180, Douglas dissenting.

23. Thomas Sowell, "Are Quotas Good for Blacks?" *Commentary* (June 1978), p. 50.

24. Thomas Short, "A 'New Racism' on Campus?" *Commentary* (August 1988), p. 50.

25. Shelley v. Kraemer, 334 U.S. 1, 21–23 68 S.Ct. 836,846 92 L.Ed. 2d 1161, 1185.

26. Cohen, "Why Racial Preference Is Illegal and Immoral," p. 44.

27. "U.S. Remains Racist, Survey Respondents Say," Greenville, South Carolina *News*, August 8, 1988.

28. Joseph Califano, "Tough Talk for Democrats," *New York Times Magazine*, January 8, 1989, p. 29.

29. Charles Murray, "Affirmative Racism: How Preferential Treatment Works against Blacks," *New Republic*, December 31, 1984, p. 22.

30. Janoviak v. Corporate City of South Bend, 750 F.2d 557, 561 (7th Cir. 1984).

31. Williams v. City of New Orleans, 729 F.2d 1554, 1565 (5th Cir. 1984), Judge Gee concurring.

32. United States v. Paradise, 480 U.S. 149,153 107 S.Ct. 1053 94 L.Ed. 2d 203,212.

33. Johnson v. Transportation Agency, Santa Clara County, 480 U.S. 616,630 107 S.Ct. 1442,1451 94 L.Ed. 2d 615, 629.

34. Wygant v. Jackson Board of Education, 476 U.S. 267,274 106 S.Ct. 1842, 1848 90 L.Ed. 2d 260,269,270.

35. Davis v. City of Dallas, 777 F.2d 205,216,225 (5th Cir. 1985). The Court cited Spurlock, 475 F.2d at 219 and Kinsey, 557 F.2d at 837.

36. "A Disgrace to the FBI," *Washington Post*, January 26, 1988.

37. Ibid.

38. Ibid.

39. Ibid.

40. Eloize Salholz with Ned Zeman, "Going after Detroit's Rogue Cops," *Newsweek*, September 5, 1988, p. 37.

41. David C. Couper, *How to Rate Your Local Police* (Washington, D.C.: Police Executive Research Forum, 1983), p. 15.

42. Ibid. See also Peter B. Block and Deborah Anderson, *Policewomen on Patrol, Final Report* (Washington, D.C.: The Police Foundation, 1974).

43. *Standards for Law Enforcement Agencies: The Standards Manual of the Law Enforcement Agency Accreditation Program* (Fairfax, Va.: Commission on Accreditation for Law Enforcement Agencies, Inc., 1984), pp. 31-1 to 32-9.

44. U.S. Department of Labor, Employment Standards Administration, WH Publication 1462, September 1988.

45. Los Angeles Police Department, *Police Officer Recruitment Plan*, prepared by the Personnel Department of the Police and Fire Selection Division, June 1987.

46. Quoted by Ordway P. Burden, "Recruiting Police from College," *FBI Law Enforcement Bulletin* (March 1988), pp. 1, 2.

47. Ibid., p. 2.

48. Ibid.

49. Ibid.

Chapter 8: Illegal Narcotics Issues

1. *The Papers of James Madison*, vol. 10, ed. Robert A. Rutland et al. (Chicago: University of Chicago Press, 1975), p. 10.

2. See, for example, Eric W. Single, "The Impact of Marijuana Decriminalization," in *Research Advances in Alcohol and Drug Problems*, vol. 6 (New York: Plenum, 1981), p. 406.

3. Lee P. Brown, "Strategies for Dealing with Crack Houses," *FBI Law Enforcement Bulletin* 57(6) (June 1988), p. 6.

4. Timothy Egan, "U.S. Agents and Drug Fight in Seattle," *New York Times*, July 15, 1988.

5. "The Legalization of Drugs" (A Policy Paper for the Police Executive Research Forum, Washington, D.C., June 6, 1988), p. 3.

6. Peter Kerr, "The Unspeakable Is Debated: Should Drugs Be Legalized?" *New York Times*, May 15, 1988.

7. *Progress Report*, National Drug Policy Board (Washington, D.C., July 1988), p. 2; citing the *National High School Senior Survey: Monitoring the Future*, conducted for the National Institute on Drug Abuse by the Institute for Social Research, University of Michigan, January 1988, tables 15 and 9.

8. Peter Kerr, "More People Found Opposing Drugs," *New York Times*, July 14, 1988.

9. George Will, "The Good Prohibition," *Newsweek*, June 20, 1988, p. 74.

10. Ovid Demaris, *The Boardwalk Jungle* (New York: Bantam Books, 1986), pp. x–xii.

CHAPTER 9: FUNDAMENTALS OF CHARACTER

1. J. O. Urmson, *Aristotle's Ethics* (Oxford: Basil Blackwell Ltd., 1988), p. 22.

2. Robert C. Wadman, Monroe J. Paxman, and Marion T. Bentley, *Law Enforcement Supervision: A Case Study Approach* (St. Paul, Minn.: West Publishing Co., 1975), pp. 34, 35.

3. Ibid., p. 36.

4. William James, *Psychology: The Briefer Course*, ed. Gordon Allport (New York: Harper and Brothers, 1961), p. 11. James's essay on "Habit" is also reprinted in *The Writings of William James*, ed. John J. McDermott (Chicago: University of Chicago Press, 1978), pp. 9–21.

5. Ibid.

6. Lawrence W. Sherman, *Ethics in Criminal Justice Education* (Hastings-on-Hudson, N.Y.: The Hastings Center, 1982), p. 17.

7. Ibid., p. 3.

8. Lawrence W. Sherman and the National Advisory Commission on Higher Education for Police Officers, *The Quality of Police Education* (San Francisco, Calif.: Jossey-Bass Publishers, 1978), p. 89.

9. Sherman, *Ethics in Criminal Justice Education*, pp. 17, 18.

10. Ibid., pp. 20, 21.

11. Immanuel Kant, *The Metaphysical Elements of Justice* (Indianapolis, Ind.: Bobbs-Merrill Company, Inc., 1965), p. 36.

12. Matthew Lipman, *Philosophy Goes to School* (Philadelphia: Temple University Press, 1988), p. 69.

13. Sherman, *Ethics in Criminal Justice Education*, pp. 3, 26, and 32.

14. Carol Schlagheck, "Ida Man Helps Ohio Patrolman," Ida, Ohio *Evening News*, February 24, 1988.

15. Urmson, *Aristotle's Ethics*, p. 77.

16. Ibid., pp. 77, 78.

17. Harper Lee, *To Kill a Mockingbird* (New York: Fawcett Popular Library, 1962), p. 34.

18. Dorothy Uhnak, *Policewoman* (South Yarmouth, Mass.: John Curley and Associates, Inc., 1963), pp. 20–22, 30.

CHAPTER 10: MORAL PROBLEMS IN TRAINING

1. William James, *Psychology, The Briefer Course*, ed. Gordon Allport (New York: Harper and Brothers, 1961), pp. 12–15.

2. Brand Blanshard, *Reason and Goodness* (London: George Allen and Unwin Ltd., 1966), p. 417, 418.

3. James Boswell, from the conversation of June 13, 1784, in *Boswell's Life of Johnson*, ed. Anne H. Ehrenpreis and Irwin Ehrenpreis (New York: Washington Square Press, Inc., 1965), p. 469.

4. "Police Blame ABC for Abrupt Raid," *New York Times,* April 11, 1988.

5. Malachi L. Harney and John C. Cross, *The Narcotic Officer's Notebook* (Springfield, Ill.: Charles C. Thomas, 1961), p. 135.

6. Ibid., p. 150.

7. *ABSCAM Ethics: Moral Issues and Deception in Law Enforcement,* ed. Gerald M. Kaplan (Cambridge, Mass.: Ballinger Publishing Company, 1983), p. v.

8. Malachi L. Harney and John C. Cross, *The Informer in Law Enforcement* (Springfield, Ill.: Charles C. Thomas, 1968), p. vii, viii, 5, and 12.

9. Ibid., p. 20.

10. Irwin B. Nathan, "ABSCAM: A Fair and Effective Method for Fighting Public Corruption," in *ABSCAM Ethics,* p. 5.

11. Sissela Bok, *Lying* (New York: Pantheon, 1978), p. 18.

12. Sanford Levinson, "Under Cover: The Hidden Costs of Infiltration," in *ABSCAM Ethics,* pp. 45, 58, and 55.

13. Mark H. Moore, "Invisible Offenses: A Challenge to Minimally Intrusive Law Enforcement," in *ABSCAM Ethics,* p. 17.

14. Harney and Cross, *The Narcotic Officer's Notebook,* p. 152.

15. Ibid., p. 242.

16. William Shakespeare, *Othello, The Moor of Venice,* I, iii, ed. Marc Eccles (New York: Appleton-Century-Crofts, Inc., 1946), p. 24.

17. Larry Lewis, "An Officer's Nightmare: Drug Role Became Reality," *Philadelphia Inquirer,* March 21, 1988.

18. Jonathan Rubinstein, *City Police* (New York: Farrar, Straus and Giroux, 1973), p. 207.

19. Gary T. Marx, *Undercover: Police Surveillance in America* (Berkeley and Los Angeles, Calif.: University of California Press, 1988), p. 107.

20. Lon L. Fuller, *The Morality of Law* (New Haven, Conn.: Yale University Press, 1964, reprinted 1975), p. 159.

21. *The Ethics of Aristotle, The Nicomachean Ethics Translated,* 10.3, trans. J. A. K. Thomson (Hammondsworth, Middlesex, Eng.: Penguin Books Ltd., 1953, reprinted 1958), p. 265.

22. William Ker Muir, Jr., *Police: Streetcorner Politicians* (Chicago: University of Chicago Press, 1977), p. 191.

23. *The Ethics of Aristotle, The Nicomachean Ethics Translated,* 3.7, pp. 96, 97.

CHAPTER 11: TRAGEDY AND CORRUPTION

1. Immanuel Kant, *Foundations of the Metaphysics of Morals* (New York: The Bobbs-Merrill Company, Inc., 1959), pp. 46, 47.

2. Albert Camus, *Resistance, Rebellion, and Death,* trans. Justin O'Brien (New York: Vintage Books, 1974), p. 5.

3. Bertolt Brecht, *Galileo,* English version by Charles Laughton (New York: Grove Press, 1966), p. 110.

4. Walter Lippmann, *The Public Philosophy* (New York: Mentor Books, 1955), p. 27.

5. *Crimes Code of Pennsylvania,* sections 502, 503 (USA: Gould Publications, 1985), pp. 19, 20.

6. David Maraniss, "Death of a Reputed Vigilante," *Washington Post*, September 21, 1986.

7. Joan Fleischman, "Ex-cop: 'I enjoyed shooting dealers,' " *Miami Herald*, April 14, 1988.

8. William Safire, "Stalker's Last Case," *New York Times*, June 30, 1986. Safire was writing in the context of his analysis of the "Stalker Affair," so named by Deputy Chief Constable of the Greater Manchester Police John Stalker in describing his investigation of alleged abuses of authority and power by the Royal Ulster Constabulary. The case is much more complex and murky than popular published accounts make it out to be, but Safire's statement of principle is nonetheless correct.

9. Robert Bolt, *A Man For All Seasons* (New York: Vintage Books, 1962), p. 43.

10. Carl B. Klockars, "The Dirty Harry Problem," in *Moral Issues in Police Work*, ed. Frederick A. Elliston and Michael Feldberg (Totowa, N.J.: Rowman and Allenheld, 1985), pp. 55–62.

11. See Edmund Burke, *Reflections on the French Revolution and Other Essays* (New York: E. P. Dutton and Company, 1951), p. 60.

12. Reinhold Niebuhr, *The Irony of American History* (New York: Charles Scribner's Sons, 1952), pp. vii, viii, 5.

CHAPTER 12: DEATH, DEADLY FORCE, GUILT

1. C. S. Lewis, *A Grief Observed*, Afterword by Chad Walsh (New York: Bantam Books, 1976), p. 16.

CHAPTER 13: TAKING OUR LIVES SERIOUSLY

1. Paul H. Appleby, *Morality and Administration in Democratic Government* (Baton Rouge, La.: Louisiana State University Press, 1952), pp. 67, 68.

2. Walter Lippmann, "A Theory about Corruption," in *Political Corruption: Readings in Comparative Analysis*, ed. Arnold J. Heidenheimer (New York: Holt, Rinehart and Winston, Inc., 1970), pp. 296, 297.

3. Lon M. Fuller, *The Morality of Law* (New Haven, Conn.: Yale University Press, 1964, reprinted 1975), p. 5.

4. Ibid., p. 8.

CHAPTER 14: FATALISM, MICROCOSMS, AND THERAPEUTIC REDUCTIONS

1. Immanuel Kant, *Lectures on Ethics*, trans. Louis Infield (New York: Harper Torchbooks, 1963), p. 126.

2. 356 U.S. 86 Albert L. TROP, Petitioner v. John Foster DULLES, as Secretary of State of the United States and United States Department of State.

No. 70. Reargued October 28, 29, 1957. Decided March 31, 1958. (*Supreme Court Reporter* [St. Paul, Minn.: West Publishing Co., 1959], vol. 78, p. 590.)

3. Howard S. Cohen and Michael Feldberg, *Power and Restraint: The Moral Dimension of Police Work* (New York: Praeger, 1991), p. 43.

4. Edwin J. Delattre and Scott R. Stripling, "Police Integrity and Public Expectations," *The Public Interest Law Review* (Durham, N.C.: Carolina Academic Press for the National Legal Center for the Public Interest, 1992), pp. 47–62.

5. Selwyn Raab, "Report Says Police Tolerate Corruption," *New York Times,* January 2, 1994.

6. Francis E. Rourke, "Urbanism and American Democracy," *Ethics,* vol. 74, no. 4 (July 1964), p. 264.

7. Ibid., p. 265, citing Josiah Strong, *The Twentieth Century City* (New York, 1898), pp. 101, 102.

8. "Texts of Letters between Clinton and Baird," *New York Times,* January 23, 1993.

9. "Baird's Withdrawal: What Some Americans Had to Say," *Atlanta Journal/Constitution,* January 23, 1993.

10. Steve Terrell, "Country's Violent Crimes Rate Ranks High," *Santa Fe New Mexican,* September 16, 1990.

11. "A Scandal in the Cloister," *Newsweek,* July 23, 1990, p. 34.

12. Carol Innerst, " 'Sensitivity' Is Buzzword at Colleges," *Washington Times,* August 29, 1990.

13. "Feminist Woes," *Crisis,* September 1990, p. 4.

14. David Streitfeld, "The Addiction Habit," *Washington Post,* August 28, 1990.

15. Ibid., citing the *Los Angeles Times.*

16. "Excerpts from Durenberger's Senate Testimony," *New York Times,* June 14, 1990.

17. M. A. J. McKenna, "Experts to Debate Measures for Getting Moms off Drugs," *Boston Herald,* September 30, 1990.

18. Don Feder, "Sex Addicts: Newest Victims," *Boston Herald,* June 18, 1990.

19. David Gelman et al., "The Mind of the Rapist," *Newsweek,* July 23, 1990, p. 46.

20. Trish Hall, "Spas to Massage Both Body and Mind," *New York Times,* July 11, 1990.

21. Edward Silver, "This Alter Ego Helps Scripts Be Psychologically Sound," *New York Times,* July 1, 1990.

22. Juan Williams, "Hard Time for Rayful Edmond," *Washington Post Magazine,* June 24, 1990, p. 20.

23. California Task Force to Promote Self-Esteem and Personal and Social Responsibility, *Toward A State of Esteem* (Sacramento: California State Department of Education, 1990), pp. vii, 2.

24. Ibid., pp. 7, 10.

25. Ibid., pp. 22, 23.

26. Ibid., p. 27.

27. From the National Assessment of Educational Progress, cited by Chester E. Finn, Jr., "Narcissus Goes to School," *Commentary,* June 1990, p. 43.

28. From the University of Michigan's Institute for Social Research, ibid.

29. Gerald J. Pine and Asa G. Hilliard III, "Rx for Racism: Imperatives for America's Schools," *Phi Delta Kappan*, April 1990, p. 595.

30. Ibid.

31. Eleanor Clift, "Peccadillo Politics and the New Rules of Conduct," *Newsweek*, April 9, 1990, p. 21.

32. Ze'ev Chafets, "The Tragedy of Detroit," *New York Times Magazine*, July 29, 1990, p. 50.

33. Jane De Hart-Mathews, "The New Feminism and the Dynamics of Social Change," *Women's America*, ed. Linda K. Kerber and Jane De Hart-Mathews (New York: Oxford University Press, 1987), p. 451.

34. Douglas Martin, "They Are Gay, and Asking God to Save Them," *New York Times*, July 21, 1990.

35. Linda Hayes Tischler, "Self-Help's Hottest Guru," *Boston Herald*, August 13, 1990.

36. Charles Krauthammer, "Defining Deviancy Up," Bradley Lecture, American Enterprise Institute for Public Policy Research, Washington, D.C., September 13, 1993.

37. Wilhelm Reich, *The Mass Psychology of Fascism*, trans. Theodore P. Wolfe (New York: Orgone Institute Press, 1946), 3d ed., p. 51.

38. Daniel Patrick Moynihan, "Defining Deviancy Down," *American Scholar*, vol. 62, no. 1 (Winter 1993), pp. 17–30.

39. Krauthammer, "Defining Deviancy Up."

40. Herbert D. Kleicker, "On Current Approaches to Drug Abuse—Progress, Problems, Proposals," *New England Journal of Medicine*, February 3, 1994, p. 362.

41. *American with Disabilities Act: Policy Guide* (Washington: Bureau of National Affairs, 1991), p. 19.

42. See Shelby Steele, *The Content of Our Character* (New York: St. Martin's Press, 1990), p. 74, quoting from Ellison's novel, *Invisible Man*.

43. Derald Wing Sue and David Sue, *Counseling the Culturally Different* (New York: John Wiley and Sons, 2d ed., 1991), p. 113.

44. Ibid., p. 117.

45. U.S. Code Title 20—Education; Chapter 26–Support and Scholarship in Humanities and Arts; Museum Services; Subchapter 1—National Foundation in the Arts and Humanities; Sec. 951 (Sec. 2), Congressional Declaration of Purpose.

CHAPTER 15: ETHICAL IDEALS, YOUTH VIOLENCE, AND GANG ENFORCEMENT

1. John Silber, *Straight Shooting: What's Wrong with America and How to Fix It* (New York: Harper & Row, Publishers, 1989), p. 75.

2. Josh Barbancl, "More Students Are Violent at Young Age," *New York Times*, December 4, 1993.

3. Larry Rohter, "Florida Governments Move to Get Teen-Ager Curfews," *New York Times*, December 23, 1993.

4. William J. Bennett, "Getting Used to Decadence: The Spirit of Democ-

racy in Modern America," Keynote address, the Heritage Foundation's twentieth anniversary, Washington, D.C., December 7, 1993.

5. Connie Fletcher, *What Cops Know* (New York: Villard Books, 1991), p. 21.

6. "Should Crime Be Color Blind? Mayors Urge Removal of Race Data from Crime Stats." *Law Enforcement News*, December 15, 1993, pp. 1, 10.

7. As William J. Bennett has written: "During last year's Los Angeles riots, Damian Williams and Henry Watson were filmed pulling an innocent man out of a truck, crushing his skull with a brick and doing a victory dance over his fallen body. Their lawyers then built a *successful* legal defense on the proposition that people cannot be held accountable for getting caught up in mob violence. When the trial was over and these men were found not guilty on most counts, the sound you heard throughout the land was relief. . . . We are losing a once-reliable sense of civic and moral outrage." "Commuter Massacre, Our Warning," *Wall Street Journal*, December 10, 1993.

8. Sidney J. Harris, "Gangs Make Martyrs of Issues," in Robert K. Jackson and Wesley D. McBride, *Understanding Street Gangs* (Placerville, California: Custom Publishing Company, 1990), p. 1.

9. Ibid., p. 11.

10. C. S. Lewis, *The Abolition of Man* (New York: Macmillan, 1947), p. 24.

11. ATF FACTS, Bureau of Alcohol, Tobacco, and Firearms, Washington, D.C., 1 (800) 726-7070 or (202) 927-8329.

12. See, for example, American University's packet, *Conflict Resolution*, "Anatomy of Confrontation," p. 4.

13. Evan Simpson, "Social Norms and Aberrations: Violence and Some Related Facts," *Ethics*, vol. 81, no. 1 (October 1970), p. 29.

14. Kathryn Girard, Janet Rifkin, and Annette Townley, *Peaceful Persuasion: A Guide to Creating Mediation Resolution Programs on College Campuses* (Amherst, Mass.: The Mediation Project at the University of Massachusetts/Amherst of the National Institute for Dispute Resolution, 1985), p. 7.

15. Ibid., p. 6.

16. Program on Negotiation at Harvard Law School, "Increasing HR Effectiveness: New HR Leadership Strategies for Managing Organizational Issues and Disputes," An Inter-University Consortium, Harvard University, MIT, Tufts University, October 15–17, 1990; April 29–May 1, 1991, p. 6.

17. Jacques Barzun, *Begin Here: The Forgotten Conditions of Teaching and Learning* (Chicago: University of Chicago Press, 1992), p. 14.

18. I am hopeful that the Police Executive Research Forum [PERF] projects on gangs and organized crime conspiracies, funded for two years late in 1993 by the National Institute of Justice and the Bureau of Justice Assistance, will prove valuable to police and sheriffs, legislators, and law enforcement agencies. PERF describes the projects as follows:

> With funding from the National Institute of Justice, PERF is conducting a 24-month project to identify the relationships between traditional and newly emerging organized crime groups and youth gangs. The study will include an extensive review of the literature; a national mail survey to identify police perceptions of the nature of criminal group relationships; structured interviews regarding the nature of links between various crime groups with law enforcement and others in two cities impacted

by chronic gang problems; and field studies consisting of interviews with gang members about the nature of criminal gangs, their structure and changes over time, such as their possible transition into groups that more closely resemble traditional organized crime. [Staff Contact: Deborah Lamm Weisel, (312) 413-7445.]

PERF has joined with COSMOS Corporation, a private sector think-tank, to develop a comprehensive problem-oriented approach to addressing the chronic gang problems that plague urban areas. The comprehensive strategy will be flexible enough to allow each locality to tailor the approach to its needs and conditions. Funded by the Bureau of Justice Assistance, the project will be divided into four separate stages. STAGE I will consist of a national assessment of gang problems and local responses throughout the United States. STAGE II will focus on developing a problem-solving model that combines enforcement, prevention, and education. The model will provide analysis guidelines for each site to use to determine the program mix that best fits local conditions and gang problems. STAGE III will consist of training and technical assistance. The PERF/COSMOS team will develop training for police and other practitioners to assess their communities' needs and the nature of their own gang problems and to implement this approach in their communities. In STAGE IV, PERF and COSMOS will develop a technical assistance implementation plan and provide initial assistance to BJA-selected demonstration sites. [Staff Contact: John Stedman.]

[See Police Executive Research Forum, "Active Projects," December 1993. PERF is located at 2300 M Street, N.W., Suite 910, Washington, D.C. 20037; telephone (202) 466-7820; FAX (202) 466-7826.]

Such projects may advance knowledge *and* draw police into closer association regionally and nationally. If they succeed in doing so, they will help to improve policing generally, and not only in gang enforcement.

Index

About the Author

EDWIN J. DELATTRE of Boston University is professor of education and dean of the School of Education and professor of philosophy, College of Liberal Arts. He is an adjunct scholar of the American Enterprise Institute for Public Policy Research in Washington, D.C., and president emeritus of St. John's College, Annapolis, Maryland, and Santa Fe, New Mexico.

He was president of St. John's College in Annapolis and Santa Fe from 1980 to 1986; director of the National Humanities Faculty from 1976 to 1980; and professor of philosophy at the University of Toledo from 1968 to 1976. Dr. Delattre received a B.A. in philosophy from the University of Virginia and a Ph.D. in philosophy from the University of Texas.

He is former chairman of the National Advisory Board of the Fund for the Improvement of Postsecondary Education; a member of the National Council of the National Endowment for the Humanities and former vice-chairman of the council; a member of the Board of Trustees of Converse College, of the Advisory Council of the Heritage Foundation's Salvatori Center for Academic Leadership, and of the Board of Directors of Quaker Chemical Corporation. He is a frequent lecturer at the FBI Academy in Quantico, Virginia, and at police academies throughout the country.

Dr. Delattre is the author of two books, *Education and the Public Trust* (1988; 2d ed., 1992) and *Character and Cops: Ethics in Policing* (1989; 2d ed., 1994) and of numerous newspaper and magazine articles on ethics in daily private and public life—including parenthood and moral education of the young, education, law enforcement, government, and business. He has also published articles on excellence in humanities and liberal arts education; on the governance of educational institutions; and on illegal narcotics, organized crime, urban gangs, and related domestic and international policy issues.